The Birmingham
Parish Workhouse
1730–1840

The Birmingham Parish Workhouse 1730–1840

Chris Upton

West Midlands Publications
an imprint of
University of Hertfordshire Press

First published in Great Britain in 2019 by
West Midlands Publications
an imprint of
University of Hertfordshire Press
College Lane
Hatfield
Hertfordshire
AL10 9AB

British Library Cataloguing in Publication Data
A catalogue record for this book is available from the British Library

ISBN 978-1-912260-14-0

Design by Arthouse Publishing Solutions Ltd
Printed in Great Britain by Hobbs the Printers Ltd

Contents

Illustrations

Acknowledgements

I should like to acknowledge the very generous contribution of Dr Ian Cawood in enabling the completion of this book by my late husband, Chris Upton, and the support and assistance of the staff at Archives and Collections, Library of Birmingham. Without this invaluable help, the publication of his book could not have been achieved and I am very grateful. I hope Chris would be pleased with the result.

Fiona Tait

Introduction

Then, shall we grumble at the Parish Rate,
If it's the Poor that makes so many great;
For sure, for them, Provision should be made,
To which the Wealthy ought to lend their Aid,
To succour those, that fall into Distress,
And chasten those, who're prone to Idleness:
For Idleness is ever a Disgrace,
And more so, if it's in a trading Place;
Yet, if Disorder has amongst them crept,
They merit Gain, who do the Fault correct;
And as it seems that some do now devise,
To build a WORKHOUSE of the largest Size;
In which the Poor may Health and Comfort find,
And forc'd to work – those lazily inclined;
When filching skulks, who stroll, or lounging lie,
By Labour there, may well their wants supply;[1]

Near to the bottom of Lichfield Street stood Birmingham parish workhouse, its clock-tower proclaiming the hours to all who dwelt on the east side of town. From the middle of the eighteenth century the building remained for more than a hundred years, until reorganisation in the 1850s removed the institution to Winson Green. There is no indication of its presence in the area today, and, indeed, the street name itself was erased from the map by the redevelopment we know as the Birmingham Improvement Scheme, under the terms of the Artisans' Dwellings Act (1875). An equally grand edifice, the Victoria Law Courts, occupies the site today; it is still a place for social control, but of a different kind.

---

1   Anon., 'Local Remarks: A Poem', *Aris's Gazette*, 21 April 1783.

Here, it would appear, in one of the most successful and progressive of towns – 'toyshop of Europe', 'first industrial city in the world' – there was an Achilles heel, a clear demonstration of inadequacy. In this new world of capitalist advance, commercial progress evidently sat cheek-by-jowl with household misery; the town that sped forward left others behind, and with credit came debit. Yet, for the town's wealthier citizens, the Lichfield Street workhouse was a symbol of pride, a manifest embodiment of their care for the poor and huddled masses, who crowded into Birmingham's ever more teeming streets. They might resent the regular visits by the collectors of levies, always demanding more of their hard-earned money, but the workhouse itself was a physical representation of where their rates were going. It was a constant reminder of those ordnances preached at them from the pulpits, both Anglican and nonconformist, each Sunday morning: to feed the hungry, tend the sick, and clothe the naked. And if there was no longer any guarantee that such behaviour would speed the donor towards heaven, the English Reformation having put paid to that promise, the values of care and responsibility still fitted well enough with the new ideas of civic pride and community.

For the poor, however, the workhouse had a very different meaning. To them the workhouse dealt with the ends of things: the end of hope, the end of independence, the end of life, the end of the line. It was the place that took them in when all else failed. If our lives are lived in light, the workhouse cast the darkest of shadows, a place where the forlorn and the bankrupt, the penniless and the dispossessed – 600 or more of them in Birmingham in bad times – slept side-by-side within its stark and comfortless wards. Charles Dickens, who knew Birmingham well, ably described the negative attitude of many of the poor towards the workhouse, when he put these words in the mouth of Betty Higden in *Our Mutual Friend*:

> Kill me sooner than take me there. Throw this pretty child under cart-horses' feet and a loaded wagon, sooner than take him there. Come to us and find us all a-dying, and set fire to us all where we lie, and let us all blaze away with the house into a heap of cinders, sooner than move a corpse of us there![2]

Yet the workhouse was also the place that gave shelter to the homeless, the one establishment that cared for the sick and the aged who had nothing. It was both infirmary and maternity hospital, school and crèche, asylum and care home. For a society that had no National Health Service, no state provision for the unemployed, no long-term plan or pension for old age and no state education for the poor, the workhouse picked up the bill.

---

2   C. Dickens, *Our Mutual Friend*, Vol. 1, London, 1865, p. 242.

For twenty years or so I have found the workhouse a fascinating place; from the safe distance, that is, of the early twenty-first century, when it could no longer threaten to take me in. Part of the attraction, as a historian, is the challenge to reconstruct the life of an institution from its official and often highly impersonal records. Since I first took an interest in them, workhouse literature and websites have proliferated, catering for a burgeoning interest among social historians and genealogists, who have found that their families were born into, or ended their days, in one. There are also now a growing number of former workhouses, at Gressenhall, Ripon, Northwich and Southwell, which have opened their doors to the public. The evolution of the Northwich museum at Weaver Hall in Cheshire is an interesting reflection of increasing public engagement with the subject. What began some years ago as a museum of the town's important salt industry, which happened to be accommodated in an old workhouse building, has more recently been re-modelled to reflect its former use more directly. The clear shift in public history away from industry and towards such social institutions is nowhere better illustrated.

Much of this attention, however, has concentrated on the period after 1834, when the Poor Law Amendment Act or 'New' Poor Law created the sprawling institutions (with equally sprawling records) known as Union workhouses, which still form the core of many of our NHS hospitals even today. The smaller parish workhouses which preceded them are often dealt with in a paragraph or two. This emphasis on the Victorian and Edwardian workhouse, perhaps inevitably, reflects where the surviving sources are richest. Poor Law Unions maintained vast quantities of records, while their humbler predecessors kept relatively few, or kept them haphazardly, and what they did keep often did not survive the take-over by the Union or the depredations of the following 180 years of change, reorganisation and war.

It is equally true that the enduring image of the workhouse, as the gateway of tears or the 'Bastille' of the poor, has diverted popular attention too much away from the wider application of the Poor Laws by the state. The workhouse was but one aspect of its work, only the tip of a much bigger iceberg. Under its various provisions the parish dealt with apprenticeships and vagrancy, with medical care and out-relief, even with work schemes for the unemployed. The workhouse may have been the first port of call for applicants, but it was, in most cases, far from the final destination. Most of the poor applicants for relief were not directed to the workhouse, much as overseers and the Poor Law Commissioners might have wanted them to be. In 1833, for example, at a time when around 1,000 persons were in residential care in the Birmingham workhouse, workhouse infirmary or Asylum for the Infant Poor, 'the number more or less dependent upon the parish', was estimated as between 16,000 and

17,000.[3] On top of that, though beyond the reach of the records, were those many thousands who would not dream, or dare, to apply directly for relief, but struggled on as best they could in the fashion of Dickens' Betty Higden.

By the late 1700s Birmingham was already growing into a mighty metropolis, dwarfing its neighbours in ambition, and in the size and speed of its growth. In the range of its institutions too, including the Poor Law, it was of a different order. While the paupers in many of the nearby parish workhouses might number no more than twenty or so, those housed in Lichfield Street were in their hundreds. In 1803–4 one third of all the indoor paupers in Warwickshire were domiciled either in the Birmingham workhouse, or in the Asylum for the Infant Poor.[4] As one of the most extensive workhouses in one of the largest (and fastest growing) towns in nineteenth-century Britain, Birmingham tells a national, as well as a local, story. It wrestled with the problems of poverty and disease, pauperism and education, in its own individual way, but in a manner which reflected (and sometimes contradicted) national trends and attitudes too. The history of the workhouse in Birmingham is not a micro-study of the national or even of the West Midlands history of workhouses. Birmingham, after all, saw the consequences of industrial change earlier than most. But, as Felix Driver wrote in his ground-breaking study of the Huddersfield Poor Law Union 'it would be quite wrong to divorce the local experience of the … Poor Law from its broader context'.[5] The effects of national Poor Law legislation were far-reaching in Birmingham as elsewhere and the shifting of attitudes and of policy priorities among those responsible for the poor in Birmingham were influenced by broader cultural and social changes across Britain and Western Europe. And the workhouse inmates themselves were far from parochial: migrants arrived from all corners of the British Isles (and beyond) to seek work in this industrial giant and (later) found themselves washed up on the stony shore of poor relief.

The story of the Poor Law, then, is of a state institution with a local heart, struggling to meet the ever-increasing demands of an ever-increasing society. We might see some of the solutions as inconsistent, sometimes unkind, overtly moralistic and often ill-informed. But the problems it addressed are no less pressing in the twenty-first century. Indeed, every time I turn on the radio I find myself back in the guardians' boardroom, and the agenda has not changed.

---

3   In 1833 C.P. Villiers found 439 inmates in the Lichfield Street workhouse, *Report from His Majesty's Commissioners for Inquiring into the Administration and Practical Operation of the Poor Laws*, Appendix A, Parliamentary Papers, XXIX, 1834, p. 32a.

4   'County of Warwick', *Abstract of answers and returns made pursuant to the Act of 43 George III relative to the expense and maintenance of the poor in England*, Parliamentary Papers, XIII, 1803–4, pp. 533–48.

5   F. Driver, *Power and Pauperism: The Workhouse System 1834–1884*, Cambridge, 1993, p. 131.

How do we solve the problem of homelessness? How can we provide affordable care for our elderly and infirm? What is the right balance between incentives to work and social support for the unemployed? How do we get people off welfare and into work? Can we improve the ways we treat mental illness? How do we break the cycle of what the Victorians called 'hereditary pauperism'? What level of public and social services are we prepared to pay for? How does local support survive when central funding is squeezed? How should we address the challenge of childhood poverty? How can we improve the life chances of children in care? And what role should the private and charitable sectors play in all of this?

When I began compiling the evidence for this book, some years ago, Great Britain was considered to be a rich country. Now it does not appear quite so affluent. Recession, the credit crunch and a series of cold, relentless winters seem to have turned the clock back to my childhood, and to the even tougher childhood of my parents. We are not so poor, so crushed by unemployment and deprivation as ordinary people were in the 1790s or the 1830s, yet the people who inhabit this book feel a little closer to me than they did a year or two ago. I can hardly say that I'm grateful for this, but the problems they wrestled with – finding a home, getting a job, paying the rent, feeding a family and securing a future for their children – still reach out from the pages of history. Ultimately, the challenges of providing for the elderly, encouraging the able-bodied into work, breaking family cycles of dependency and protecting the poor have not changed or gone away. We may surely learn from the past as we prepare for the future.

I would like to thank all those archivists, librarians and museum curators who have helped in the making of this book. The staff of Birmingham Archives and Collections, Library of Birmingham, have dealt with a constant barrage of request slips for three years and more, and have done so with a cheery professionalism at all times. My wife, Fiona Tait, has read through all the chapters in this book, as always a touchstone of its accuracy and readability. With their help, I hope that I have brought life to an ancient institution, helped its inmates and its staff to walk in the daylight once more. Wherever I have been able to, I have given them names; it is the least I could do. You may not care to live in the same world, but it merits our attention and our sympathy nonetheless.

Chris Upton, 2015

1

The Birmingham Poor Law

As a kind tree, perfectly adapted for growth, and planted in a suitable soil, draws nourishment from the circumjacent ground, to a great extent, and robs the neighbouring plants of their support, that nothing can thrive with its influence; so Birmingham, half whose inhabitants above the age of ten, perhaps, are not natives, draws her annual supply of hands…[1]

In June 1832 a clock and watch repairer from Rowley Regis in the Black Country, Thomas Anson by name, died in the infirmary ward at Birmingham workhouse. The man was already suffering from chronic ill health, and so the inquest into his death did not detain the coroner long. But with cholera menacing the town, the authorities were rather more diligent than usual. What interested the coroner, and the reporter from the *Birmingham Journal* deputed to cover the story, was the presence of this outsider at the workhouse in Lichfield Street.[2] There was, after all, a perfectly serviceable workhouse in Rowley. The man's arrival itself could hardly be called unexpected: the town of Birmingham was full of migrants and job-seekers, and some inevitably found themselves at the workhouse, if only briefly, before they were sent packing back to their native parish. What was unusual was the evidence supplied by one of Thomas Anson's neighbours in the Black Country. Anson had, apparently, declared his intention to go to Birmingham workhouse, 'because it was better than the workhouses of other places', and so he made his final journey. It was a glowing testimonial from the most unexpected of places.

In its social provision, Birmingham workhouse was, indeed, more innovative, and perhaps more generous, than most of its neighbours: that certainly was its reputation locally. Charles Pelham Villiers prefaced his report to the Poor Law Commission in 1834 with the town's good name ringing in his ears:

---

1   W. Hutton, *The History of Birmingham*, 6th edn, Birmingham, 1836, p. 67.

2   *Birmingham Journal*, 7 July 1832.

The poor are commonly said to be provided for here under a management superior to that of other places. To a certain extent this is the case; the disorder visible in other parishes is not to be observed here.[3]

The editor of the *Birmingham Advertiser* was of similar mind:

It would be difficult to find throughout all England any parish in which the Poor Law, and the parochial affairs of the town generally, are more beneficially and prudently managed than in Birmingham.[4]

Writing in 1836, James Guest might easily have had the clock repairer from Rowley in mind when he proudly declared: 'One would think that situation could not be so despicable, which is often wished for, and often sought, that of being one of the poor of Birmingham.'[5]

Good provision, however, came at a cost. It was just as true to say that Birmingham had a reputation for higher rates. By the nineteenth century, estate agents were using the lower levies in Aston, by way of contrast with its bigger neighbour, to promote their properties across the parish boundary. In 1834, according to Villiers, the total levies in Birmingham cost almost eight times as much as those in Aston, though the population was only three times larger.[6]

Yet poor relief in the town was still subject to the same constricting financial restraints as anywhere else, and, if anything, exposed to greater pressures. Behind every benevolent overseer and guardian stood an irate ratepayer, breathing down his neck and complaining about the price he paid for such 'superior management'. In addition, as Villiers himself admitted, the administration of poor relief in a manufacturing town like Birmingham was a far more complex business than it was in an agricultural area. Villiers singled out 'the fluctuating character of manufacturing employment ... and the alternation of high and low wages' as two chief reasons for the problem.[7] Steering the Poor Law through these unpredictable waters was no easy matter.

The town of Birmingham stood in a highly ambiguous relationship with its Poor Laws. Here was a place that grew and prospered on the

---

3   *Report from His Majesty's Commissioners for Inquiring into the Administration and Practical Operation of the Poor Laws*, Parliamentary Papers, XXIX, 1834.

4   *Birmingham Advertiser*, 19 May 1834.

5   Hutton, *History of Birmingham*, p. 364.

6   *Report from His Majesty's Commissioners for Inquiring into the Administration and Practical Operation of the Poor Laws,* Appendix A, Parliamentary Papers, XXIX, 1834, p. 56a.

7   *Ibid.*, p. 22a.

back of migration, its innumerable workshops, and promise of limitless employment, drawing in labour from across the Midland counties and beyond. Without a single boundary change the population of the town grew seven-fold over the course of the eighteenth century, from around 11,000 in 1700 to 73,670 in 1801.[8] Over the same period the population of Coventry had merely doubled, while the national population had risen by around fifty per cent.[9]

Birmingham's headlong growth had been a matter of remark from the time that William Camden had seen it 'swarming with inhabitants and echoing with the sound of anvils' back in the 1580s.[10] When the La Rochefoucauld brothers passed through the town in 1785, Birmingham's teeming streets were even more marked:

> You can have little idea of the crowds of people going by in the streets all the time: there is as much life as in Paris or in London. You can hardly walk on the pavements without being obliged to step off.[11]

In this hotbed of inward migration and laissez-faire capitalism the laws of settlement were dead in the water, let alone the Corporation and Test Acts. As the barrister, John Morfitt, told Samuel Pratt in 1802:

> Thus circumstanced, Birmingham covets not the oppressive honours of a corporation … She throws her arms wide open to all mankind, inviting strangers of all descriptions into her hospitable bosom. In many places it is more difficult to pass the artificial boundaries of a parish than an arm of the sea, or Alpine hill; but Birmingham regards not the narrow policy of our laws of settlement, nor does she anxiously trouble herself with who are and who are not likely to become chargeable.[12]

Such generosity of spirit did not necessarily go down so well with the Poor Law's administrators, nor with Birmingham ratepayers in the middle of a recession. What became of these migrants when times were hard and jobs were few? Was the 1662 law of settlement and removal not a useful measure to fall back on?

---

8 G.E. Cherry, *Birmingham: A Study in Geography, History and Planning*, Chichester, 1994, pp. 22, 33.

9 E.A. Wrigley and R.S. Schofield, *The Population History of England, 1541–1871: A Reconstruction*, Cambridge, 1981, pp. 208–9.

10 W. Camden, *Britannia*, London, 1586, p. 505.

11 N. Scarfe, *Innocent Espionage: The La Rochefoucauld Brothers' Tour of England in 1785*, Woodbridge, 1995, p. 114.

12 S.J. Pratt, *Harvest Home, Consisting of Supplementary Gleanings, Original Dramas and Poems, Contributions of Literary Friends and Select Re-publications*, Vol. 1, London, 1805, p. 265.

This chapter will cover the history of the Birmingham Poor Law from the 1720s to 1840. It is worth recognising, at the outset, that any account of any workhouse, be it a contemporary or a modern one, is only true and accurate for a single point of time. It takes only a little delving into the minutes of guardians and overseers, or into the financial records of the workhouse itself, to realise that the organisation was in a state of constant flux. The names of officials and the numbers of inmates obviously altered frequently, but so did the nature of the paupers' labour, their diet and the rules governing their behaviour, and how the individual parts of the workhouse site itself were utilised. More importantly still, public attitudes to poverty and disability, to the treatment of children and those with mental illness, were similarly subject to change, and that was mirrored in the policies of the men who ran the Poor Law. No general description can therefore be true for more than a matter of months. This has not deterred modern historians from writing such overviews and from attempting to portray, either locally or nationally, 'life in the workhouse', but to do so is often to undermine its accuracy and exaggerate its universality. It needs rather more care than that. If questioned as to the conditions in the workhouse, one ought really to ask when, where and for whom.

The records of Birmingham workhouse are far from complete, but they are extensive, more so than any other Midland institution under the Old Poor Law. It would be worthwhile at the outset, therefore, to outline what does survive and what does not, at least prior to the mid-nineteenth century.

We can reconstruct how and when the workhouse was built from the so-called Town Books – records of public meetings called by the parish vestry – which begin in 1723, and from the evidence in the Warwickshire Quarter Sessions. There is also a single volume recording payments both for the workhouse itself and to the outdoor poor, covering the period 1739 to 1748. No other dedicated volume as early as this survives. From 1803 onwards, however, we have the minute books of the parish overseers, who shared responsibility for the running of the workhouse with the guardians of the poor. More importantly still, there are the minute books of the 108 elected Birmingham guardians, which begin with their appointment in July 1783. In addition, there are four volumes of accounts – cash books – which record payments for all aspects of poor relief from 1799 to 1836, and a single volume summarising investigations into settlement. There are, of course, national records in which the Birmingham workhouse is mentioned as well, such as the census and the records of the Home Office. From a combination of these sources we can begin to put flesh on the bones of the Birmingham Poor Law and to re-construct its operation.

What the surviving minute books are not, as a cursory reading of them quickly makes clear, is a full account of meetings of the overseers and guardians.

The books record the outcome of deliberations, but not the discussions themselves. The parish clerk would certainly have made a fuller record, prior to a 'fair copy' being entered in the official minute books, but this has not been preserved. What mattered to the clerk and to the officers were the decisions that were reached, not the arguments which preceded (or prevented) them. A revealing exchange, recorded by the *Birmingham Advertiser*, took place at a routine public meeting to approve the parish constables' accounts in July 1835 after the institution of the 'New' Poor Law. Questioned by James Oram, himself a former guardian, the workhouse clerk admitted that the draft minutes of the guardians' and overseers' meetings were routinely destroyed, and that this had been the practice 'since before he [Oram] was born'.[13] The meeting voted unanimously to stop this practice, but it is unlikely that it had the power to enforce a change in policy.

This may simply reflect a sensible attempt to limit the mounting pile of paperwork in the clerk's office, but it may well also indicate a concerted attempt to manage how news of the proceedings of meetings was presented. The board of guardians was just as riven by factionalism as was the Birmingham political scene as a whole. The board's instinct was not to parade its dirty linen in public, or to make its deliberations widely accessible, unless it was absolutely forced to do so.

We should also register that the way meetings of the guardians were conducted, their regularity and range, also varied enormously. The records of these meetings are merely the top of a mountain of paper, however. Internal accounts, day books and inventories for the workhouse must once have been kept; records from the infirmary, and the minutes of the various committees into which the guardians were organised, but these are now lost. There were also, since they are mentioned elsewhere, registers of inmates and an 'obituary book', which recorded deaths in the house. Workhouse masters were also required to keep a journal; one survives from Wolverhampton, but nothing from Birmingham.

Understanding the workings of the Poor Law in any parish, therefore, involves much patient reading between the lines, and piecing together disconnected fragments of evidence. The best period for scrutiny at Birmingham is undoubtedly from 1818 onwards, when a serious financial scandal involving the governor and the workhouse finances was uncovered, leading to a root-and-branch overhaul of the way the Birmingham Poor Law operation was run and, more importantly, how it was reported and monitored. From this point onwards, the guardians' minutes, and the reports they contain, could hardly be more helpful.

---

13   *Birmingham Advertiser*, 30 July 1835.

There are, of course, more centralised records to add to the mix. As the cost of the Poor Law grew nationally over the course of the eighteenth and nineteenth century, so the activities of the parishes came under greater governmental scrutiny. In 1776, 1803–4 and 1818, and again in the run-up to the Amendment Act of 1834, parochial officers were required to submit statistics of their expenditure to Westminster. These returns are often treated as the gold standard of historical evidence by historians of the Poor Law. Close comparison between the local records and these national surveys, however, reveal them to be less accurate, and less comprehensive, than we would like them to be. Birmingham's returns for its indoor poor in 1803–4, for example, do not include the pauper children who were maintained in the Asylum for the Infant Poor. The inclusion of the Asylum children would have doubled the published number of paupers.[14] With the eyes of Parliament upon them, parish officers were clearly ready and willing to bend the rules to their advantage.

On-site inspections were no more likely to be strictly accurate. The round of visits undertaken by the assistant commissioners in 1834 was itself bound to be selective. Charles Pelham Villiers, who undertook the local audit, had as his area of operation not only Warwickshire and Worcestershire, but also parts of Gloucestershire and North Devon.[15] The assistant commissioner was also subjected to considerable lobbying whilst he was in town. In Birmingham Villiers was buttonholed both by Henry Knight and George Edmonds, who had their own axes to grind. Knight was campaigning for the provision of parochial schools for the poor and Edmonds was demanding a more democratic election of guardians.

Not all such national surveys were commissioned by Parliament. Sir Frederick Morton Eden's three-volume account of the poor, undertaken in 1794–6, was conducted independently, but was similarly reliant on questionnaires, and local returns.[16] Nevertheless, Birmingham's response was remarkably fulsome, supplying to Eden or his agent workhouse statistics for a four-year period, dietary tables and overseers' accounts for no less than ten years (1786–96). Most notable are the mortality returns from the workhouse, which would otherwise be lost.[17] Eden also received returns from the parish of Sutton Coldfield, but not from what would become the other Birmingham parishes. As with the

---

14   *Abstract of answers and returns made pursuant to the Act of 43 George III relative to the expense and maintenance of the poor in England*, Parliamentary Papers, XIII, 1803–4.

15   *Report for His Majesty's Commissioners for Inquiring into the Administration and Practical Operation of the Poor Laws*, Parliamentary Papers, XXIX, 1834.

16   F.M. Eden, *The State of the Poor*, 3 vols, London, 1797.

17   Eden, *The State of the Poor*, Vol. III., London, 1797, pp. 737–53. (The page numbering in the original text is inconsistent.)

parliamentary enquiries, Eden was at the mercy of his correspondents, whether that was the workhouse master or the vestry clerk, and their evidence must always be tested against what the internal records themselves tell us.

Eden's work was intended to provoke and inform a national debate on the condition of the labouring classes, though there was hardly much need to raise the topic locally; it was rarely out of the news. Extrinsic to the local records of the guardians and overseers, but of equal importance, is the coverage of Poor Law issues in the Birmingham newspapers, principally in *Aris's Birmingham Gazette* (from 1741) and the *Birmingham Journal* (from 1825). Both papers were published weekly, at least until the abolition of Stamp Duty in 1855. How the poor rates were spent and the conditions within the workhouse were of abiding interest to journalists, editors and the general public, as the fierce battle in the 1820s to gain access to guardians' meetings showed.

Once newspapers succeeded in breaking through this veil of secrecy, their reports of meetings are frequently much fuller than the minutes of the guardians and overseers themselves. For reasons already described, the men from the press preserved a more extended account of discussions than the cursory summaries in the minute books. If the way the news was reported carries the accusation of political spin, it was no more slanted than the arguments of the officers themselves. In addition, the newspapers often printed more complete sets of Poor Law accounts than the ones which survive within the parish records themselves. Those annual accounts were always carried on the front page; such was the enduring appeal of Poor Law expenditure to the reading public.

While the *Gazette* and the *Journal* were the local newspapers with the largest circulation, they were far from the only ones on sale in the town, or read in the pubs and coffee houses. A bewildering variety of other publications came and went, all reflecting different shades of political opinion, and driven forward with a characteristic Brummagem energy. Samuel Sidney (the pseudonym of Samuel Solomon, the Birmingham-born travel writer) commented ruefully in 1851 that 'the only sign of Birmingham's ancient literary pre-eminence is to be found in several weekly newspapers, conducted with talent and spirit far beyond average'.[18] The *Birmingham Advertiser* (published from 1833) claimed at the outset to stand mid-way between the political stance of the more conservative *Gazette* and more radical *Journal*, though its position moved steadily towards the Tories. The paper's grandstanding campaign against the New Poor Law provoked the wrath of the guardians at Aston for 'attempting to excite discontent and turbulence among the class whom the Law is intended

---

18   S. Sidney, *Rides on Railways*, London, 1851, p. 79.

to protect, to improve and to benefit'.[19] The fact that the proprietor of the *Advertiser* was Rev William Riland Bedford, rector of Sutton Coldfield, by then a part of Aston Union, only served to stoke the fires of controversy.

The *Midland Representative* (published from 1831) had in its sights wider political reform. *Swinney's Birmingham & Stafford Chronicle* took a more regional approach to issues, whilst George Edmonds' *Weekly Recorder* or *Register* (covering only 1819) served as a platform for its author's campaign to shake up local government and the running of the Poor Law. Joseph Allday's Peelite *Monthly Argus* (1829–34) combined both political conservatism with a strong impulse to reform the way the poor were treated. The subtle shades of Birmingham's rainbow politics are no better demonstrated than in its press, but they do show that, in Asa Briggs' words, 'Birmingham of the 1820s was a city where politics ... were taken seriously.'[20]

In addition, once the activities of the Poor Law came to be opened up to more acute public scrutiny, the press regularly provided the battleground where issues of ill-treatment, parsimony or over-expenditure were fought out. The letters column became, as well as a place of pseudonymous rumour and innuendo, the place where the authorities justified their actions in the court of public opinion. The guardians thus had an uneasy relationship with the local press (as local government still does today), but a divorce was never possible. They needed the space in newspapers to tender for goods and services, to advertise for staff, to announce public meetings and publish their accounts for public scrutiny.

Few topics in town were likely to raise the temperature more than the workings of the Poor Law. Whether it be lavish expenditure – real or perceived – by the overseers, the high-handedness of the guardians, the ill-treatment of workhouse inmates or the level of childhood mortality, all issues generated passionate argument, a debate that the officials themselves felt duty-bound to enter. Many were the meetings of guardians which ended with an instruction to the clerk to dash off a reply to the paper in answer to some scurrilous attack. Indeed, dissident guardians themselves, unhappy with some decision or other of the board, sometimes went public to air their grievances.

These letters and editorials merit close attention, though the polarised nature of political debate makes them far from easy to interpret and dissect. No more so than in the early 1830s, when the cause of political freedom – the Reform Bills and Chartism – sucked almost every aspect of public life into the maelstrom. Indeed, from the mid-1810s onwards political engagement in

---

19   Archives and Collections, Library of Birmingham. GP AS/2/1/1 Aston Guardians' minutes, 26 June 1836.

20   A. Briggs, *Press and Public in Early Nineteenth-century Birmingham*, Oxford, 1949, p. 18.

the town grew exponentially, impacting directly on the way poor relief was delivered. The elections of guardians were contested, the levies challenged, and conditions within the house investigated. Campaigners like George Edmonds, a veteran of the Great Reform Bill meetings, turned their attention increasingly towards the Poor Law, and broadcast their views both in the weekly papers and in their own self-published pamphlets.[21]

The workhouse, the internal workings of the Poor Law, its cost and its scope were active topics of conversation and controversy throughout the period. If the nature of historical evidence means that the voices of the recipients of poor relief – the poor themselves – are largely silent, they are replaced by the sound of the chattering classes. George Edmonds and Joseph Allday stand at opposite poles of political opinion, but many in between ventured opinion and commentary and constructive criticism. The actor, playwright and poet Samuel Jackson Pratt, who appears to have settled in Birmingham from about 1802, was at the centre of one group of opinion makers. His anthology of contemporary 'gleanings', *Harvest Home* (1805), contains the eyewitness testimony of Pratt himself, the barrister John Morfitt, the bookseller and poet William Hutton, and the pseudonymous pamphleteer Job Nott, supplemented by evidence solicited from the workhouse master.[22] That a work primarily literary in intention devotes so much space to the lives of the poor, and the subject of poor relief, is testimony to the centrality of this ongoing dialogue.

Evidence from the law courts can be equally enlightening, from the proceedings of the Public Office or Quarter Sessions themselves, or from the reporting of cases in the local press. The local magistracy had a key role to play in the enactment of the Poor Law, whether that was to force the officers to take responsibility for a family when they were reluctant to do so, or to punish a trouble-maker in the workhouse, or to chastise a dishonest claimant. Such proceedings were, in disciplinary cases, a final resort, but a reminder that the Poor Law was, at the end of the day, a matter of law. On top of that, any sitting of the Quarter Sessions, in whatever county they were held, had a great pile of settlement cases on which to adjudicate, as Poor Law Unions, and parishes before that, sought to shift the financial responsibility for a pauper onto another union or parish. It was a costly, time-consuming and unedifying routine.[23]

There is one other important source referred to in this study, and that is the diaries of the Congregationalist missionaries, working in Birmingham's

---

21   For example, G. Edmonds, *George Edmonds' appeal to the labourers of England: an exposure of aristocrat spies, and the infernal machinery of the poor law murder bill*, London, 1836.

22   Pratt, *Harvest Home*, Vol. 1.

23   See N. Landau, 'Who was Subjected to the Laws of Settlement? Procedure under the Settlement Laws in Eighteenth-Century England' *Agricultural History Review*, 43:2, 1990, pp. 139–59.

back streets in the late 1830s. Other nonconformist churches engaged with Birmingham's poor – the Unitarians and Methodists among them – but the Congregationalists were the earliest to leave their journals behind. A handful of men – Messsrs Derrington, Sibree, Clay and Finigan – trod those streets, and they vividly communicated the conditions in which the town's poor were living.[24] Unlike most of their class, who were content to read about deprivation and hardship in the newspapers, the work of the missionaries from Carrs Lane, inspired by the preacher, John Angell James, took them into the very houses and courts of those whom economic progress had largely left behind. Their journals offer a unique insight into conditions, as well as an important reminder that many of the poor (perhaps the majority) struggled on without the assistance of the Poor Law, relying instead upon charity, the occasional pay day and the pawnshop.

The year 1840 was chosen as a concluding date for this study in order to incorporate the transition from the Old Poor Law to the New, but the change of emphasis from parish to union, from overseers to guardians, from outdoor to indoor relief, was of little direct importance to Birmingham. Birmingham was established as a Poor Law Union by its own Act of Parliament in 1782, and the great Amendment Act of 1834 had little immediate effect upon it. The city of Coventry was similarly protected.[25] The Birmingham guardians took the trouble to write to their MPs, suggesting that the new Act was doomed, but in most aspects they could keep it at arm's length. Few of the circulars and instructions sent out by the Poor Law Commissioners, dutifully read and inwardly digested in the neighbouring Unions of Aston and Kings Norton, detained them long. Nevertheless, since 1834 is always held up as one of the great watersheds in English social history, it seemed churlish not to acknowledge it.[26] More important in the industrial Midlands, I suspect, was the crippling economic slump which happened to follow immediately after.

At the heart of the English Poor Law, be it in Birmingham or elsewhere, lay a conundrum. How could society meet its Christian duty of care towards the poor, and yet avoid making them comfortable with their lot? To use a metaphor, how could a safety net for the vulnerable be prevented from becoming a hammock for the idle? Where did self-help end and social care begin? John

---

24 Edwin Derrington (1801–85) was allocated streets in the Aston area. Peter Sibree (1797–1863) was minister at the Ebenezer Chapel in Steelhouse Lane. Thomas Finigan's journal has recently been published by the Birmingham Irish Heritage Group. Mr Clay has not been identified.

25 W.B. Stephens (ed.), *A History of the County of Warwick: Vol. 8: The City of Coventry and Borough of Warwick*, London, 1969, pp. 276–7.

26 Although John Langford candidly noted that 'the year 1834 was very uneventful' in Birmingham. J.A. Langford, *A Century of Birmingham Life*, Vol. 2, Birmingham, 1871, p. 563.

Cadbury, Quaker confectioner and Birmingham guardian, expressed it succinctly (and revealingly) in 1829, in the course of a heated debate over the number of surgeons the parish should be employing:

> He [Cadbury] wished to see the condition of the poor really ameliorated; but he doubted if extending the system of parochial relief was the most judicious means of accommodating so desirable an end.[27]

The evangelical revival, which affected all sects of the Protestant faith in the early nineteenth century, did not merely promote philanthropy. It also required the wealthy to ensure that the consequence of their generosity should not be the moral degradation of the recipients.[28] The chapters which follow will trace that fine line between care and cost, between carrot and stick, between protection and deterrent.

Finally, for those new to the complexities of Poor Law legislation and operation, it may be worthwhile outlining, in general terms, how the system evolved. This is necessarily a brief summary, but it may help to make sense of the more detailed and place-specific discussions that follow.

We may begin with the Poor Law legislation of 34 Elizabeth I, often referred to as the 1601 Great Poor Law Act, which established the template for more than two hundred years of social provision. Under the 1601 Act the parish became the linchpin of the Old Poor Law, on whose shoulders the burden of responsibility was to be carried. It had a duty of care towards all of those who, for a variety of reasons, were unable to support themselves. This included the aged and infirm, those with physical or mental disabilities, the sick, the single mother, the orphaned or illegitimate child, and the unemployed. The Act specifically sub-divided the poor into three main classes: the able-bodied, the sick and infirm, and those referred to in the legislation as 'sturdy beggars'. The parish, and more particularly annually appointed parish officers known as overseers, took responsibility for meeting the needs of these three groups, supplying them with cash, clothing or shoes, or tools to enable them to work. They might also provide them with accommodation, perhaps in an almshouse, a cottage owned by the parish, or (by the early eighteenth century) in a workhouse. The funds for such provision came from the ratepayers, who paid poor rates or levies in proportion to the value of their property.[29]

---

27 *Birmingham Journal*, 28 November 1829.

28 A.J. Kidd, *State, Society and the Poor in Nineteenth-Century England*, Basingstoke, 1999, pp. 70–1; D.W. Bebbington, *Evangelicalism in Modern Britain: A History from the 1730s to the 1980s*, London, 1989, pp. 121–2.

29 P. Slack, *The English Poor Law, 1531–1782*, Basingstoke, 1990, pp. 51–8.

Parish responsibility for an individual or a family was determined by what was known as settlement. This might be in the parish of one's birth, or of a parent's later residence; settlement might also be obtained by working, or being hired to work, in a parish (in normal circumstances for a full year), or by renting a house for a minimum length of time. Much of the time of parish officers, workhouse clerks and others was taken up with establishing settlement, and parishes engaged in open warfare over which of them bore responsibility for an individual or family. As we have said, in many cases the final decision rested in the hands of the justices at the Quarter Sessions.

Finally, parish officers were empowered under the 1601 Act to find work for the children of the poor, typically by drawing up apprenticeship indentures for a fixed term of years.[30] This might be within the parish boundaries, or with an employer outside the parish, and many of Birmingham's neighbouring parishes found employment for their young people in the manufactories of the town, or even in the coal mines of the Black Country. Again, apprenticeships were drawn up with the approval of the local magistracy.[31]

These were the arrangements laid down in 1601. But this set out an overall framework; it did not determine every single piece of parochial policy. Some parishes (such as Birmingham and Aston) made an early decision to erect a workhouse; others waited as late as the 1820s. Some retained a centralised control over the poor in the workhouse; others 'farmed out' the labour of the poor, using an outside contractor to supervise them, set them to work and profit from their industry. Differing decisions were also taken over the treatment of the mentally and physically ill: whether to retain them in the workhouse or send them for treatment in a private asylum or public hospital.[32]

Given the breadth of its responsibilities, the parish was obliged to pay others to undertake some of its duties. It needed to pay for a parish doctor to examine and treat the sick, whether in their own homes or in the workhouse. The workhouse itself needed staffing and supervision, at the very least by a master and matron. A parish constable or other official might be deployed to round up vagrants, transfer paupers to another parish, or track down absentee fathers or mothers. The expectation was that a family was responsible for its own kith and kin, and the parish was legally obliged to step in only if the family was absent, or financially incapable of bearing that burden. In some cases intervention by a local magistrate forced the parish to do so.

We ought finally to say something about how the Poor Law system in Birmingham (and elsewhere) was paid for. As Samantha Williams has recently

---

30   J. Lane, *Apprenticeship in England, 1600–1914*, London, 1996, pp. 1–3.

31   *Ibid.*, pp. 132–9.

32   G.W. Oxley, *Poor Relief in England and Wales, 1601–1834*, Newton Abbott, 1974, pp. 80–1.

commented, there have been few studies 'of ratepaying, the proportion of the parish paying the rate, the wealth distribution of ratepayers and their familial characteristics'.[33] Poor rates or levies were raised according to the rateable value of property, which was periodically re-assessed. The rate was paid by the house owner, though s/he may well have passed on the cost to tenants. The 1783 Local Act specified that Birmingham levies were to be assessed at two shillings in the pound 'on the annual value of the property', though this was far from universally applied.[34] In 1816 there were nineteen levies at sixpence in the pound; in 1819 eleven levies at one shilling in the pound; and in 1829 three levies at two shillings.[35] The need for a new levy was determined by the overseers (the one responsibility that remained solely theirs), and then approved by the magistrates. Only eight levies in twelve months would feel like a very good year indeed. When the poet and innkeeper, John Freeth, chose that number as proof of Birmingham's peaceable and cost-effective state, he was being very economical with the truth:

> Trace all the towns the kingdom round,
> One, only one, stands fair to view,
> Where sixty thousand souls are found,
> Govern'd by only constables two;
> Whilst levies eight
> The work complete,
> Who of the management can complain?[36]

The actual number of levies was almost always greater than this, and twenty levies signified a year of particular hardship. Eden's accounts, highly questionable in their accuracy, show the number of 'double levies' increasing from eight in 1786 to twelve in 1790, and the amount of revenue collected as rising from £100,000 per year to £155,000.[37] Nor did this represent the peak of demand. In the year ending in April 1818, according to the accounts published by George Edmonds, there were no less than 33 levies.[38] Yet the £53,157 raised in that year came nowhere near to meeting all the outgoings, which amounted

---

33   S. Williams, *Poverty, Gender and Life-Cycle under the English Poor Law, 1760–1834*, Woodbridge, 2011, p. 71.

34   *Report from His Majesty's Commissioners for Inquiring into the Administration and Practical Operation of the Poor Laws*, Appendix A, Parliamentary Papers, XXIX, 1834, p. 58a.

35   *Aris's Gazette*, 11 January 1830.

36   J. Horden, *John Freeth (1731–1808): Political Ballad-Writer and Innkeeper*, Oxford, 1993, p. 186.

37   Eden, *State of the Poor*, Vol. III, pp. 744–8.

38   Archives and Collections, Library of Birmingham. 65627 BCOL 41.1 Vol. 4, G. Edmonds, *Letter III to the Inhabitants of Birmingham*, Birmingham, 1819, p. 30.

to £62,312. In many instances the overseers asked for double levies, the equivalent of a rate of four shillings in the pound. In 1822–3 there were sixteen double levies, raising a total of £51,005.[39]

Collecting was undertaken door-to-door by two paid assistant overseers, who were obliged to hand over the money once they had amassed more than £20. There were always, of course, rates that were not collected, as is the case with the council tax today. A combination of factors – conscientious objection, tax avoidance and simple hardship – might lead to non-payment. In such cases, goods could be seized, and, more often than not, were auctioned outside the door of the offender. In cases of severe hardship the overseers might grant relief from the levies for a fixed period. The Birmingham vestry clerk told the assistant commissioner in 1833 that 19 per cent of the levies were never collected.[40] There is little evidence that Birmingham householders objected to the paying of poor rates in principle; it was their frequency that irked them. Church rates, which went directly to the Anglican Church, were another matter entirely and were the source of constant complaint in a town with a strong nonconformist population.

Not everyone, however, was liable to pay. Initially, only houses rated at £10 or above were assessed. This equated to a weekly rent of some 4s a week, and for much of the eighteenth and early nineteenth century the actual rent for a back-to-back house was much lower than this, often as little as 1s 6d a week. Indeed, one might argue that the main inducement for property developers and builders to build so many back-to-back houses in the town (as many as 10,000 courts of them) was the fact that they fell below the rating threshold. Over in Handsworth the vestry moved in 1794 'to discourage by every legal means the building of small houses'.[41] It was not simply that such houses did not pay levies; their occupiers, by residence, could also qualify for parochial support, and were the most likely to do so. Thus the early nineteenth century building frenzy populated the city with the very people most likely to claim, yet who did not need to pay.

The economics of this was that Birmingham's Poor Law finances resembled an inverted pyramid, a vast and expensive superstructure, resting on the shoulders of a small number of households. The *Gazette* reported in January 1817 that of the 18,082 residential properties in the town, only 3,893 (less than

---

39   Archives and Collections, Library of Birmingham. 89104A, Birmingham Scrapbook 3, Birmingham Workhouse Accounts 1822–3.

40   *Report for His Majesty's Commissioners for Inquiring into the Administration and Practical Operation of the Poor Laws*, Appendix A, Parliamentary Papers, XXIX, 1834, p. 31a.

41   Archives and Collections, Library of Birmingham. DRO 86/109 Handsworth Vestry minutes, 1784–1822.

one quarter) were assessed for the poor rate, and 'of those which do pay, some pay one in two levies, some one in three'.[42]

Yet the cost of Birmingham's poor relief continued to grow exponentially. William Hutton's *History of Birmingham* produces figures to show that the cost of poor relief almost doubled between 1676, when it was £329, and 1700, and again over the first half of the eighteenth century. In the second half of the century expenditure rose even more rapidly, from £1,168 in 1750 to £22,000 in 1810. James Guest, who edited a subsequent edition of Hutton in 1836, shows a further doubling in the poor rates between 1810 and 1834.[43]

Various means were adopted to square this circle, by selling annuities and by borrowing, the annuities themselves amounting to personal loans by investors. And approval for yet one more levy could always be squeezed out of the magistrates. Yet this situation could not continue (and continue to grow worse) indefinitely, though it took all of four years for a reassessment to be forced past both local and Parliamentary opposition.[44] Hutton, for one, argued that extending the poor rate to lower properties would unduly penalise the small investor, who had put his savings in bricks and mortar. In 1821, however, after much lobbying and heated argument, Parliament approved the rating of all houses valued at £6 and above.[45] The avowed intent was not only to augment the levies, but also to discourage the building of small houses, much as Handsworth had done 30 years before.[46]

The move necessitated the appointment of no less than twelve new assistant overseers to collect the levies from this much expanded property band.[47] A little over 58 per cent of all Birmingham houses were rated at under £10 a year. The vestry clerk in 1833 estimated the number of such properties at 13,945.[48] As a result, Birmingham's parochial finances were miraculously transformed. Parochial relief remained expensive, but now it began to look affordable. Nor was this an end to the issue. The 1831 Guardians' Act extended rating to all properties in the town. There would still be exceptions, those who through personal circumstances were unable to pay, but exceptions were what they now would be.

---

42 *Aris's Gazette*, 27 January 1817.

43 Hutton, *History of Birmingham*, pp. 366–8.

44 *Aris's Gazette*, 16 July 1817.

45 *Aris's Gazette*, 29 January 1821.

46 *Aris's Gazette*, 24 February 1817.

47 The power to appoint salaried assistant overseers had been granted under one of the recent Sturges Bourne Acts: *An Act to Amend the Law for the Relief of the Poor*, 1819, 59 Geo. III c.12.

48 *Report for His Majesty's Commissioners for Inquiring into the Administration and Practical Operation of the Poor Laws*, Appendix A, Parliamentary Papers, XXIX, 1834, p. 58a.

This, then, was the delicate balance between need and obligation at the heart of the Birmingham Poor Law, painstakingly constructed and endlessly modified. We must now consider the evolution of the building which, more than any other, came to symbolise it.

2

'The residence of a gentleman': The Birmingham Workhouse

The workhouse may be deemed the Nursery of Birmingham, in which she deposits her infants for future service: the unfortunate and the idle, till they can be set upon their own basis, and the decrepid [*sic*], during the few remaining sands in their glass.

William Hutton[1]

William Hutton tells us that the Birmingham parish workhouse was built in 1733.[2] This date has been accepted in all subsequent histories of Birmingham, including the *Victoria County History*.[3] Hutton, however, was writing some fifty years after the event, and had not been living in Birmingham at the time; he first saw the town, he tells us, on 14 July 1741, and finally came to settle there in 1750 or 1751. Nor did Hutton have access to the parish records, it appears. In short, and not for the only time in his writings, he got it wrong.[4] Whatever Birmingham's first historian might have thought of Birmingham's original workhouse, or the moral justification for such institutions in general, the town was hardly acting unilaterally in opening one. By the time the Birmingham workhouse was built in the 1730s there were already such 'nurseries' in Bilston, Bromsgrove, Halesowen, Walsall and Wednesbury, to consider only those parishes within the West Midlands. Other towns such as Bristol, Exeter and Hereford had opened workhouses as early as 1696.[5]

---

1   W. Hutton, *The History of Birmingham*, 6th edn, Birmingham, 1836, p. 224.

2   *Ibid.*, pp. 216–17.

3   W.B. Stephens (ed.), 'Political and Administrative History: Local Government and Public Services' in *A History of the County of Warwick: Volume 7: The City of Birmingham*, London, 1964, p. 321.

4   Hutton, *History of Birmingham*, p. 45.

5   G.W. Oxley, *Poor Relief in England and Wales, 1601–1834*, Newton Abbott, 1974, pp. 80–1.

The Act of Parliament empowering parishes to build workhouses, either individually or in combination (Knatchbull's Act), was passed in 1723 and was the first iteration of the so-called 'workhouse test':

> Poor person or persons ... shall be kept in any such house or houses for the better maintenance and relief of such poor person or persons who shall be there kept or maintained and In case any poor person or persons of any parish town, township or place where such house or houses shall be so located or hired, shall refuse to be lodged, kept or maintained in such house or houses, such poor person or persons so refusing shall be put out of the book ... and shall not be entitled to ask or receive collection or relief.[6]

The Act was permissive, however, not compulsory, and few parishes across the West Midlands initially took up the offer. Indeed, such a direct response to the Act appears to have been limited to the two parishes of Birmingham, St Martin's and St Philip's, though the parishes of Aston and Sutton Coldfield followed suit shortly after.[7] The Town Books, which record the joint actions of the two Birmingham parishes, offer us a limited chronology for the process. That the Town Books themselves begin in 1723 suggests an immediate decision to form a union for the purposes of poor relief, though the books themselves cover a variety of other parochial matters as well: pew allocations in St Martin's, maintenance of church plate, and the auditing and passing of the accounts of the constables, churchwardens and overseers. In fact, the Birmingham Town Books in general represent decisions taken by meetings of the town inhabitants, summoned to assemble by the vestries of the two parishes. By way of comparison, the three Coventry parishes united for the purposes of poor relief only in 1801.[8] Prior to that, each ran a separate workhouse.

At a public meeting, held on 16 May 1727, it is reported in the Town Book that the church officials and inhabitants of Birmingham:

> ... do think it highly necessary and convenient that a publick work house be erected in or near the said town to employ and set to work the poor of Birmingham ... for their better maintenance.[9]

---

6   *An Act for Amending the Laws relating to Settlement, Employment and Relief of the Poor*, 1723, 9 Geo. I, c. 7.

7   The second parish of St Philip's had only recently been created in 1708, prior to the erection of the church, now cathedral, in Temple Row.

8   *Abstract of answers and returns made pursuant to the Act of 43 George III relative to the expense and maintenance of the poor in England*, Parliamentary Papers, XIII, 1803–4; *An Act for the Better Relief and Employment of the Poor in the Several Parishes ... of the City of Coventry*, 41 Geo. III, 1801.

9   Archives and Collections, Library of Birmingham. CP B/286011 Town Book, 16 May 1727.

That telling phrase, 'for their better maintenance', became the gloss on all subsequent Acts associated with the Old Poor Law in Birmingham. 'Setting the poor to work' was a phrase directly lifted from the wording of Knatchbull's Act. Clearly Birmingham, a rapidly growing town of industry, was far more comfortable with the idea of a blanket test for those seeking relief and some exchange of labour in return for food and shelter (ideas that only became widely accepted nationwide in the early nineteenth century) than the more traditional, organic communities where kinship and mutual dependence continued to facilitate effective Christian charity and generous poor rates.

No further mention of the objective to construct a workhouse was made for more than three years, until another meeting declared its aim 'to obtain next sessions an Act of Parliament for erecting a work house to be paid out of the public levies'.[10] One assumes that no such step was taken, or indeed was necessary, for the 1723 Act already empowered the parishes to do so. Conrad Gill's claim that such an Act was obtained in 1731 is clearly erroneous.[11] In December 1733 (again in the Town Book) the wording of the May 1727 minute is repeated, with the addition that the poor rates for the following year were all to be paid in a single levy in order to provide the funds for such a move.[12] Such an action was unprecedented, and it is doubtful whether the magistrates would ever have countenanced it. Two more months passed before a list of 21 names, along with all the overseers and churchwardens of the two parishes, were drawn up 'for effectual looking after and governing the work house hereafter to be built'. Public meetings were held in March and April to consider the purchase of land and the 'order of building'.[13]

At the April 1734 meeting, three named individuals, Jonathan Johnson, John Willinger and Samuel Avery, were appointed as 'carpenters and masons', to be paid at an unspecified daily rate, and John Blum was nominated as surveyor of the work.[14] It was immediately after this meeting (16/17 April 1734) that indentures were drawn up between representatives of the parish and a local builder, George Bridgens, for the sale of land between Lichfield Street and what was then known as Whitehalls Lane, later to be called Steelhouse Lane. The cost, amounting to £119 18s 3d, 'being money raised by the inhabitants of the town and parish', must represent all that had been collected thus far.[15] It does not, by any means, represent the total income from a year's levies.

---

10   *Ibid.,* 10 November 1730.

11   C. Gill, *History of Birmingham,* Vol. I, Oxford, 1952, p. 68.

12   Archives and Collections, Library of Birmingham. CP B/266011 Town Book, 3 December 1733.

13   *Ibid.,* 11 February 1734.

14   Archives and Collections, Library of Birmingham. CP B/266011 Town Book, 3 April 1734.

15   *An Act for Better Regulating the Poor within the Parish of Birmingham,* 23 Geo. III c. 54, 1831.

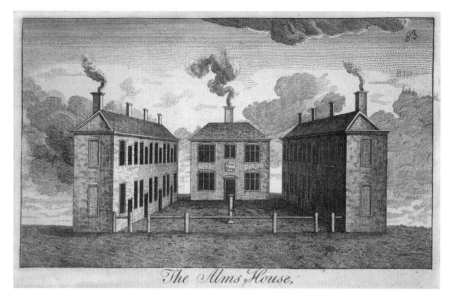

The Alms House.

Figure 2.1 The Birmingham Workhouse, in three buildings. Archives and Collections, Library of Birmingham: MS 897 Volume 1 No. 83

A monthly public meeting was to be held to examine the progress and cost of the work, though no such meetings are recorded in the Town Books, and there is no indication in the surviving records of when the work was completed. It was not yet 'sett on foot' in August 1734, when the parish officials attempted to poach Samuel Whitley, the master of the Wolverhampton workhouse, for the Birmingham workhouse, at an annual salary not exceeding £25. This appointment was not entirely cut-and-dried, in that Whitley's assistance was also sought to 'procure a proper person to do the business of a master', if he was unwilling to take up the position himself.[16] We must guess, therefore, that the workhouse in Lichfield Street opened at some point soon after this, late in 1734 or in 1735. The earliest surviving accounts for the Birmingham workhouse (a single volume, covering 1739–48) begin in August 1739.[17] Hutton's comment that the building cost £1,173 3s 5d to erect cannot be verified from the surviving evidence.[18]

Unfortunately, this is not the end of William Hutton's confusion, or of his successors'. The historian's proud description of the workhouse, 'which a

---

16   Archives and Collections, Library of Birmingham. CP B/266011 Town Book, 7 August 1734.

17   Archives and Collections, Library of Birmingham. CP B/380973 Accounts of the Birmingham Workhouse and Record of Out-Relief to the Poor, 1739–48.

18   W. Hutton, *The History of Birmingham*, 2nd edn, Birmingham, 1783, p. 216.

stranger would rather suppose was the residence of a gentleman, than that of four hundred paupers', is sufficiently vindicated by the engraving that accompanies Hutton's text. It shows a two-storey building, with attic or dormer windows, and two wings, together with a central bell-tower supporting a weather-vane and clock. Hutton tells us that the left wing, 'called the infirmary', was added in 1766, at a cost of £400, and the right wing, a 'place of industry', in 1779 at a cost of £700. We might add that James Guest's edition of Hutton's work, edited and updated posthumously, alters the date of the right-hand wing to 1799.[19]

Here again, Hutton's dates for the two wings, perhaps because they are so confidently priced, have always been accepted as accurate. Yet the maps of Birmingham tell a very different story. William Westley's first plan of the town, dated 1731, shows the space at the north-eastern end of Lichfield Street unoccupied. By 1750, the date of Samuel Bradford's plan, the workhouse is already shown with its two wings, and a small block behind, which appears to be labelled 'infirmary', though we ought not to put too much confidence in labels, which were often positioned for the convenience of the printer. Thomas Hanson's plan of 1778 likewise shows a building with two wings. By this date the workhouse buildings are shown as occupying the whole site bounded by Lichfield Street (also spelt 'Litchfield' on some maps) to the south (with a frontage to the street of 65 yards) and Steelhouse Lane to the north. The label 'infirmary' has migrated across the road to the far side of Steelhouse Lane, almost certainly for convenience of printing. All the evidence, then, suggests that the Birmingham workhouse was first constructed with its two wings already attached. At this point, according to the returns submitted to Parliament, the house could already accommodate 340 residents, making it by some distance the largest workhouse in Warwickshire.[20] As early as the 1790s Frederick Eden was finding the failure to provide a detached site for the workhouse a major design fault, a problem only increased by the later annexation of adjacent property and expansion of the infirmary. That aside, he declared the place 'clean, and tolerably convenient'.[21]

If the workhouse was first erected 'to set the poor to work', what employment could be provided there? We know that the inmates were undertaking some kind of work by 1740, when the workhouse accounts record a payment of 14s 9d 'paid to encouragement – money for people that work in the house', though

19   Hutton, *History of Birmingham*, 6th edn, p. 362.

20   *Reports from Committees of the House of Commons*, first series, IX, 1774–1802, p. 287.

21   F.M. Eden, *The State of the Poor*, Vol. III, London, 1797, p. 737.

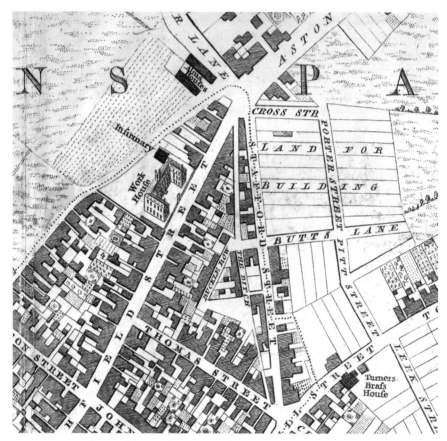

Figure 2.2 Part of map of Birmingham surveyed by Samuel Bradford, 1750, showing the Workhouse and its infirmary on Lichfield Street. Archives and Collections, Library of Birmingham: MAL 14002

this may only refer to domestic duties.[22] There is also a subsequent payment for 'the repairing of the twisting mill'.[23] In short, the inmates were making string. Pack-thread (strong thread used for securing parcels or packages) was still being made by the paupers in 1754, when the overseers were planning to erect new buildings for this manufactory. A town meeting put a stop to this idea, at least in the short term.[24] R.K. Dent misjudges the tone of this entry: the meeting was not a protest against the manufacture of pack-thread in itself, or of

---

22   Archives and Collections, Library of Birmingham. CP B/380973 Accounts of the Birmingham Workhouse and Record of Out-Relief to the Poor, January 1740.

23   *Ibid.*, January 1746.

24   Archives and Collections, Library of Birmingham. CP B/286011 Town Book, 24 September 1754.

any other article, only against the cost to the ratepayers of additional building to accommodate such activities.[25]

Here too William Hutton's account is clearly confused. According to Hutton, the manufacture of pack-thread was introduced into the workhouse in 1754, and the spinning of mop-yarn in 1766. Neither of these dates can be correct. We must assume that Hutton did not know much about the early activities of Birmingham workhouse, and that his informant, whoever that was, mis-remembered much.[26] All of William Hutton's remarks, we should add, were made in the context of ever-increasing poor rates. Whatever the overseers did, he moaned, 'the levies still increased'.[27] And in that, at least, Hutton was perfectly accurate.

As all the maps confirm, then, Birmingham's first workhouse stood with its main gate and façade facing onto Lichfield Street, that is, on the left side of the street as one headed north-eastwards out of town. It was, at least until the opening of the Public Office in Moor Street in 1807, the most striking public building in the town and one of very few to have had a clock. An entry in the surviving eighteenth-century accounts records a payment of 12s 6d to Thomas Brown 'for cleansing both ye clocks', probably the one on the central bell tower and a smaller time-piece inside.[28] Time-keeping, inside or out, had an essential role to play in measuring out the paupers' days.

Architecturally, there was little in the overall design of the Birmingham house which was innovative. The poorhouse in Lichfield Street looked much like other workhouses built at Chatham and Hull at this time, and a similar cupola could also be seen at Liverpool workhouse, St George's in Hanover Square in London and at Exeter. The latter also boasted a clock.[29] The central bell-tower and clock probably have their origins in the design of almshouses, which in a sense were the seed-bed from which the workhouse system itself grew. One such set of almshouses, provided by Lench's Trust, already stood nearby in Steelhouse Lane. That bell, of course, would have had a salutary psychological effect on the area too, a mournful sound recorded by the novelist, George Gissing, whose career, he always anticipated, was itself but one step from the workhouse:

The various sounds which marked the stages from midnight to dawn had grown miserably familiar to him; worst torture to his mind was the chiming and striking of clocks. Two of these were in general audible, that of Marylebone parish church, and that of the adjoining

---

25 R.K. Dent, *The Making of Birmingham*, Birmingham, 1894, p. 107.

26 Hutton, *History of Birmingham*, 2nd edn, pp. 363–4.

27 Hutton, *History of Birmingham*, 6th edn, p. 371.

28 Archives and Collections, Library of Birmingham. CP B/380973 Accounts of the Birmingham Workhouse and Record of Out-Relief to the Poor, 4 November 1748.

29 K. Morrison, *The Workhouse: A Study of Poor-Law Buildings in England*, Swindon, 1999, pp. 11–30.

workhouse; the latter always sounded several minutes after its ecclesiastical neighbour, and with a difference of note which seemed to Reardon very appropriate – a thin, querulous voice, reminding one of the community it represented.[30]

What is self-evidently true is that Birmingham's workhouse was not hidden away, and William Hutton's comments on its gentlemanly appearance were not misplaced. In his perambulation of the town, William West referred to the institution's 'considerable magnitude ... well suited to the extent of the town and its population'.[31] Nor was Lichfield Street itself some insignificant backwater, though there is no doubt that it was considerably decayed by the 1870s, when Joseph Chamberlain's Improvement Scheme (under the terms of the Artisans' Dwellings Act, 1875) swept it from the map. In the eighteenth and early nineteenth centuries, however, Lichfield Street was quite different. Indeed, in 1827, when the overseers were worrying about the state of the pavement outside the workhouse, they described the road thus:

Lichfield Street is the great thoroughfare from York, Manchester, Sheffield, Derby, Lichfield and other places of the north to the Royal Hotel, the News Room, St Philip's, the Post Office and the residences of the professional gentlemen.[32]

By the latter was meant the physicians and surgeons, whose houses and surgeries were invariably located in Old Square and Temple Row. The workhouse carts and 'the carriages of the nobility and gentry' did, indeed, share the same stretch of road.[33] The very presence of the workhouse, however, had an inevitably depressive effect upon the neighbourhood, and by 1839 even the comparatively low rent of three shillings a week was considered too high for the houses 'in the court above the infirmary'.[34] In 1837 the town missionary, Thomas Finigan, whose district included Lichfield Street, was declaring it '... the very worst part in all Birmingham. The courts abound with poor prostitutes, with idle fellows, with wretched beggars, rag-pickers and bone-gatherers.'[35] It was not only Lichfield Street that Finigan had in mind; the neighbouring streets of John

30 G. Gissing, *New Grub Street*, London, 1891, chap. 9, p. 108.

31 W. West, *The History, Topography and Directory of Warwickshire*, Birmingham, 1830, p. 222.

32 Archives and Collections, Library of Birmingham. CP B/660984 Birmingham Overseers' Minutes, Vol. 3, 18 September 1827.

33 Archives and Collections, Library of Birmingham. GP B/2/9/1/1 Birmingham Guardians, Estates Committee minutes, 1839.

34 *Ibid.*

35 Archives and Collections, Library of Birmingham. MS 3255 Thomas Finigan's Journal, 7 August 1837, pp. 40–1. There is also a transcript of the diary, published by the Birmingham Irish Heritage Group: T.A. Finigan, *Journal of Thomas Augustine Finigan*, Birmingham, 2010.

Street, Thomas Street and London-Prentice Street were, if anything, even more run down. Steelhouse Lane too, by the mid-1830s, was being described as 'one of the most disorderly streets in town, from the numbers of lower orders of Irish that infested it'.[36] As early as 1818, one of the Lichfield Street residents described its atmosphere as 'contaminated'.[37] It was this steady decline in the social standing, the rateable value and the life expectations of its inhabitants, which paved the way for Chamberlain's Improvement Scheme itself.

If the surroundings were not grim enough already, there was the growing problem of 'trampers', collecting in the evening for admission to the workhouse casual ward, and by 1840 the authorities were seeking help from the chief constable to control and direct this crowd.[38] Indeed, it had become one of the duties of the newly formed Birmingham police force to arrest 'those who linger about the town to the annoyance of the inhabitants', and deliver them to the workhouse. The instinct to re-define casual poor relief as a 'law and order' issue is a significant innovation at this time.[39] There was an additional 'annoyance' on Lichfield Street on Fridays, when out-relief was paid. Street hawkers, selling 'useless articles to the poor', gathered in front of the workhouse to relieve the re-enriched paupers of a little of their new money.[40]

Nevertheless, Birmingham's workhouse would continue to occupy this site until 1852, when a new workhouse (and later an infirmary) were built on Birmingham Heath, now known as Winson Green. But that is not to say that the institution erected in 1734 was not subject to change, both inside and outside. It was, in fact, in a constant state of expansion and modification, as surviving records readily demonstrate. The sheer number of individuals requiring indoor relief in the rapidly growing town made such adaptation unavoidable. Nor was its continuation in Lichfield Street as late as 1852 a matter of universal acceptance. The guardians and overseers occasionally, and the polemical writers of pamphlets often, advocated removing the house to a more spacious site and they were doing so less than 50 years after it went up. A pamphlet of 1782 put forward the first proposal, at a time when the current premises was already overcrowded. The anonymous author claimed that, at

---

36 *Aris's Gazette*, 25 August 1836.

37 'H.W.S.', *Plain Truth, or a Correct Statement of the Late Events Relative to the Birmingham Workhouse*, Birmingham, n.d. [1818?], p. 32.

38 Archives and Collections, Library of Birmingham. CP B/660987 Birmingham Overseers' Minutes, Vol. 6, 14 April 1840.

39 See A. Eccles, *Vagrancy in Law and Practice under the Old Poor Law*, Aldershot, 2012, pp. 115–38.

40 Archives and Collections, Library of Birmingham. CP B/660987 Birmingham Overseers' Minutes, Vol. 6, 14 April 1840.

this time, the workhouse was crammed with 630 inmates.[41] This was the first of many such protests over the years. Ten years later Job Nott likewise proposed a new poorhouse:

> This house ought to be built in a way that the poor might be divided; for it is shocking that a reduced decent person should be obliged to herd with the vilest and dirtiest of the human species. There should be work-rooms, also, and every body obliged to work that can.[42]

In 1783 Birmingham obtained an Act of Parliament (23 Geo. III c. 54) 'for the better management of the poor and to provide a proper workhouse'. The Local Act declared the current workhouse 'greatly insufficient' to receive the numbers of paupers applying for admission. The 1783 Act put forward four good reasons for a new building: better accommodation for the sick, diseased and infirm; more systematic employment of the industrious; correction of the idle and profligate; and the education of the infant poor 'in habits of industry, religion and honesty'. In suitable conditions, the Act continued, the parish might even profit from their labour. This last clause, it must be said, was probably more designed to sell the Bill to the ratepayers than to establish the ground rules for the new institution. It also demonstrates that Birmingham overseers were influenced by the campaigning work of Thomas Gilbert, MP for Lichfield, who had introduced a bill into parliament in 1782 for the creation of poor law unions which would then build good quality workhouses across the country.[43]

The possibility of replacing Lichfield Street must have been a topic of active discussion in the drafting of the Local Act, and it remained so after its passing. The *Gazette* reported in March 1783 that a public meeting was held to canvass support for three alternative sites. The rector of St Martin's offered a piece of land, said to be between 18 and 20 acres, near the Sand Pits, at £8 a year rent. Two more possible locations on wasteland to the west of the town, at Key Hill or on Birmingham Heath, were also considered.[44] But the discussions apparently went no further. Every ambitious proposal, whether to move the workhouse, build a separate lunatic asylum or a new infirmary, floundered in the face of ratepayer resistance and political suspicion, or became bogged down in endless

---

41 Anon., *The Present Situation of the Town of Birmingham Respecting its Poor, considered. With a Proposal for Building a New Workhouse*, Birmingham, 1782, p. 9.

42 'Supplementary Gleanings, Collected in the Years 1782 and 1783 on the Warwickshire Station, including the Communications of J. Morfitt Esq. from S.J. Pratt', in S.J. Pratt, *Harvest Home, Consisting of Supplementary Gleanings, Original Dramas and Poems, Contributions of Literary Friends and Select Re-publications*, Vol. 1, London, 1805, p. 290.

43 D. Owen, *English Philanthropy, 1660–1960*, Cambridge, MA, 1964, p. 86.

44 *Aris's Gazette*, 3 March 1783.

arguments about the cost, as did many other parishes which attempted to set up a 'Gilbert Union'. No such arguments are extant in the official records, though an anonymous poem published in the *Gazette* in April 1783 gives some hint of the tenor of public debate:

> And as it seems that some do now devise
> To build a workhouse of the largest size,
> In which the poor may health and comfort find,
> And forc'd to work those lazily inclin'd ...
> Then, as such blessings may attend the scheme,
> 'Tis strange that men the motive should misdeem,
> Or strive to quash what (fully understood)
> So pregnant does appear with public good.[45]

Thus the idea was shelved, the opportunity missed, and the authorities continued to pursue a policy of 'make do and mend'. This was perhaps the only middle course to be found between accusations of reckless expenditure on the one hand, and of penny-pinching inhumanity on the other. Unanimity and the Poor Law never marched hand-in-hand. A further Bill 'to amend the Act of 23 George III' did not even reach the Commons.

Ultimately it was the public meeting itself which acted as the major stumbling block to reform and relocation. Unincorporated towns such as Birmingham relied on public meetings, in reality a gathering of ratepayers, to direct public policy, unlike those parishes that did enact Gilbert's Act and managed to replace the overseers with paid 'guardians' of the poor, chosen by the leading ratepayers of the Union.[46] The so-called Town Books represent the outcome of such assemblies. It was a public meeting that launched the workhouse in the first place and later authorised the first Sunday Schools in the town; even the opening of a humble soup shop was felt to require the endorsement of a general meeting.[47] But the body was inherently conservative when it came to spending money, and many a bright idea withered when tossed into the public arena. It took the Birmingham Guardians Act of 1831 for that obligation to win public support to be discreetly removed from the town's Poor Law arrangements, as other Unions had managed under Gilbert's Act after 1782. After a century of acting as a quasi-sovereign body in parish affairs, the town meeting was thus shunted into a siding. It had, in the words of the Commissioners' Report of

---

45   *Aris's Gazette*, 21 April 1783.

46   A. Brundage, *The English Poor Laws, 1700–1930*, Basingstoke, 2002, p. 21.

47   *Aris's Gazette*, 11 January 1830.

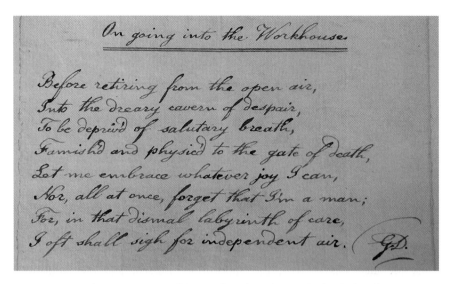

Figure 2.3 Poem by George Davis of Birmingham (*c*.1790–1819) who died in the Workhouse. 'On going into the Workhouse', 'the dreary cavern of despair'. Archives and Collections, Library of Birmingham: MS 3456, p. 51

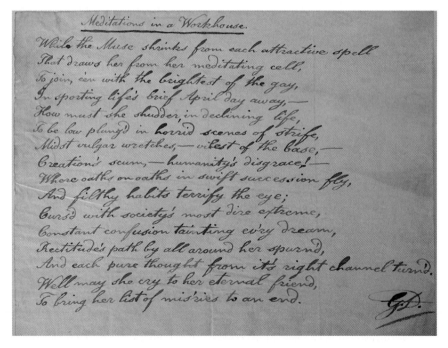

Figure 2.4 Poem by George Davis of Birmingham (*c*.1790–1819) who died in the Workhouse. 'Meditations in a Workhouse', 'in horrid scenes of strife, midst vulgar wretches, – vilest of the base – Creations's scum – humanity's disgrace!' Archives and Collections, Library of Birmingham: MS 3456, p. 55

1832, become 'very defective'.[48] Then, and only then, could the guardians begin to think seriously about finding an alternative to Lichfield Street. The Act of 1831, building on the benefit of hindsight, provided the legal foundation for the move to Winson Green, empowering the guardians to identify land, lease-hold or free-hold, and to borrow sums to build on it.

Perhaps the greatest challenges of all faced by the Birmingham guardians were the alarming fluctuations in workhouse admission, and in the overall size of the institution. When required to submit average statistics of occupancy to Parliament in 1803–4, the parish clerk was quick to point out that the figure given (360) took no account of the peaks and troughs of demand:

> This was the average number of poor in the house from Easter 1802 to Easter 1803. Before that period the poor in the house were a more fluctuating body, there being in the house from five to seven or eight hundred, and at one period during the year 1801, upwards of one thousand.[49]

The lack of distinction between classes of inmates, an inevitable consequence of overcrowding, was the most common criticism of what was on offer in Lichfield Street. As a result, in contemporary parlance, the deserving and the undeserving poor rubbed shoulders, and privacy and comfort were entirely absent. George Davis, Birmingham's very own workhouse poet, who died within its walls in 1819, no more valued the presence of many of his fellow inmates than the guardians did. In a poem probably datable to 1816, Davis laments his lot, driven from the open air 'into that dismal labyrinth of care'.

> Midst vulgar wretches – vilest of the base –
> Creation's scum – humanity's disgrace –
> Where oaths on oaths in swift succession fly,
> And filthy habits terrify the eye.[50]

Such complaints inevitably increased at times of highest pressure, itself a reflection of external economic forces. Occupancy statistics, released to the press or minuted at public meetings, help to chart those overall peaks and troughs. One peak coincided with the recession of 1795, made all the more

---

48 *Ninth Annual Report of the Poor Law Commissioners, Appendix A: Reports of Assistant Commissioners, No. 2, Mr Power and Mr Weale's Report on Birmingham*, London, 1843, p. 234.

49 *Abstract of answers and returns made pursuant to the Act of 43 George III relative to the expense and maintenance of the poor in England*, Parliamentary Papers, XIII, 1803–4.

50 Archives and Collections, Library of Birmingham. MS 3456 [413435] Poems of George Davis, 1790–1819.

severe by an extreme winter and the high price of bread. In September 1795, when there were still 403 paupers in the house, the overseers congratulated themselves on having reduced their numbers 'to two-thirds of what they were a few months ago'.[51] That claim turned out to be rather premature. Setting aside seasonal variations, the numbers in the house continued to grow, reaching a peak of 663 in January 1798, necessitating the construction of an asylum for the infant poor in Summer Lane to which children over the age of four were transferred.[52] After that, the overseers stopped releasing weekly figures to the press. A figure supplied to Samuel Pratt by the workhouse master, George Hinchcliffe, shows the number of inmates reaching an unprecedented 1,094 in July 1801.[53] This demonstrates that Birmingham conformed to the national trend of a sharp increase in the poor relief burden in the 1790s, caused by bad weather and poor harvests as well as war and the political disruption in continental Europe.[54]

There was little to be done to stem the flow of admissions to the house at times like this. Yet the judicious application of the law might limit applications for out-relief a little. In July 1786 the Birmingham vestry voted to refuse applications from anyone who kept a dog.[55] This was not a policy, it has to be said, limited to Birmingham, but it reflected the widespread assumption (not without foundation) that the labouring classes kept dogs, not as pets, but to earn them money, either by hunting with them or fighting them. Two years later, anyone found guilty of 'tippling', or seen in a state of drunkenness, had his or her payment withdrawn.[56] Alongside these changes, the parish circulated lists of absent fathers, and threatened to prosecute anyone found to be harbouring a pregnant woman.[57]

The mid-1810s represented the second crisis of this kind. Problems of overcrowding, probably more sporadic than permanent, dogged the authorities constantly during the post-Waterloo depression of trade.[58] As a temporary measure, in 1817 premises were taken in Water Street to provide extra 'sleeping rooms'.[59] Whether the overcrowding in 1819 was as bad as the campaigner

51 *Aris's Gazette*, 14 September 1795.

52 *Aris's Gazette*, 8 January 1798.

53 Pratt, *Harvest Home*, Vol. 1, p. 377.

54 A.J. Kidd, *State, Society and the Poor in Nineteenth-Century England*, Basingstoke, 1999, p. 168.

55 *Aris's Gazette*, 11 July 1796.

56 *Aris's Gazette*, 15 October 1798.

57 *Aris's Gazette*, 26 August 1799.

58 D. Eastwood, *Governing Rural England: Tradition and Transformation in Local Government, 1780–1840*, Oxford, 1994, p. 130.

59 Archives and Collections, Library of Birmingham. CP B/660983 Birmingham Overseers' Minutes, Vol. 2, 22 July 1817.

George Edmonds alleged is hard to say, but his report carries a certain vivid realism about it:

> The old women eat and drink and sleep all in one room and to increase the noisome stench of the place, there are a large number of them, and they have large fires. There also opens into this room another small room. I saw also some sweet children, six in one bed, and as they were disposed at the head and feet of the bed, I thought there only wanted an old sow, to lie in the middle, and then the degrading picture would be complete.[60]

A detailed report on the state of the house in December 1816 does, indeed, confirm that 177 children and three adult women were sharing just 25 beds in the 'children's sleeping room'. At this point the workhouse as a whole contained 244 beds, shared by 260 males, 265 females and 250 children. In every room, other than in the infirmary, beds were being shared, even in the lying-in ward. In the 'old garret', for example, 82 men and 20 boys shared the 32 beds, whilst in the 'new garret' 78 men and 27 boys slept in 34 beds.[61] A newspaper report from May 1816 suggests that there were 941 inmates in the house at this time, falling to 752 by October 1817.[62] The respite in 1817 and 1818 was followed by another surge in numbers in the summer of 1819. Once more, according to Edmonds, the workhouse was 'rapidly populating'. 'In the last month,' he added, 'three hundred to four hundred were added to the poor.'[63] The numbers in the adjacent infirmary were also growing, reaching 110 by July.[64]

The overcrowding reported in 1819 mercifully turned out to be a high-water mark. As alternative means to support the able-bodied were explored, such as temporary labour schemes to employ them at a minimum wage outside the workhouse, so the numbers occupying the workhouse slowly fell. By 1834 the average number of inmates declared in the guardians' annual reports had been reduced to 377 in 1833/4,[65] to 363 in 1835/6[66] and to 360 in 1836/7.[67] By October 1836 Henry Knight, then chairman of the board of guardians, was able to claim that there were no longer any able-bodied inmates in the house at all, other than eight individuals (two male and six female), who were retained

---

60   G. Edmonds, *Letter VII to the Inhabitants of Birmingham*, Birmingham, 1819, p. 112.

61   Archives and Collections, Library of Birmingham. CP B/660983 Birmingham Overseers' Minutes, Vol. 2, 24 December 1816.

62   *Aris's Gazette*, 20 October 1817.

63   *Edmonds' Weekly Recorder*, 26 June 1819.

64   *Edmonds' Weekly Recorder*, 3 July 1819.

65   *Birmingham Journal*, 5 July 1834.

66   *Birmingham Journal*, 25 June 1836.

67   *Birmingham Journal*, 24 June 1837.

as nurses or domestic servants.[68] 'Were they to be dismissed,' warned Knight, 'hiring labour would cost more.' Henry Knight's report provides a useful snapshot of the ages and classes of the residents at this point in time.

	Male	Female	Total
70 years and over	29	22	51
Aged 50–70	30	28	58
Lame and blind	16	3	19
Insane and idiotic	41	59	100
Lying-in		2	2
Women with infants		10	10
Infants	5	7	12
Infirmary	29	30	59
Aged 7–12	11	7	18
Able-bodied	2	6	8
Total	163	174	337[69]

However, that improved situation also proved to be temporary. By 1838, as Birmingham fell once more into recession, along with the rest of the country, the numbers of inmates began to rise yet again, reaching an annual average of 474 in 1838.[70] The recession kicked in with remarkable speed and ferocity early in the summer of 1837. A group of Birmingham merchants and manufacturers warned Lord Melbourne in March that 'unless remedial measures be immediately applied, a large proportion of our population will immediately be thrown entirely out of employment'.[71] The warning appeared to be justified as Knight reported the number of new applications for relief as rising from 219 in mid-May to 733 by mid-June.[72]

The situation had probably eased somewhat by 1839, when an average of 400 inmates occupied the house.[73] Nevertheless, the report presented to the guardians in July 1839 by the new workhouse committee revealed a less than attractive picture. There were, they said, five wards in the house, 'parcelled into thirty chambers', along with seven apartments in the infirmary and nine in the

68 *Birmingham Journal*, 15 October 1836.

69 *Birmingham Journal*, 15 October 1836.

70 *Birmingham Journal*, 23 June 1838.

71 *Edinburgh Review*, vol. 65, no. 131, April 1837, p. 82.

72 *Birmingham Journal*, 17 June 1837.

73 Archives and Collections, Library of Birmingham. GP B/2/1/4 Birmingham Guardians' minutes, 2 July 1839.

lunatic asylum. With an occupancy rate of six to ten persons to each chamber, it seems that the problem of overcrowding had largely been overcome. But it had been replaced, in the committee's eyes, by equally pressing concerns about poor ventilation and the lack of adequate supervision.

> In addition to two or three very small courts, the only ground for exercise is a space about twenty yards square, surrounded by the workhouse on all sides. And three of the four sides very lofty as to preclude the free circulation of air.[74]

The whole building, with the exception of the recently completed infirmary and insane wards, they called dilapidated. Nor were these defects that could be solved by a judicious lick of paint. 'The walls in several places,' commented the committee, 'are in a decayed and dangerous condition, and the floors and roofing unsound.' Robert Weale, the assistant Poor Law commissioner, entirely concurred. 'The workhouse in Lichfield Street,' added Weale, 'is an old building and very ill-adapted to the purpose to which it is applied.'[75] Yet the new workhouse to address these shortcomings (and many others to boot) would not be forthcoming for a further thirteen years. This is puzzling as Felix Driver has demonstrated that the Poor Law Commissioners were active in pressuring Unions to update or replace their workhouses in the years 1835–49, with £588,000 authorised to be spent on altering existing workhouses to suit the demands of the 'New' Poor Law.[76] Birmingham, as a 'Local Act' Union, already in existence, may simply have evaded the control of the Poor Law Commission until the workhouse scandals of the mid-1840s forced a more systematic response to the inadequacies of workhouses from both central and local authorities.

The workhouse finally relinquished in 1852 would have looked very different to the one first erected in 1734 and shown in the early engravings. As we will see elsewhere, a new infirmary was completed in 1794, and new insane wards in 1835. In addition, what amounted to a new chapel was built in 1821, to designs by Thomas Rickman.[77] A local artist added the royal coat of arms (gratis) as a finishing touch in July 1822.[78] The parish authorities also continued to nibble away at adjacent property in Lichfield Street and Steelhouse Lane with a view to expansion. In 1835, however, having purchased 70 and 71 Lichfield Street and

---

74   *Ibid.*

75   *Ninth Annual Report of the Poor Law Commissioners*, London, 1843, p. 145.

76   F. Driver, *Power and Pauperism: The Workhouse System 1834–1884*, Cambridge, 1993, pp. 73–81.

77   Archives and Collections, Library of Birmingham. CP B/660983 Birmingham Overseers' Minutes, Vol. 2, 21 December 1821.

78   Archives and Collections, Library of Birmingham. CP B/660984 Birmingham Overseers' Minutes, Vol. 3, 30 July 1822.

Figure 2.5 The Birmingham Workhouse, with adjoining buildings. Archives and Collections, Library of Birmingham: MS 897 Volume 1 No. 88

the court of houses behind, the vestry elected to rent them out and pocket the cash, rather than spend money converting them into extra accommodation. This was still the case in 1852.[79] Each of the front houses brought in rent of £20 a year, and the seven back houses were rented out at 3s a week. Yet for all the problems of ageing buildings, along with the need for separate medical provision for those who were physically or mentally ill, and the lack of clear differentiation between classes of inmates, the guardians were remarkably successful in managing the numbers of paupers resident in Lichfield Street. Every possible means – tighter criteria for admission, separate provision for children, work schemes for the unemployed and so on – was deployed to keep numbers under control.

There were, as we have seen, periods of high demand for relief, indoor and outdoor, directly linked to the performance of the economy. Were there also seasonal factors to take into account? From January 1826 to 1840 the numbers of inmates appear each quarter in the guardians' minutes (in January, April, July and October), allowing us to map the rise and fall much more closely. The pattern these figures reveal, we may assume, reflected the wider economic climate, the cost of food, the availability of employment and therefore the ability of the poor to support themselves without recourse to the overseers. Seasonal illnesses could also lead to increased demand. The total of inmates

---

79   Archives and Collections, Library of Birmingham. GP B/2/9/3/1 Birmingham Guardians' Estates and Law Committee minutes, 1849–53.

invariably rose from October to January, and continued to rise through to April, falling through the summer months, levelling off around October, and rising again thereafter. The fall in numbers over the summer months had two probable causes. Firstly, the warmer weather meant that the homeless were less inclined to swap the streets for the casual ward. Secondly, the availability of agricultural work provided employment on the farms outside Birmingham. 'The approaching harvest,' commented the *Gazette* in July 1816, 'will find work for thousands'.[80] There were also a number of ways by which the parish sought to reduce the numbers of resident paupers. Able-bodied men were deployed to the labour colonies at Key Hill and Winson Green after 1801, but, conversely, some who had been sent to private lunatic asylums returned to live in the house. The attraction of the workhouse as a place of last resort probably also varied in accordance with the regime. Nor, we can guess, did the exact rules for admission to in-house and outdoor relief remain constant throughout the period. No evidence survives to clarify the particulars of this.

Finally, it should be added that these general figures for occupancy in no way indicate the levels of traffic into and out of the workhouse, at least in the earlier period. Surviving records do not measure the rate of admission and discharge, except for two years in 1812–13. In those years the average number of inmates remained almost constant: 442 at Easter 1812 and 449 at Easter 1813. Yet the number of admissions per year averaged over 1,000 persons. It would appear from this that the length of time able-bodied persons spent in the workhouse was often very short indeed. In the 1770s, the period covered by the one surviving admission and discharge register, a new inmate was admitted to the house every two days or so, but this was matched by an equal rate of discharges.[81] Each admission told a story, if only we had them to read, and concluded a set of negotiated decisions taken by pauper, overseer and clerk. How great was the need? How full was the house? An exchange between the bench at the Public Office and Elizabeth Cox in March 1840 reveals the thinking of one 'incorrigible old offender', as the reporter from the *Birmingham Journal* called her. The magistrate in question was Harry Gem, credited with the invention of lawn tennis. He would undoubtedly have enjoyed the match.

Cox: Send me to gaol, as I would rather spend twenty years in gaol than one week in the workhouse.

Gem: How do you know the difference between the two places?

Cox: Because I have tried them both.

---

80   *Aris's Gazette*, 8 July 1816.

81   Archives and Collections, Library of Birmingham. GP B/19 Birmingham Pauper Admission and Discharge Register, 1767–76.

Gem: Well, the magistrates will now send you to the House of Correction for one calendar month.

Cox: Oh, send me for two!

Gem: No, the magistrates will now only send you for one month. But if you come again, they will send you for three.

Cox: God spare your life, I'll be here again![82]

This constantly contracting and expanding institution required considerable skills of management and financial adroitness to control, not to mention the wider demands of poor relief outside the house. Both the Birmingham guardians and the overseers had a formidable job on their hands, and the paid employees even more so.

---

82   *Birmingham Journal*, 21 March 1840.

3

A Day in the Life

In 1830 an anonymous official picked up a copy of the printed regulations of Birmingham workhouse (copies of which were widely distributed) and added, in pen, a brief description of the institution (see Appendix 1). Before the Royal Commission began to collect reports a couple of years later, such overviews rarely existed. The document thus provides us with an invaluable snapshot of the daily life of the parish workhouse almost a century after its creation.[1] At the moment the anonymous writer took up his pen the workhouse in Lichfield Street contained 478 pauper inmates (198 men, 195 women and 85 children). Most of the children would have been no more than four years old; older children were sent to the Asylum for the Infant Poor in Summer Lane, where, in 1830, there were 340 residents. The figure for the workhouse proper represents a considerable reduction from the high-point of 800 or so, reached in the winter of 1800.[2] A new deluge of applications would begin when the local economy dipped again in the middle of the decade.

The 1830 document, together with snippets of information in the minute books, allows us, albeit tentatively, to reconstruct a typical day in the Birmingham workhouse in the early nineteenth century. The hand-written document indicates the various ways that the guardians and overseers provided the poor with labour. We can divide this into in-house labour and outside work (the latter discussed in greater depth in chapter 13). The women in the house were given domestic work to perform and an institution housing almost 500 people provided plenty of that. No women at this time were employed in any manufacturing work. For the men the work was more varied. A handful of

---

1   Archives and Collections, Library of Birmingham. MS 2126/EB9/1829 Regulations of Birmingham Workhouse (with annotations dated 1830). See Appendix.

2   Archives and Collections, Library of Birmingham. GP/B/2/1/1 Birmingham Guardians' minutes, 30 November 1800.

them (the writer suggests between thirteen and seventeen) were sent daily to the flour mills on Steelhouse Lane, where they operated hand mills to grind the corn. The rest of the males spent their working hours either about the house or in outside work.

A few of the boys were sent out to work in the town's factories, bringing their wages back with them, but most were apprenticed out once they were old enough. The parish still owned the sand mine at Key Hill, where more of the male inmates, along with those applying for casual relief, were sent to dig sand and then wheel it to the parish wharf. The rest of the able-bodied men were engaged in stone-breaking or road-making, the casual poor being paid one shilling a day for this. Children in the asylum were not spared useful toil either. At this date 124 children were working in the pin manufactory next door, 11 were engaged in glass polishing and 56 were making lace. The cost of accommodating each pauper in the house was estimated at 2s 11d per week and in the asylum at 1s 11d, though any productive labour would partly offset these costs. The writer of the report does not enumerate or mention the many paupers who were either in the infirmary or were too old or too young to work. It was the productivity (or lack of it) of the able-bodied which interested him. The author also sets down, since they were freely available and published in the local press, the Birmingham Poor Law accounts for the year ending Lady Day 1830. The salaries itemised here are complicated by the fact that not only the cashier, but also the governor and governess, died during that year and indeed there is an expenditure of £136 13s 6½d on 'public funerals' for the three individuals concerned. Wages are recorded for the governor and governess, cashier, house and vestry clerks and their assistants and for the visitors to the out-poor and assistant overseers. Visitors were employed to attend the out-poor in their own homes 'and to get information generally as to the real necessities of the applicants for relief'.[3] Such work might also include interviews with employers, if individuals were in part-time employment. Such is the sum of the information provided by the anonymous writer sometime in 1830. At the back of the volume, taking advantage of a few more blank pages, the same man berates and lambasts the way the grammar school in New Street was being run and managed. Overall, the two sections sound like the *cri de coeur* of one of the ratepaying middle classes, squeezed by ever-increasing poor rates on the one side and failed by the education system on the other. It was ever thus.

As we have already pointed out, the Poor Law itself was in a constant state of reorganisation, but much of the workhouse routine remained the same. The workhouse was, indeed, a place of routine. Whether that felt comfortable or

---

3   *Report from His Majesty's Commissioners for Inquiring into the Administration and Practical Operation of the Poor Laws*, Appendix G, Parliamentary Papers, XXIX, 1834, p. 289g.

suffocating depended upon the individual inmate, but it was certainly a matter of reassurance to the guardians. Once they had established the arrangement, it was principally only deviations from it that came to their attention. The rules drawn up by a sub-committee of guardians in 1783 and subsequently printed set the pattern.[4] These regulations were also posted up in various parts of the house and, in deference to the illiterate, read to a large crowd of inmates in the long room on at least one occasion.[5] Further rules were issued in 1820 and 1841 and, though they list additional staff and duties, they show that the general running of the house had altered remarkably little.[6]

The morning began with the ringing of the workhouse bell at a quarter to six in the summer (an hour later in the winter) and all rose from their beds and trooped downstairs, except for the old and infirm, who were permitted to lie in until after breakfast. At six o'clock, once the workhouse master had handed the gate keys to the porter, the main gate was opened and those able-bodied paupers who were employed in the various factories of the town (outworkers, as they were called) set off to work. They would be back in time for supper, but not before and so the pantry man gave them their midday allowance of food (bread and cheese) to take with them. Although it is not specified in the rules, this must also have been the moment for slopping-out in the yard and for a brief wash with cold water from the pump. On Fridays, the day of payment for out-relief, a queue of claimants would have been forming outside the workhouse gate soon after six. At seven o'clock sharp one or more of the overseers was in his seat to interview the out-poor and make (or refuse) an order for relief. This could easily take up the rest of the morning.[7] He would, at least, have had tea or coffee to keep him going, until that allowance was eventually revoked.

Work in the clothing manufactory began at six o'clock for indoor paupers as well, most of whom would be female. A superintendent made sure that the work rooms (of which there were never enough) were sufficiently supplied with material and the work was conscientiously performed. Each worker's output was noted in a book. While the paupers were downstairs working, their sleeping apartments were being aired and washed. The latter took place three times a week in the summer, only once a week in the winter, but the windows of the dormitories were invariably opened wide to let in the cool (but not

---

4   Archives and Collections, Library of Birmingham. 49736 B.Col 41.11 Vol. 2 *Orders and Rules to be Observed in the Birmingham Workhouse*, Birmingham, 1784, no pagination.

5   Archives and Collections, Library of Birmingham. GP/B/2/1/1 Birmingham Guardians' minutes, 5 January 1784.

6   Anon., *Regulations for Conducting the Affairs of the Birmingham Workhouse*, Birmingham, nd. [1820?]; *Rules and Regulations of the Guardians of the Poor of the Parish of Birmingham*, Birmingham, 1841.

7   *Aris's Gazette*, 3 March 1806.

necessarily fresh) Birmingham air. It was the job of the governess to see that all wards were thoroughly washed, and she and her husband were directed to inspect each ward daily. At nine o'clock the bell rang again and all went into the long room, as the dining hall was called, for a breakfast of six ounces of bread and two pints of milk porridge. By the 1830s breakfast on two days of the week (Sundays and Thursdays) consisted of two pints of sweetened rice milk instead.[8] Half a pint of milk was thickened with rice or oatmeal and then watered down again. The governor was always on hand to say grace (both before and after meals), to ensure good order and to check that no one took their allowance of bread away. The pantry man had probably been cutting up the bread and cheese for some hours and weighing it to make sure all received their correct allowance. The children took their breakfast elsewhere, under the watchful eye of the governess. As far as was possible in this crowded house, children and adults were kept apart.

Once the half-hour of breakfast was over, work began again and continued through until one o'clock, when the bell rang for the dinner hour. This was the main meal of the day and the only one to include meat. Not every day was a meat day, but when there was meat the pantry man and the house clerk carved it and put it on plates for the diners, again under supervision from the governor. By the 1830s three days of the week included meat (six ounces of beef) and potatoes, with three-quarters of a pint of beer to wash it down. On two days there was bread and soup with beer; the remaining two days provided suet pudding and beer.[9] The beer brewed at Birmingham, as in many institutions, was what was usually called 'small beer' or 'table beer', with a low alcohol content. But in a town that still relied principally on artesian wells and springs for its water supply, beer was decidedly less dangerous to drink. Ale, roughly twice as strong and made with a larger quantity of malt, was reserved for a special occasion such as Christmas Day. As for the soup, this was the perfect way to use up left-overs from the carving of the meat. It was also popular with the medical men, who considered it nutritious, warming and easily digested. The Birmingham recipe for 86 gallons of the stuff, helpfully outlined in the Guardians' minutes, consisted of 84 pounds of bones, half a peck of (dried) peas, four ounces of pepper, with celery and mint 'as we have it' and water. This would have made sufficient for 344 servings.[10]

The children were served meat as well, but in reduced portions, cut into smaller pieces by women while the governess looked on. The scene in the long

---

8   Archives and Collections, Library of Birmingham. GP B/2/1/4 Birmingham Guardians' minutes, 17 October 1838.

9   *Ibid.*

10   *Ibid.*

room would have indicated just what a disparate community the workhouse contained. Here were the able-bodied, the aged and infirm and those with mental health problems all crammed together in a single room. Anyone who did not respond quickly enough to the summons of the bell missed their meal and only those 'judged incapable' were permitted to consume their allowance elsewhere. They were required to send down a ticket, with their name and ward number and their food was sent up. For the patients in the infirmary wing, there was often a different diet, as specified by one of the workhouse physicians. Mutton replaced beef and rice pudding substituted for the bread and cheese or the soup. They were also given a reduced ration of half a pint of beer. On occasions, if the medical officer prescribed it, the sick were given wine (as a stimulant) instead of beer or water to drink. The wine supplied was normally raisin wine, which appears in the overseers' accounts for 1786–8, though port wine was also used.[11]

Manual work commenced again in the afternoon and continued until the bell sounded for supper at seven o'clock. There was probably an hour or so between work finishing (at least in the winter) and supper, a time for conversation and exercise in the yard. The yard itself, sub-divided for males and females and surrounded on all sides by high walls, would have served to emphasise what an enclosed and isolated world this was. Since the workhouse was lit only by candles, it was impossible to carry on sewing after the daylight disappeared. By eight o'clock the outworkers had returned and were given their supper, which was rarely anything more than bread and cheese or porridge, though they did get larger portions. If there was dripping available after the cooking of the beef, this went on the bread instead of cheese. On two days of the week supper consisted of broth 'with bread cut into it'.

The bell summoning all to bed sounded at ten o'clock in the summer and an hour earlier in the winter and since all fires and candles were extinguished at this time there was little to stay up for. The rules firmly stated that anyone seen 'lurking about the premises after the retiring bell' forfeited their breakfast for a first offence and would be confined 'at the discretion of the governor' for any subsequent lurking. And so, once the master had done his rounds to ensure all were in bed, the workhouse on Lichfield Street was dark and quiet until the next bell sounded eight long hours later. Since the keys were now back in the hands of the master, there would be no coming and going until dawn. While much of Lichfield Street continued late into the night, the pubs open, the traffic trundling past, the night watch on patrol, the workhouse slept. All that could be heard, perhaps, was the cry of a baby or a woman in labour. This entire daily routine could not have taken place without considerable help from the many inmates who were recruited to domestic duties. There were ward-keepers, who

---

11   F.M. Eden, *The State of the Poor*, Vol. III, London, 1797, pp. 744–5.

took out bedding for washing and ensured that candles and fires were out by ten o'clock; there were cooks and others to serve the food and draw the beer; and female servants who undertook cleaning and replaced candles and soap and other articles. The superintendent and the seamstress, who cut out material for the work rooms, were also probably inmates. The rewards for their labour were those 'perquisites' – tea and coffee, perhaps, or an extra allowance of food.

It was expected that the paupers in the workhouse should be well and truly grateful for the kind and generous treatment they received, and that expectation of gratitude is implicit in George Sims' famous ballad 'In the Workhouse: Christmas Day', published in 1877:

> Oh, the paupers are meek and lowly
> With their 'thank'ee kindly, mum's. [12]

It was also hoped that such appreciation would be spontaneously expressed, but if it was not, it was one of the duties of the workhouse governor on his rounds occasionally to exhort his charges 'to a good behaviour and a grateful sense of their comfortable situation'.[13] Likewise, those successfully discharged from the infirmary were directed by the apothecary 'to return thanks to the committee of guardians on the Monday preceding their discharge'.[14] Those who bit the hand which fed them, then, were doubly culpable and duly suffered the consequences. A good example of what might easily happen took place in December 1783 and the criminal evidence was set out, almost forensically, before the guardians.[15] The workhouse porter, Alexander Craig, manning the gate onto Lichfield Street as was his duty, spotted one James Price about to walk out. 'Suspecting that he had bread and cheese concealed about him', Craig led the culprit to the kitchen and the governess, Mrs Craddock, was called. Bread and cheese were found 'nearly all round him' under several waistcoats, shirt and 'in his bosom'. Since Price then had to be strip-searched, a male clerk was summoned, it being entirely inappropriate for the governess to be present while Price's trousers were removed. Two more large pieces of bread were found 'between his breeches and his shirt, within the waistband'. James Price was next asked to produce his box and several allowances of bread were discovered therein. Finally, the governor (the man with the scales) was on hand to weigh the loot, which amounted to seven pounds of bread and cheese on Price's person and a further six pounds in

---

12   G.R. Sims, *The Sunday Referee*, December 1877.

13   *Orders and Rules to be Observed in the Birmingham Workhouse*, Birmingham, 1784.

14   *Ibid.*

15   Archives and Collections, Library of Birmingham. GP B/2/1/1 Birmingham Guardians' minutes, 29 December 1783.

his box. For his misdemeanours James Price was sentenced by the guardians to fifteen lashes at noon on the following Wednesday.

The story highlights a number of interesting aspects of workhouse life, not least the fact that each pauper was issued with a box (kept under the bed?) in which to keep any valuables (surely very few) that he or she possessed. It would also have held any paperwork, such as an apprenticeship indenture or contract of work, which proved his settlement. Such boxes are never mentioned elsewhere in the records. Was Price simply storing up his daily allowance of bread and cheese to sell outside (though this was itself against the regulations) and getting hold of others' as well? It would have been almost impossible to root out this practice entirely: the workhouse was full of provisions and inmates were frequently recruited to help with their distribution. Nor was it difficult, as we have already seen, to smuggle items out of the institution entirely. If the public chastisement of James Price was intended to discourage others, it was immediately shown to be ineffective. The following month Mary Colley received 'ten lashes on her bare back with a cat and nine tails' for carrying out provisions to sell and Martha Price was confined 'in the dark hole' for twenty-four hours for the same offence.[16] This, we should add, was exactly half what Mary Fisher received for 'disobeying orders and profane swearing' on the same day. Some crimes were much more serious than theft. What was referred to as the 'low diet' for workhouse offenders did not lack for nutrition, but was monotonous and no attempt was made, as with the normal menu, to vary the daily fare. Breakfast on a low diet was milk porridge and bread, dinner was bread, broth and pudding, and supper was gruel or milk porridge and bread. This is the sole mention of gruel, that mainstay of workhouse literature, in the Birmingham records. It was, in fact, no more than a watery version of the porridge.[17] This flexibility in definition and nomenclature may explain a striking discrepancy here between Frederick Eden's report and the internal Birmingham records. Eden's summary of the dietary in 1796 specifies gruel as the workhouse breakfast for each day of the week.[18] The Birmingham staff preferred to call it porridge or pottage.

It was not only what paupers took out of the workhouse that was a problem; it was also what they failed to bring in. The obligation was that inmates who went out to work in one of the town's manufactories should bring back their wages and hand them over to the cashier. Typically, at least at this date, the pauper was permitted to keep back for himself two pence in every shilling 'by way of encouragement'. However, the temptation to hang on to more of this cash (or to

---

16   *Ibid.*, 7 January 1784.

17   *Report from His Majesty's Commissioners for Inquiring into the Administration and Practical Operation of the Poor Laws*, Appendix A, Parliamentary Papers, XXIX, 1834, p. 33a.

18   Eden, *State of the Poor*, Vol. III, p. 737.

spend it) proved irresistible to Joseph Bright in 1789. Bright had been working for a local cooper for seven weeks and had earned £3 3s 2½d, of which only 14s found its way back to the workhouse. For this Mr Bright was sent to the town dungeon in Peck Lane.[19] Not that this was the end of the story: shortly afterwards Bright broke out of the prison and escaped over the wall 'in the night season'. No more was heard of him. No doubt it was the abject failure of the justice system here which induced the guardians to adopt an internal solution to the next such theft. A week later one James Glover was found guilty of the same offence. He was ordered to be confined for two days and nights and fed on bread and water,

> And be chained by his right leg to a post in the open garden from twelve noon till two o'clock on Friday next and to be handcuffed with his hands behind and a label affix'd to his breast with the following: 'For cheating the overseers of the poor of my wages'.[20]

Externally earned wages did not only find their way into the pockets of the workers. In 1822 the workhouse gatekeeper, William Suffolk, was accused of receiving the wages of one of the boys employed outside the house. Mr Suffolk did not wait for his punishment; he absconded.[21] The cash books record payments for the transfer of 'disorderly paupers' from the workhouse to the town gaol in August 1801, but their offences cease to appear in the guardians' minutes after the 1780s.[22] Disciplinary matters, it would appear, were devolved entirely onto the master and he must have kept a punishment book to record such crimes, but it too no longer survives. In more serious cases of indiscipline, however, the magistrates at the Public Office were there to intervene and in any instance of criminal damage or refusal to accept the authority of the master, this is where the culprit would go. To take one example from many, in March 1834 a 'travelling pauper', by the name of William Alderson, was taken before the Public Office 'for refusing to work after being given accommodation and fed in the workhouse the previous night'.[23] The result of Alderson's refusal was a three-month spell in the house of correction at Warwick, where hard labour was unavoidable. The pauper's defence, that he was given not so much a bed for the night as a 'resting-place by the fire', cut no ice, but probably reflects the poverty of accommodation for the casual poor. In another case from the same

---

19   Archives and Collections, Library of Birmingham. GP B/2/1/1 Birmingham Guardians' minutes, 1 July 1789.

20   *Ibid.*, 8 July 1789.

21   Archives and Collections, Library of Birmingham. CP B/660984 Birmingham Overseers' Minutes, Vol. 3, 27 September 1822.

22   Archives and Collections, Library of Birmingham. GP B/3/1/1 Birmingham Guardians' Cash Books, 20 August 1801.

23   *Birmingham Advertiser*, 6 March 1834.

year, Jane Hart was sentenced to twenty-one days in the house of correction for 'disorderly conduct' in the workhouse.[24] Recourse to the Public Office, however, was relatively rare because of the costs involved; in most circumstances misbehaviour could be dealt with in-house.

The inmates might, on occasion, take a calculated decision as to where it was preferable to be incarcerated. In February 1832 three women, Mary Bell, Mary Martin and Harriet Reddis, were in the refractory ward on a bread-and-water diet for breaking the windows of their 'apartment'. Unhappy with this outcome, they elected to 'mill the glaze' (as they termed it) of this room too. Inevitably this took them before the magistrates and thence to the Warwick house of correction for twenty-one days.[25] In the same month, an applicant for out-relief, Louis Stokes, was ordered to stand in the stocks for an hour, after presenting himself at the workhouse 'so drunk he could hardly stand'.[26]

The magistrates' court was always the final recourse for the overseers or the workhouse master, when faced with refractory behaviour or defiance in the poorhouse. In 1833 Henry Wilson and William Davison received twenty-one days for refusing to work at the corn mills after a night in the workhouse.[27] Such punishments were not always confined to the inmates. Anne Heritage, a nurse in the lying-in ward at the workhouse, was similarly sent to the house of correction for twenty-one days for stealing bread to give to the women.[28] It appears that Anne and her husband, who worked as a barber at the workhouse, both had a culpably generous attitude towards their charges. Two years earlier John Heritage had been taken to court for forging signatures on recommendations for relief. On this occasion the overseers agreed not to prosecute if Heritage published (and paid for) an apology in the newspaper.[29] On the other hand, the magistrates might equally choose to overrule the overseers and order relief when it had been initially refused. Again, one such example may be allowed to stand for many. In October 1825 an unnamed woman with child, said to have been a 'respectable farmer's daughter, seduced away to Birmingham and abandoned', had been refused relief by the authorities. The justices overturned this decision.[30] The Public Office, then, stood as the final court of appeal in Poor Law cases locally. Disagreement between parishes or Unions, over settlement, perhaps, were dealt with at the appropriate Quarter Sessions.

---

24   *Birmingham Advertiser*, 26 June 1834.

25   *Midland Representative & Birmingham Herald*, 18 February 1832.

26   *Midland Representative & Birmingham Herald*, 25 February 1832.

27   *Birmingham Journal*, 5 October 1833.

28   *Birmingham Journal*, 24 November 1832.

29   *Birmingham Journal*, 18 December 1830.

30   *Birmingham Journal*, 8 October 1825.

It goes without saying that no inmate could leave the workhouse without permission and this could only be granted by the master. No written record of such temporary absences survives and we only hear of them when something went wrong. In December 1836, for example, an unnamed old woman was allowed out 'to visit her friends' but returned drunk and subsequently collapsed and died.[31] A pauper who absconded without leave was technically guilty of theft, for he or she left 'wearing the workhouse clothes'. Cases of this kind can be found throughout Poor Law records and usually ended up in the local house of correction. However, unless there was a particular reason for taking the matter to court, the workhouse clerk at Birmingham often turned a blind eye to the offence. A workhouse uniform was cheaper to replace than the cost of recovering it in the courts. In a rare exception, in 1837 John King was prosecuted at the Public Office, because he had absconded no less than five times and on each occasion had sold the clothes he was wearing, returning 'almost naked'.[32] It was not only clothing from the workhouse that could find a ready market. In Birmingham's poorest quarters anything which could be turned into hard cash was fair game. The town's pawnbrokers had a key role to play in such transactions, accepting out-relief tickets dispensed in lieu of out-relief and converting them into money. In 1814 the overseers threatened retribution on any who took part in this exchange.[33]

From as early as the 1601 Act it had been the parish obligation to provide accommodation for what the Act called 'the sturdy beggar' (who found accommodation in what was referred to as the 'casual ward') and Birmingham's overseers had, by various means, been dealing with casuals as far back as we have records to read. The terminology applied to this group evolves but is almost always unsympathetic. In the earliest surviving Birmingham Poor Law accounts they are referred to as 'vagrants' and in 1743 Widow Ball was paid 3s 6d for 'subsisting a big bellyd vagrant' for seven days.[34] They were still known as such in 1812, when the workhouse master, George Hinchcliffe, paid out almost £13 in relief to 'vagrants' over a three-month period.[35] By 1819 the vocabulary had widened: a vagrant was also either 'a rogue, a vagabond or incorrigible rogue' and there was a bounty of five shillings (paid for out of parish funds) for anyone who took such a person before a Justice of the Peace. Lodging-

31 *Birmingham Journal*, 31 December 1836.

32 *Birmingham Journal*, 14 October 1837.

33 *Aris's Gazette*, 31 October 1814.

34 Archives and Collections, Library of Birmingham. CP B/380973 Accounts of the Birmingham Workhouse and Out-Relief to the Poor, 1 April 1743.

35 Archives and Collections, Library of Birmingham. GP B/3/1/2 Birmingham Guardians' Cash Books, 20 June 1812.

house keepers, of which Birmingham had many, were also fined for harbouring them.[36] By 1820 the vagrants had been joined by 'impostors and travelling beggars', whose 'laxity of morals' and 'want of cleanliness' were, in the eyes of the overseers, only too evident in the cheap lodging-houses.[37] The language of the overseers reflected, in part, that of the various Vagrancy Acts passed in these years, but what was seen as a growing social problem required a local solution too. The committee, therefore, agreed to establish a 'vagrancy office' with a lodging-house attached, to which all such characters were to be directed. The office would accept 'only such as have been examined and appear proper objects'. The fact that this house was to be supervised, not only by the overseers and surgeons, but also by the head borough, the prison keeper and the parish constable, shows that this particular class of paupers were perceived as a threat to good order, as well as a health risk. Whether temporary accommodation for vagrants was actually established at this point is unclear, but by 1831 such a house was certainly in operation, probably to cope with an overspill from the workhouse, and the owner, John Booth, was being paid to look after them.[38] The arrangement was finally terminated in December 1832 and the vagrants returned to the workhouse 'as formerly'.[39]

Dealing with vagrancy was never solely a Poor Law issue and necessarily involved cooperation with the police, the magistrates and other relevant bodies. A branch of the Mendicity Society, founded in London in 1818, was established in Birmingham in 1830, with the intention 'to rid the streets of beggars ... not so much by relief as investigation'.[40] When its members detected what they saw as 'imposition', they took the culprits to the police court, or delivered deserving cases to the overseers. In their first year of surveillance the society delivered 96 impostors to the Public Office on Moor Street and a further 267 into the hands of the parish officers. A mendicity office, run by volunteers, remained in operation for most of the 1830s, the first port-of-call for those found begging in the streets.[41] But the society remained chronically short of funds and, in a marketplace full of worthy causes, was considered less deserving than many. In most instances vagrants were directed straight to the casual ward of the

---

36 Archives and Collections, Library of Birmingham. CP B/660893 Birmingham Overseers' Minutes, Vol. 2, 10 December 1819.

37 *Ibid.*, 17 March 1820.

38 Archives and Collections, Library of Birmingham. GP B/3/1/4 Birmingham Guardians' Cash Books, 18 February 1832.

39 Archives and Collections, Library of Birmingham. CP B/660895 Birmingham Overseers' Minutes, Vol. 4, 11 December 1832.

40 *Birmingham Journal*, 2 April 1831.

41 Archives and Collections, Library of Birmingham. CP B/660896 Birmingham Overseers' Minutes, Vol. 5, 1 May 1838.

workhouse and here the principle of 'less eligibility' was enacted more keenly than anywhere else in the system. The casual ward at Lichfield Street was the bleakest and least comfortable room in the house and little money was ever spent on it. It appears to have adjoined the internal courtyard, a low, single-storey structure, where beds were shared and the roof leaked. In spite of the ward's clear role as a deterrent, the vagrants would not be going away and, indeed, by 1822 were increasing considerably.[42] By 1827 the more familiar term of 'tramp' or 'tramper' was widely in use and so they remained here on in. It was at this point that the guardians began to record the numbers of tramps 'entertained' in the house. A total of 1,148 (724 men and 424 women) were relieved in the quarter ending September 1830, suggesting an intake of some twelve a day.[43] Quarterly statistics for the numbers of tramps 'boarded and lodged' appear sporadically in the guardians' minutes from this point onwards, though not often enough to detect an overall pattern. Vagrancy may well have been related to employment trends, but not exclusively so. In July 1832 the number reaches a quarterly high of 2,095 persons,[44] reducing to 395 in April 1836.[45] The figure then rises to a further peak of 1,674 in April 1840, before falling back later in the year.[46] The temporary drop in the figure in 1836 may well be related to the introduction of hand mills (as an additional deterrent) into the workhouse. At this time able-bodied applicants for relief, including the tramps, were required to do two hours' work on the mills in the morning before they were allowed to leave.[47] This tougher regime appears to have coincided with the appointment of Thomas Alcock as master of the workhouse in 1829. Under Alcock, not only were the casuals required to work for their subsistence, the bed and board offered them was also reduced to a bare minimum. No fires were provided in the ward and the men were obliged to sleep on bare boards, only the women being allowed the comparative comfort of straw. Two meals were offered to the casuals, one in the evening and breakfast the following

---

42   Archives and Collections, Library of Birmingham. CP B/660894 Birmingham Overseers' Minutes, Vol. 3, 9 August 1822.

43   Archives and Collections, Library of Birmingham. GP B/2/1/3 Birmingham Guardians' minutes, 30 October 1827.

44   Archives and Collections, Library of Birmingham. GP B/2/1/3 Birmingham Guardians' minutes, 3 July 1832.

45   Ibid., 13 April 1836.

46   Archives and Collections, Library of Birmingham. GP B/2/1/4 Birmingham Guardians' minutes, 7 April 1840.

47   Archives and Collections, Library of Birmingham. GP B/2/1/3 Birmingham Guardians' minutes, 24 February 1836.

morning,[48] but by 1840 supper was limited to 'a little bread and water'.[49] This was probably the minimum the law would allow.

Casual accommodation, as we have said, was in two rooms (for males and females) in the backyard of the workhouse and they were far from salubrious. In 1831 John Cadbury had cause to complain of

> the close and offensive state of the back yard comprising the tramp rooms. These receptacles of filth and wretchedness expose the whole house to contagion and fever.[50]

In making the accommodation as unwelcoming as possible the parish risked infecting the whole establishment and various alterations were subsequently made to improve the overall conditions. Whether Birmingham's home-made version of 'less eligibility' was effective is open to question. The guardians thought it was, but the figures they gathered hardly helped their case. In the year up to Lady Day 1839 a total of 3,080 vagrants had been relieved; in the year to March 1840 the figure had risen to 4,605.[51]

The monthly break-down of the figures was no more favourable. The average monthly intake in the casual ward from January to October 1840 was 307 men and 92 women. As we might expect, applications peaked in the winter months, when any kind of roof over one's head, even a workhouse roof, was preferable to a night on the streets. A total of 365 male vagrants were admitted in January 1840, falling to 249 admissions in July. The overseers attributed the reduction in numbers in 1840 to the deterrent effect of the Birmingham police, who were inspecting the tramps as they left the workhouse.[52] One police constable told the Birmingham magistrates in June 1840 that it was his duty 'to go every morning to the tramp room at the workhouse to inspect the tramps'. It was during one morning inspection that PC152 recognised 'by his gait' that one of the inmates was an army man and therefore likely to be a deserter and hauled him before the court.[53] Police involvement, however, cut both ways. By 1840 (under the regime of the police commissioner imposed by the government) they were also under orders to round up any tramps found wandering the streets of Birmingham or the neighbouring parishes and bring them to the

---

48 *Ibid.*, 21 July 1829.

49 *Birmingham Journal*, 7 November 1840.

50 Archives and Collections, Library of Birmingham. CP B/660895 Birmingham Overseers' Minutes, Vol. 4, 8 November 1831.

51 *Birmingham Journal*, 7 November 1840.

52 Archives and Collections, Library of Birmingham. GP B/2/1/4 Birmingham Guardians' minutes, 7 July 1840.

53 *Birmingham Journal*, 27 June 1840.

workhouse. Since begging was itself illegal, no additional powers were needed for this. Over a twelve-month period from March 1839 to March 1840 a total of 4,905 vagrants were thus deposited at the workhouse door.[54] These visitors stayed, on average, three or four nights in Lichfield Street before moving on.[55]

The above monthly figures for vagrancy, that is, occupancy rates in the casual ward of the workhouse, were compiled in 1840, when the Birmingham guardians were fighting a rear-guard action over what they saw as an underhand attempt to impose the New Poor Law upon the town. Birmingham, having its own Local Act, was not yet subject to the 1834 legislation. Ultimately the argument boiled down to a statistical debate over the relative tightness or laxity of the Birmingham system towards vagrancy, compared with that of a neighbouring Poor Law union such as Aston. The debate was triggered by a negative report by Robert Weale, the Poor Law Commission's Midland agent, highlighting what he saw as a rise in pauperism in the town, which Weale attributed to the inadequacy of the Local Act. 'Birmingham,' he commented, 'was now a great place of refuge for mendicants and beggars, who infest the local countryside.'[56] The Birmingham guardians felt duty-bound to contest such a claim. The number of tramps in the casual ward, they argued, had actually decreased over the past decade and cited the introduction of hand mills into the workhouse as one of the reasons. Weale had exaggerated the problems, they argued, in order to justify the repeal of the Local Act. It was also true that, as the largest conurbation in the area, the town saw considerably more cases of vagrancy and homelessness than any of its neighbours. In times of distress it was better to seek solace in the city than in the villages around it and the homeless flooded in, sleeping rough in the brick-yards, begging in shop doorways, queuing at the soup kitchens. More often than not, as Henry Knight pointed out, it was not the rich who helped out the poor, but the poor themselves. 'If a poor child was lost,' Knight asked his fellow guardians, 'who took its hand and fed it? Was it the rich? No, it was the poor woman, who had, perhaps, hardly food for herself.' The tramps' accommodation at Lichfield Street, then, represented the obverse to Birmingham's phenomenal growth over the previous century, a place for the poorest of the poor, a casual ward for life's casualties.

---

54 Archives and Collections, Library of Birmingham. CP B/660897 Birmingham Overseers' Minutes, Vol. 6, 14 April 1840.

55 *Birmingham Journal*, 7 November 1840.

56 *Birmingham Journal*, 14 November 1840.

4

Putting Names to the Nameless Poor

> In many places it is more difficult to pass the artificial boundaries of a parish than an arm of the sea, or an Alpine hill, but Birmingham regards not the narrow policy of our laws of settlement…
>
> John Morfitt[1]

The rightful recipients of poor relief in Birmingham and elsewhere were carefully differentiated. Firstly, there were those described as the 'indoor poor', who lived in the workhouse. A steadily declining number of these were able-bodied, as the workhouse increasingly became the refuge for the elderly and infirm, the mentally and physically sick, and for single women who were offered the lying-in ward, usually for the last month of their confinement. Secondly, there were those who remained at home and received outdoor relief, an altogether larger and more disparate group. Such has been the attention devoted to the workhouse in recent years that this latter group have not been so thoroughly investigated, yet they received equal attention in Sir Frederick Morton Eden's trail-blazing survey of England's poor in 1797. Eden is unable to supply a figure for the indoor poor in Birmingham but is much more precise about those in receipt of out-relief: in June 1796 they comprised 684 old and infirm widows, 550 soldiers' wives, 13 seamen's wives, 143 bastard children, 1,522 legitimate children, and militia men's wives and children at nurse (number not stated). Total of persons receiving out-relief, 4,660. As the number in the family is not specified, it is not possible to ascertain the exact number of the poor, but if the number in the General Hospital and charity schools be included, it is probable that one-fifteenth of the population of Birmingham, or even a twelfth, if the number of soldiers

---

1   S.J. Pratt, *Harvest Home, Consisting of Supplementary Gleanings, Original Dramas and Poems, Contributions of Literary Friends and Select Re-publications*, Vol. 1, London, 1805, p. 265.

raised in Birmingham in the last three years is deducted from the population, was in receipt of regular or occasional charity.[2]

No snapshot like this should be generalised beyond the moment it is taken. Eden's visit happened to coincide with a high level of military mobilisation, during the war with France and when the Birmingham economy was also in the doldrums. From the earliest days of the Poor Law, it had been a duty of parishes to support the wives and family of the militia or regular army, and any such woman could apply to any parish for relief: the laws of settlement did not apply. In the late 1790s such numbers were abnormally high, and Eden's overall estimate reflected that fact. Overall, numbers inevitably grew in step with the town. In June 1818 the new workhouse governor, William Cheshire, took the opportunity, as new brooms often do, to make a statistical declaration of the extent of dependency in the town.[3] At this point there were 603 residents in the workhouse, and a further 420 children in the Asylum for the Infant Poor. Cheshire's figures for the out-poor still reflected the classes current in Eden's time.

1st class (aged & infirm & widows)	927
2nd class (soldiers' wives & families)	80
3rd class (families requiring permanent relief)	537
4th class (illegitimate children)	384
Non-parishioners paid by other parishes	370
Wives and children of militia men on permanent duty	8
Persons and families requiring occasional relief	1,071[4]

The workhouse governor's figures, reported in *Aris's Gazette*, need a little glossing. It seems likely that the numbers refer to households, rather than individuals, which is how the records would have been kept. With peace came a huge diminution in the parish's obligation to maintain the families of men in the army, but that is more than made up for by the growth in casual relief. It was this class, the able-bodied poor, who would cause the overseers the most difficulty, their numbers rising and falling with the economy. To those who held the purse-strings, each of these family units represented a cost incurred by the parish. In Eden's day, old men and widows received 1s a week, which might rise to 2s or 2s 6d in 'cases of great age and infirmity'. The allowance for a child averaged 1s 6d. Much more detailed figures for the outdoor poor also exist from 1838, when the reformist guardian, Henry Knight,

2   F.M. Eden, *The State of the Poor*, London, 1797, pp. 326–7.

3   *Aris's Gazette*, 6 June 1818.

4   *Ibid.*

put forward proposals to re-classify them.[5] Like most Poor Law authorities, Birmingham sub-divided its outdoor poor into four classes, categories which reflected their overall need (in the guardians' eyes) and the extent of parish responsibility. The first class (often referred to as 'pensioners') comprised those who were 'aged and infirm'. In the week Knight chose to examine (in December 1837) there were 859 persons of this first class, consisting of 88 married couples, 110 single men and 661 single women. Each received, on average, 2s 6d a week, or 5s for a married couple. Such a rate of pay in the 1830s might just have allowed a single man or woman to pay the rent for a back-to-back, but not to buy food and clothing. The second class consisted of soldier's wives. This group too had declined markedly from Eden's time. In December 1837 there were only 19 such cases in Birmingham. The third and largest class were those called 'casual poor', and they too were sub-divided into those with tickets and those without. A ticket, bestowed by an overseer or even by a ratepayer, gave the recipient semi-permanent status, though this might sometimes be reviewed, and still required the person to apply directly to the workhouse on Friday mornings, with occasional home visits by the workhouse visitor. If the applicants were too ill to attend, an unofficial system existed whereby 'broker women' collected their tickets, claimed their allowance at the workhouse and took the money back to them, charging a small fee for doing so. Such broker women could well be leaving the house with up to £50 in allowances.

Henry Knight counted 884 applicants in this 'casual poor' category in 1837, and broke the number down more precisely. Of these 884 cases, the largest group by far were widows without children, who numbered 388. Knight saw no particular reason why all these women should be treated so favourably, arguing that widowhood alone (without reference to age or infirmity) should not automatically bestow such privileged (and permanent) status. Three-quarters of the 884 cases (661 women) were widows, and 98 were married couples with or without children. The remainder was made up of orphans (33), unmarried men (23) and widowers (17).

The casual poor *not* given tickets would also have to call at the workhouse on Friday mornings, where, in Knight's words, they were:

... subjected to such interrogation and repulsive scrutiny as is deemed expedient to prevent persons from unnecessarily and improperly becoming burdensome to the parish.[6]

---

5   Archives and Collections, Library of Birmingham. GP B/2/1/3 Birmingham Guardians' minutes, 13 February 1838.

6   *Ibid.*, 13 February 1838.

Such interrogation would, we assume, have been repeated each week until the applicants ceased to apply for relief or were awarded a ticket. Knight counted 946 individuals in this class, and also broke the number down into smaller groups. The largest group here were the 634 married couples, both with and without families, followed by the 201 widows. The point of mentioning children was that their relief would be at a higher level if there was a child in the family, and higher still for more than two children. This whole group would be the one which fluctuated most widely, since unemployment or temporary illness was the most likely reason for their visit to the workhouse. It should be noted that vagrants or tramps were not included in any of Knight's figures. Their daily appearance was counted and accounted for separately. They were not part of what Henry Knight was examining, that is, the underlying and long-term structure of pauperism in the town. The fourth and final class were those termed 'illegitimates' or 'bastards'. Most children of this status would have found their way to the Asylum of the Infant Poor in Summer Lane, but those who were looked after by a family member, other than their mother or father, would have fallen into this category. In December 1837 there were 199 such children. Additional to the above and not given a specific class, were the so-called 'out-parishioners', paupers for whom Birmingham was responsible, but who lived outside the parish. Henry Knight counted 217 of these.

The casual poor, then, amounted to 1,830 family units, though a much larger number of individuals, once we include children. If we use the multiple of 2.5, the figure used by the workhouse clerk, the overall number was probably around 4,500. Add to this figure of those in the other classes, and allow for children, and we can estimate that approximately 10,000 people, out of a total Birmingham population of some 130,000, were receiving relief in 1837. This should be set alongside the in-house population (comprising the workhouse, the infirmary and the Asylum for the Infant Poor) of around 1,000. Compared to Birmingham's experience over the previous twenty years or so, these were very high numbers indeed. From the early summer of 1837, a time of widespread unemployment in manufacturing, applications reached record levels, as did the occupancy rate in the workhouse. Henry Knight's proposal (there is no evidence whether it was accepted by the guardians or not) was to re-brand the four classes according to marital status and the presence of a dependent family. Knight's first class was to consist of single persons, followed by widows or widowers with families, married couples without a family and (fourthly) married couples with children. Knight also sought to abolish the system of 'brokering'. Those unable to go to the workhouse should, he thought, be relieved at home by the parish visitors.

The official figures presented by Knight no doubt represent only the tip of the iceberg of deprivation in Birmingham in the late 1830s. A meeting of the General Benevolent Society in December 1830 was told by an unnamed 'reverend gentleman' that he and his colleagues had visited 3,700 families in the parish, 'in a state of utmost destitution and distress, who receive no parochial relief'.[7] These were the families who were, to all intents and purposes, on the breadline, but who devised survival strategies which did not involve a visit to the workhouse on Friday mornings. Such people are frequently mentioned by the town missionaries and described by Henry Knight in his report:

> Our population, generally speaking, is by no means debased by a spirit of pauperism, but will endure privations, and part with furniture and clothing to provide food, rather than apply for parish relief ... During the warmer part of the year, bedding, clothing etc. was pledged to provide food, to such an extent that long before the close of the year the funds of the pawn-brokers were exhausted, and their store-rooms filled with those necessary articles of comforts.[8]

Once all furniture was gone, the family withdrew into a single room and made do with whatever crates and sacking they could find. As soon as they found work which was far from easy in the later 1830s, they could redeem their property and inhabit their house again. Entering one such house in Garrison Lane, Edwin Derrington commented:

> I found all the family then in the house seated upon a piece of board, raised at each end by bricks. This was the only seat in the house. Upstairs, I looked round for the bed, but could not discover it, untill [sic] I looked behind the door, where I saw a few rags and a sheet from the Relief Fund. The other chamber door being opened ... I saw a few loose flocks which the girl said they could not get anything to put them in.[9]

On the same day Derrington visited families in similar condition in Great Barr Street:

> Many families ... have no dependence but the pawn shop, and when the furniture is gone and their boxes are empty [they] have no recourse. Some have been out of work for nine, twelve or fourteen months. One family of eight persons depend upon the earnings of two children who bring five shillings a week.[10]

---

7   *Birmingham Journal*, 25 December 1830.

8   Archives and Collections, Library of Birmingham. GP B/2/1/3 Birmingham Guardians' minutes, 13 February 1838.

9   Archives and Collections, Library of Birmingham. CC1/61 Congregational Town Mission, 2 February 1838.

10 *Ibid.*

The extent of such underlying poverty is, sadly, unquantifiable. Reluctance to enter the workhouse or otherwise 'apply to the parish' was common, but of no concern whatsoever to the authorities. The town missionary, Peter Sibree, described one such family, 'who had seen better days', living in Duke Street:

> The wife had been a member of the Baptist Church at Coventry, the husband long out of work and the wife greatly afflicted. They were unwilling to go into the workhouse, after having enjoyed so many comforts by their own industry, but I found they had been nearly starved to death for want of food. Indeed, her husband but a few days ago, without knowing me, had been asking at my own door in Aston Road for a crust of bread.[11]

If independence of spirit lay behind this family's reluctance to 'go into the house', elsewhere it was often an unwillingness to allow the family to be broken up. Thomas Finigan described one such example and the deprivation which inevitably followed, in January 1838:

> In one court called Dog and Duck Yard there was a family named Bloor. The father was a gun barrel maker, but out of employment for more than nine months. The husband and wife could not bear the idea of separation from each other, nor from their children, which would be the case, they considered, if they went into the workhouse, and they preferred accepting two or three shillings in a week and remain as outdoor poor. This, they tell me, was at last denied them, and sooner than go into the house they preferred suffering. I found the woman stretched on a sort of bedstead. Bed or blanket there was none, fire or candle there was none, nor was there a morsel of food in the house for thirty hours before my visit. And then the little that was procured was by the sale of three plates, a tea pot and an old chair for one shilling.[12]

Nevertheless, Finigan persuaded the family to enter the house and Mrs Bloor was admitted to the workhouse infirmary. Henry Knight reported the same reluctance, at the very moment he was quantifying the tidal wave of applications that arrived in June 1837. 'As long as a penny or a rag remains,' he told his fellow guardians, 'the great mass of the labouring poor avoid the workhouse as they would the pest-house.'[13]

As Henry Knight's figures implied, the overseers needed access to vast quantities of ready cash each week. We might guess around £350. In reality,

---

11   Archives and Collections, Library of Birmingham. CC1/71 Congregational Town Mission, 14 January 1839.

12   Archives and Collections, Library of Birmingham. MS 3255 Thomas Finigan's Journal, pp. 9–10, 9 January 1838.

13   *Birmingham Journal*, 17 June 1837.

Figure 4.1
Birmingham
Workhouse penny,
1812, face and reverse.
Author's own.

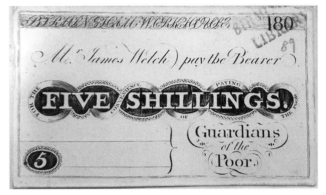

Figure 4.2 Paper token
to pay the bearer five
shillings. Archives and
Collections, Library of
Birmingham: MS 897
Volume 1 No. 89

Figure 4.3 Paper
token for one
pound. Archives and
Collections, Library of
Birmingham: MS 897
Volume 1 No. 86

however, an alternative form of currency circulated. Until the system was declared illegal by the government, the workhouse printed notes and made copper tokens. These notes and coins circulated in the town as unofficial money and many traders accepted them as payment, but they could also be redeemed and turned into hard currency on application at the workhouse. In addition, the parish printed cards to the value of 5s and 2s 6d (the commonest weekly payments), which were signed and handed out to the outdoor poor.[14]

---

14   Archives and Collections, Library of Birmingham. GP B/2/1/1 Birmingham Guardians' minutes,
     15 December 1803.

Figure 4.4 Paper token showing the Workhouse, with woman and children, 'For the Convenience of the Poor', to pay the bearer two shillings and sixpence. Archives and Collections, Library of Birmingham: MS 897 Volume 1 No. 96

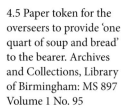

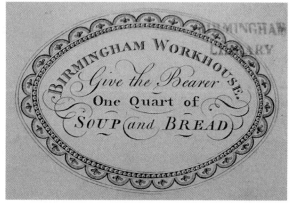

4.5 Paper token for the overseers to provide 'one quart of soup and bread' to the bearer. Archives and Collections, Library of Birmingham: MS 897 Volume 1 No. 95

Such cards were, however, also made illegal by the Promissory Note Restriction Act, when the government was seeking to squeeze the money supply.[15] They were also easy prey to forgery and fraud, especially in a town as adept at counterfeiting as Birmingham. Payment in kind was probably the cheapest form of relief and the least subject to abuse. At various points the overseers experimented with supplying clothing or shoes and by giving out tickets for food. A pair of shoes, of course, together with decent clothing, allowed an able-bodied person to seek work, but, as with most aspects of poor relief, demand outstripped supply. Over a period of two weeks in October 1832, for example, the overseers supplied 176 pairs of shoes to the out-poor, compared to only 35 pairs in the same period in 1831.[16] Over one year in 1812 to 1813 the guardians recorded a sum of

15 Archives and Collections, Library of Birmingham. GP B/2/1/2 Birmingham Guardians' minutes, 9 September 1808.

16 Archives and Collections, Library of Birmingham. CP B/660895 Birmingham Overseers' Minutes, Vol. 4, 23 October 1832.

£1,005 paid out in clothing.[17] One reason for the high cost, in the eyes of the parish authorities, was that ratepayers themselves had the right to write notes of recommendation for any poor person who asked them. As far as we can tell, these notes were only for shoes or clothing, not for cash. In 1830 the overseers sought to close this surprising loophole in their system, warning ratepayers 'to be very particular in investigating cases of persons who apply to them'.[18] Payment in kind was just one of many ways the overseers attempted to target outdoor relief more effectively and (by implication) less widely. In 1811 relief was refused to any applicant who owned a dog.[19] The same policy was adopted in West Bromwich in 1816. In 1820 a list of all those receiving relief was published, and a copy sent to every ratepayer.[20] The strategy was to encourage those who paid for relief to look out for what today would be called 'benefit fraud'.

All hand-outs, be they of clothing, bread, money or cards, took place on Friday mornings, the traditional day for relief across the country. Indeed, the casual poor were known as 'Friday paupers'.[21] On that day Lichfield Street was very busy indeed, as casuals, broker women and sellers of cheap articles to the poor crowded together in and around the house. Given the physical condition of many of the Friday paupers, poor old Lichfield Street was hardly a welcoming destination. In 1827 the overseers lamented the state of the rutted road and uneven pavement in front of the workhouse:

> to which great numbers of poor persons resort on Friday and other days, many of whom, from their infirm condition, are in great danger of accidents from the irregularity of the pavement.[22]

In 1821 awnings had to be put up in the front courtyard of the workhouse to shelter the poor while they queued.[23] These were later slated and leaded to make

---

17   Archives and Collections, Library of Birmingham. GP B/2/1/2 Birmingham Guardians' minutes, 1 June 1813.

18   Archives and Collections, Library of Birmingham. CP B/660895 Birmingham Overseers' Minutes, Vol. 4, 26 October 1830.

19   Archives and Collections, Library of Birmingham. CP B/660892 Birmingham Overseers' Minutes, Vol. 1, 26 November 1811.

20   Archives and Collections, Library of Birmingham. CP B/660893 Birmingham Overseers' Minutes, Vol. 2, 7 April 1820.

21   Archives and Collections, Library of Birmingham. CP B/660892 Birmingham Overseers' Minutes, Vol. 1, 26 November 1811.

22   Archives and Collections, Library of Birmingham. CP B/660894 Birmingham Overseers' Minutes, Vol. 3, 18 September 1827.

23   Archives and Collections, Library of Birmingham. CP B/660893 Birmingham Overseers' Minutes, Vol. 2, 14 September 1821.

them more permanent.[24] There were one or two unsuccessful attempts to change the day of payment, but Friday it remained, even when that day was Good Friday. An argument over this was reported in the minutes for 1833, throwing interesting light on what the overseers saw as their mission. As usual it was a debate first raised in the local press. William Neville had written a letter, requesting pay day to be brought forward to the Thursday of Holy Week 'that tomorrow might have been observed in a devotional manner'. It was left to Samuel Timmins, then the chairman of the overseers, to respond, and his reply has all the elements of what would later be known as Birmingham's 'civic gospel':

> The overseers will continue the practice of their predecessors, feeling that a devotion of their time on this day to the relief of the poor would be attended by approving consciences, and they trust also the approbation of their Creator.[25]

If the workhouse was, in the opinion of many, the place of last resort, it was also, for many, the only place of resort. Statistics for the size of the workhouse 'family' are presented throughout this study, the highs and lows reflecting a better or worse economic climate, as well as the policies of the guardians and overseers towards the able-bodied. Who lived in Lichfield Street and how did they end up there? It would be quite reasonable to ask these questions of the Poor Law, but remarkably difficult to answer them. The concern of the guardians, overseers and their paid officials was always with statistics, with the numbers resident and the cost to the ratepayers. The names of those admitted to, and discharged from, the workhouse would once have been written down, but they were of negligible value to those who managed the system and have therefore not been preserved. Of much more importance to the managers of the system was the age and gender profile of the inmates, how many were able-bodied and how many required some kind of intensive care, whether in the infirmary or wards for the aged. In March 1836, for example, the guardians requested a report on the numbers of inmates defined as elderly, that is (in contemporary definitions) over sixty years of age. The figures given were of 37 men and women over sixty years, 28 inmates over seventy years and 15 inmates over eighty years.[26] As Felix Driver has commented 'the workhouse system was clearly not designed for paupers; it was rather designed for their management'.[27]

---

24 Archives and Collections, Library of Birmingham. CP B/660894 Birmingham Overseers' Minutes, Vol. 3, 2 November 1824.

25 Archives and Collections, Library of Birmingham. CP B/660895 Birmingham Overseers' Minutes, Vol. 4, 9 April 1833.

26 *Birmingham Journal*, 12 March 1836.

27 F. Driver, *Power and Pauperism: The Workhouse System 1834–1884*, Cambridge, 1993, p. 3.

The lack of detailed information about the inmates is a matter of deep regret to family historians and it frustrates any initial attempt to reconstruct the lives of Birmingham's poor.

So how can we uncover or understand the experience of individual inmates, when even their names were not recorded? There is one set of records which allow us to dig a little deeper. The Settlement Act of 1662, later amended and refined, facilitated the removal of paupers from the place they were living to their parish of legal settlement.[28] Under the terms of the Acts, settlement was defined either as the pauper's parish of birth (where his or her parents were legally settled), or where settlement had been obtained, either by apprenticeship, employment for twelve months or by renting a house at £10 a year or more. To the pauper involved, this meant a rent of 4s a week or over. The parish found to be responsible for the individual under any of these terms was legally obliged to take him back, unless the person was too incapacitated to be removed thither. And, even in this latter case, the parish where the pauper was living had to be reimbursed for the cost of relief. Much litigation and bickering inevitably followed from all this. In 1838 Birmingham was paying for 217 such cases.[29] In 1833 the assistant commissioner was informed that Birmingham paid, on average, £300 in removing paupers, and the annual cost of court cases over settlement amounted to £281.[30]

A good example of the complexities of settlement came before the Public Office in December 1833, proceedings 'which excited sympathy from the magistrates and all present'.[31] The case concerned a woman by the name of Gilbert, who had worked as a domestic servant at Sandwell Hall. Here she had met and later married, a fellow servant called George Gilbert, a Catholic; the woman herself was a Protestant. The two married in a Catholic church but omitted to have the marriage confirmed in an Anglican church. The couple subsequently moved to London, where their first child was born and then to Wolverhampton, where a second child came along. There was nothing, thus far, to bring the family to the attention of the overseers, let alone the magistrates. However, while Mrs Gilbert was pregnant with their third child, George Gilbert was knocked down by a stage-coach in Birmingham, rendering him incapable of paid employment. And it was then that issues of settlement and entitlement became important. The two children had

---

28 A. Brundage, *The English Poor Laws, 1700–1930*, Basingstoke, 2002, pp. 10–11.

29 Archives and Collections, Library of Birmingham. GP B/2/1/3 Birmingham Guardians' minutes, 13 February 1838.

30 *Report for His Majesty's Commissioners for Inquiring into the Administration and Practical Operation of the Poor Laws*, Appendix A, Parliamentary Papers, XXIX, 1834, p. 58a.

31 *Birmingham Advertiser*, 12 December 1833.

settlement in London and Wolverhampton, while their father was legally settled in Birmingham. Mrs Gilbert, because she had not married by the rites of the Established Church, was not matrimonially tied to her husband's parish. Her settlement, therefore, reverted to West Bromwich, where she had been employed. Thus the support (the chargeability) of the family was shared between four different parishes. Although Mr Gilbert remained in hospital in Birmingham, his wife was sent to West Bromwich, but allowed to keep the children 'for nurture'. There can hardly be a better example of how the old (and Anglican) Poor Laws flew in the face of the reality of nineteenth-century migration patterns and religious diversity.

When a pauper, therefore, was admitted to a workhouse, or received out-relief, it was necessary to interview the individual as to his legal settlement. If settlement was found to be elsewhere, the pauper would be returned to the parish responsible. If the individual could not be removed (either through age or physical condition), then the parish responsible was legally obliged to pay for his or her upkeep. That first examination, therefore, was of crucial importance. One such volume of examinations survives in the Birmingham records before 1840.[32] The examinations, under the terms of the Settlement Act, had to be conducted before two magistrates. The people so inspected were self-selecting, in that they were unable to be removed through infirmity or sickness and in many cases had to be interviewed at home by the parish clerk, who took their biographies before the authorities. Otherwise a family member made representation on their behalf. The volume which survives commences on 22 October 1838 and contains short life stories of both outdoor and indoor paupers, all of whom had lived away from Birmingham at some point in their lives. It was this fact which made an examination as to settlement necessary. There were 460 or so interrogations in the twenty-six months before the end of 1840, averaging around 17 a month. A total of 25 of these cases to the end of 1840 involve individuals, some with families, who were residing in Birmingham workhouse, and details of 12 of these are given below. They represent, as it were, the casualties of the mass migration to Birmingham during the eighteenth and early nineteenth century, which had raised its population from some 24,000 in 1750 to 130,000 in 1840. In addition, and in the absence of any other such records, these personal accounts provide a useful cross-section of the kind of people living in the house. They are also, it must be said, unrepresentative, in that the majority of the workhouse inmates had probably never lived anywhere other than in Birmingham. In these cases, no examination would be necessary and their lives are consequently lost to us.

---

32   Archives and Collections, Library of Birmingham. GP B/12/2/1 Examination of Paupers re their Place of Settlement, 1838–46.

Much has been made by scholars in recent years of working-class autobiographies, in most cases charting the successful rise of an individual from a background of discouragement and hardship.[33] Such works are self-selecting, of course. The literacy of the writer distinguishes him or her from the majority of his class. Here, then, are other stories to set alongside them.

The earliest interview was with Ambrose Williams, aged sixty-nine years. He was in the workhouse, along with his son, John, whose age is given as nine years. The father described himself as 'ill, lame and unable to work' and this had probably been the case for some years. Ambrose was a native of Coreley, in Shropshire, but had moved to Solihull in his forties and rented a house at £11 per annum. By 1831, however, Ambrose was living in Tewkesbury, Gloucestershire, together with his wife and three children. However, being unable to support themselves there, they had been removed back to Solihull. From here they headed to Birmingham. Ann Williams, his wife, had since died and Ambrose was being paid 5s per week out-relief from Solihull.[34]

Hannah Ivory, aged thirty-six, was living in the workhouse with her three youngest children, Job (aged eleven), Reuben (aged seven) and Simeon (aged three). Hannah hailed originally from Market Drayton in Shropshire, but at the age of twenty (in the early 1820s) had moved to Birmingham, where she married James Ivory, who likewise came from the Shropshire town of Whitchurch. The couple had four children, the oldest of whom, Ambrose, was now sixteen years old. James Ivory died in 1836 and his widow and three of their children entered the workhouse. Since James Ivory had never served an apprenticeship in Birmingham and they had rented a house at less than 3s 6d a week, Hannah's legal place of settlement would still have been Market Drayton.[35]

Maria Buckerfield was single and nineteen years of age. She was born in Wolverhampton, but after the death of both of her parents, she had been looked after by her grandfather, along with her two brothers. Her grandfather later received payments as an out-door pauper. Maria came to Birmingham in 1836 and was now pregnant and still unmarried. The birth of the child was expected imminently and, no doubt, she was directed to the lying-in ward.[36]

---

33 R. Gagnier, *Subjectivities: A History of Self-Representation in Britain, 1832–1920*, Oxford, 1991; J. Simmons, *Factory Lives: Four Nineteenth-Century Working-Class Autobiographies*, Plymouth, 2007; J.R. Atkinson, *Victorian Biography Reconsidered: A Study of Nineteenth-Century 'Hidden' Lives*, Oxford, 2010; M. Hewitt, 'Diary, Autobiography and the Practice of Life History', in D. Amigoni (ed.), *Life Writing and Victorian Culture*, Aldershot, 2006, pp. 21–40.

34 Archives and Collections, Library of Birmingham. GP B/12/2/1 Examination of Paupers re their Place of Settlement, p. 10.

35 *Ibid.*, p. 14.

36 *Ibid.*, p. 44.

Richard Barker was examined as to the settlement of his daughter, Margaret, who was very ill in the workhouse. Richard was born in Herefordshire in about 1775, but while he was still very young his parents had moved to London and lived in Shoe Lane, where his mother died in St Bride's workhouse in 1801. Richard had married and he and his five children had been living in Birmingham at least ten years. The parish of St Bride's had been relieving them for much of this time.[37]

James Williams was examined as to the settlement of his grandson, Joseph Williams, who was eighteen months old. James was born at Camp Hill, Birmingham in 1787 and had served an apprenticeship to a trader in Bradford Street. The family had lived in nearby Green Street, where their son, John, and grandchild, Joseph, were born. Shortly after his birth, Joseph's father had been sent to prison and his mother had deserted him. James Williams, now in Moseley Street, was unable to care for the child, who was now in the house.[38]

Thomas Parsons was six years old and born in Birmingham. His father and mother, John and Elizabeth Parsons, were originally from Harborne and had moved to Birmingham, but in 1827 they were removed back to Harborne. By 1833, when Thomas was born, they had returned to Birmingham. Since that time Elizabeth Parsons had been sent to prison and her husband, John, was awaiting transportation.[39]

Rebecca Smith was in the insane ward at Lichfield Street, and her husband, Philip, spoke on her behalf. They had married at Alrewas, Staffordshire, in 1821 and had two children, who were living with their father in 17 Court, Edmund Street. Little is said of Rebecca herself, but Philip's own testimony tells us something of the life of a jobbing builder at this time. At the age of seventeen Philip had served a brief apprenticeship to a bricklayer in Alrewas, before being hired (at the age of twenty-two and still single) by a plasterer in Great Haywood for a period of three years. Philip Smith's contract stated that he would earn 12s a week in the first year, 13s in the second year and 14s per week in the third. For this his hours of work were from 6am to 6pm, referred to as 'the usual hours of trade'. After this time Philip worked at several other places both in Staffordshire and beyond. For seven months he had worked as far afield as Thrybergh Hall near Rotherham.[40]

Thomas Otway, aged thirty-eight years, was in the workhouse with his two children, John (nearly eight) and Edward (nearly six). He was now 'very ill', but his recall of dates and ages indicates a much firmer grasp on his own life-story

---

37   *Ibid.*, p. 52.
38   *Ibid.*, p. 58.
39   *Ibid.*, p. 89.
40   *Ibid*, p. 120.

than many of his fellow inmates. Thomas was born at Uffculme in Devon and had married Maria Otway at Bedminster in 1829. In 1831 the family had moved to Bristol, where Thomas worked as a tailor, the same trade as his father. They rented a house at £30 per annum (11s 6d a week), indicating a good level of income, if it was correct. In 1833 they were renting another house in the same parish (St James, Bristol) at £17 a year (or 6s 6d a week). In 1835 Maria Otway died and in the following year Thomas and his sons moved to Birmingham.[41]

James Lister was forty-one years old. Born in Nottinghamshire, his parents took him to London, where they rented an expensive house (at £100 per annum) in Marylebone. At the age of fourteen, James worked for his uncle at Paddington wharf as a delivery clerk. In 1827 he married in Dronfield near Sheffield, and he and Catherine Lister had six children, John, Frederick, Edward, Elizabeth, Maria and Charlotte, all aged between ten years and six months. Now out of work, he was in Birmingham workhouse, together with his wife and the children.[42]

John Wright was four years old and an orphan. His grandmother presented evidence on his behalf. His mother, Eliza Wright, bore him illegitimately in the workhouse at Chaddesley Corbett in Worcestershire. Eliza later died in Kidderminster workhouse. Mary Wright, his grandmother, looked after the child in 8 Court, Milk Street, in Birmingham for three years, but 'she is not able to keep it any longer'.[43]

James Green was sixty-seven and a native of Bromsgrove, Worcestershire. For six years he was apprenticed to a nail maker there. After his first marriage he lived in Wigan, but was maintained by the overseers of Bromsgrove, 'who sent him money to bury his first wife'. By 1825 he was back in Bromsgrove workhouse with his two children. He was there for three or four months. In (approximately) 1830 James married again, this time in Birmingham. Now 'lame of one arm' and unable to work, he and his wife, Elizabeth, were in the workhouse.[44]

John Blount, aged forty-seven, was 'insane, unfit to go at large and in the house'. His wife, Sarah Blount, presented the evidence. Sarah was born in Birmingham, married John in Harborne and bore him four children, 'three of whom are now with her'. John Blount served an apprenticeship to a shoemaker in Bewdley, Worcestershire. The family had rented a house and bakehouse in that town for more than five years, leaving for Birmingham in September 1840.[45]

The 25 biographies mentioned earlier record 45 persons (26 males and 19 females), roughly ten per cent of the inmates of Birmingham workhouse at

---

41   *Ibid*, p. 125.
42   *Ibid*., p. 146.
43   *Ibid*., p. 266.
44   *Ibid*., p. 272.
45   *Ibid*., p. 449.

the end of the 1830s. Of this number 19 were children, 3 were elderly (under the Poor Law definition of being over sixty years), 3 were lying-in and 4 were described as being 'of insane mind'. For the older children, the workhouse was probably a temporary home, before long-term decisions on their future were taken. The geographical origins of the inmates were wide, both in terms of place of birth, but also where they had previously lived or worked. Nevertheless, most of the paupers were born in the West Midland counties, Shropshire and Worcestershire featuring most prominently of all.

The stories vividly highlight the difficulty of enforcing settlement, many returning to Birmingham after having been sent back to the parish responsible for them. They also show the remarkable mobility of the working-classes by the early Victorian period. Workhouses and out-relief feature regularly in the accounts, and 17 of the 25 cases involve some degree of prior Poor Law experience, sometimes stretching back more than one generation. If the overseers needed evidence to support their theory of 'hereditary pauperism', it was here in abundance. We have followed these 45 people into the various wards of Birmingham workhouse. What their experience was there one can only infer from the overall picture, as set out in the other chapters of this book. But in an institution so driven by numbers, Ambrose Williams and his companions can, at least, give the workhouse a human face.

5

The Ghost of a Workhouse

In chapter 2 a rough chronology, admittedly imprecise in some details, was established for the creation of the Birmingham workhouse in Lichfield Street. It is this institution, with its many ups and downs, which will occupy the pages of much of the rest of this book. However, it could also be argued that the erection of the workhouse in 1734 or 1735 marked, not the beginning of a process, but the end of one. The workhouse in Birmingham had a back story – a ghost, as it were – and one with a remarkably long and chequered history. And to uncover that we must take a sideways step from the Poor Law and into the criminal law.

Firstly, we need to examine more carefully the provisions of the Elizabethan Poor Act of 1601. The legislation of 43 Elizabeth had set out, in its twenty tightly argued paragraphs, a template for more than two centuries of Poor Law provision. Yet the 1601 Act was itself the culmination of a series of Elizabethan Poor Acts, enacted in 1572, 1576 and 1597, which laid down the terms under which the poor were to be treated across England and Wales. In essence the Act of 43 Elizabeth did little more than combine and streamline those earlier statutes. Both the 1597 and 1601 Acts placed upon the shoulders of parochial overseers and local Justices of the Peace the burden of enacting the legislation. It made the newly established overseers and churchwardens responsible, not only for supporting the poor, but also for 'setting to work all such persons married or unmarried, having no means to maintain them, or no ordinary and daily trade of life to get their living by'.[1] As for the kind of labour the legislators envisaged, money raised from the ratepayers was, at least in part, to be spent on 'a convenient stock of flax, hemp, wool, thread, iron, and other necessary ware and stuff to set the poor on work'. The 1601 Act goes on to urge parish officials

---

1   *An Act for the Relief of the Poor*, 1601, 43 Elizabeth I c. 2.

to erect, build and set up in fit and convenient places of habitation, in such Waste or Common, at the general charges of the Parish, or otherwise of the Hundred or County as aforesaid, to be taxed, rated and gathered, in manner before expressed, convenient houses of dwelling for the said impotent poor, and also to place Inmates or more families than one in one cottage, or house.[2]

Whipping sturdy beggars 'until his body was bloody' back to 'the place of his birth' was made law in the 1597 Act.[3] But the 1601 Act also required, 'the said Justices of Peace or any of them, to send to the House of Correction or common Gaol, such as shall not employ themselves to work'. As can be seen, there is no specific reference in the 1601 Act to 'workhouse', although this is referred to by name in the 1576 legislation. However, the later Act does contain most of the elements which we would later associate with such a building: a place to 'set the poor on work', together with the materials that this labour might demand, alongside a 'place of habitation' for one or more of the 'impotent poor', perhaps living communally. There is reference, both in 1576 and 1601, to a 'house of correction', where those unwilling to undertake parochial work would find themselves compelled to do so. In order to examine the origins of the Birmingham workhouse, we need to look more closely at this institution as well.

Under the 1576 Act a house of correction was mandated for each county, to which were to be sent (in the terminology of the time) rogues, vagabonds, vagrants and 'lewd women' and there set to work.[4] By 'lewd women' the Act principally meant women who had given birth outside marriage. A subsequent Act of 1609 underlined the punitive nature of this institution, and it was as a place of punishment that the house of correction developed.[5] The power to erect, maintain and control a house of correction lay with the Justices of the Peace in each county.[6] By the eighteenth century, however, the house of correction had become the regular destination for minor offenders of a more general kind, despatched there either by magistrates sitting locally in so-called Petty Sessions, or at the Quarter Sessions of the county. Normally located close to the county gaol, a house of correction or bridewell (named after the first such house on the Fleet River in London) delivered a short, sharp shock of hard labour for

---

2   *Ibid.*

3   N. Longmate, *The Workhouse*, new edn, London, 2003, p. 14.

4   *An Act for the Relief of the Poor*, 1575, 18 Elizabeth c. 3. Lincoln, London and Norwich had already created such establishments. A.L. Beier, *The Problem of the Poor in Tudor and Early Stuart England*, London, 1983, p. 27.

5   *An Act for the due execution of divers laws and statutes heretofore made against rogues, vagabonds and sturdy beggars, and other lewd and idle persons*, 1609, 7 James I c. 4.

6   R. Jütte, *Poverty and Deviance in Early Modern Europe*, Cambridge, 1994, pp. 169–70.

a period of up to six months or so.[7] In 1794, for example, two Birmingham men were sent to the house of correction at Warwick 'for performing plays for hire' in a house in Deritend.[8] In August 1801 Eleanor Simons was arrested for keeping a house of ill fame in Birmingham, and Elizabeth Breedon 'for resorting thereto'. In this case too, both women were sent to the bridewell at Warwick.[9] In January 1802 Hannah Hodgkins was one of two women directed to the house of correction 'for pretending to tell fortunes'.[10] In some circumstances the bridewell might also be used to accommodate prisoners awaiting trial at the next Quarter Sessions. The earliest mention of a house of correction at Warwick dates from 1625, though it and the county gaol were subject to regular re-building, and, on at least one occasion, re-location over the following two centuries.[11]

If the house of correction had clearly become part of the penal system by the later 1700s, that role was considerably more problematic in the preceding century. Neither parochial officers nor Justices of the Peace saw or maintained any clear distinction between 'setting the poor to work' and penalising those who refused to do so. Indeed, as Ratcliff and Jonson point out, the Warwickshire house of correction itself contained pauper lunatics in the 1630s.[12] That is, the workhouse and the house of correction were seen as one and the same, and no doubt equipped with the same 'convenient stock' of materials to keep the inmates occupied. The minutes of the Warwickshire Quarter Sessions themselves refer to the building beside the county gaol as the 'workhouse' and 'house of correction' interchangeably.

What was true at Warwick was equally true elsewhere, as the house of correction model was rolled out across the whole county. In 1625 the inhabitants (by which is generally meant the ratepayers) of Stratford-upon-Avon petitioned the Quarter Sessions, and were granted the right to:

> erect and build a house of correction or workhouse, wherein to set the said poor on work and for punishing of those idle and lewd people that will not work within the said parish and other wandering and idle persons that resort to the said parish.[13]

---

7   S. McConville, *A History of English Prison Administration*, London, 1981, pp. 22–48.

8   *Aris's Gazette*, 22 December 1794.

9   *Aris's Gazette*, 31 August 1801.

10 *Aris's Gazette*, 18 January 1802.

11 'The Borough of Warwick: Introduction: The County Town', in W.B. Stephens (ed.), *A History of the County of Warwick: Vol. 8: The City of Coventry and Borough of Warwick*, London, 1969, pp. 447–51.

12 S.C. Ratcliff and H.C. Johnson (eds), *Warwick County Records Vol. VII, Proceedings in Quarter Sessions 1674–82*, Warwick, 1946, p. cviii.

13 S.C. Ratcliff and H.C. Johnson (eds), *Warwick County Records Vol. I, Quarter Sessions Order Book 1625–37*, Warwick, 1935, p. 11.

That the terminology had become extremely slippery is evident enough from the records, for a century later, in 1726, upon a further petition from Stratford, the Quarter Sessions granted a second order for a house of correction in the town, and accepted that the master of the workhouse should also be master of the house of correction.[14] Further so-called houses of correction were later sanctioned at Coleshill (1658), Chilvers Coton (1691), Atherstone (1725), Tanworth-in-Arden (1732) and Solihull (1740). And in the case of both Atherstone and Tanworth, the same individual ran both the house of correction and the workhouse.[15] The previous volume of Quarter Sessions' minutes records an agreement between the churchwardens of Rugby and John Cox and his wife to maintain the poor 'in the workhouse there'.[16]

It might be possible to add the parish of Fillongley to the list, though here the matter becomes even more contentious and involved an adjudication by the Quarter Sessions in 1635. According to the submission made at the Trinity Quarter Sessions for 1635, the parish of Fillongley had for some time made use of a building referred to as 'Church House' for accommodating the poor. By 1635, however, a section of the ratepayers:

> were and are desirous that the said house should be committed and employed for a place wherein the poor of the said parish should be set on work and there inhabit in case they were destitute of other habitation.

Indeed, such a course of action had already taken place by the time the matter came to court

> the same house having been for some time lately employed for this purpose the poor thereby were the better kept for work and small children who formerly lived idly and unprofitably were brought to get means for their relief by their own labour.

The dispute at Fillongley was over whether a salaried overseer, that is, a workhouse master, should be appointed to manage this activity more effectively, or whether the building should simply be rented out, and the profits taken for parish use. The Justices sitting at Warwick approved the plan for the continued

---

14   Shakespeare Birthplace Trust, ER1/75/5 Order of the County Sessions for a House of Correction at Stratford, 11 January 1725/6.

15   Warwickshire County Record Office, QS0039/5 Warwick Quarter Sessions minutes 1721–56, 15 October 1725, 3 October 1732.

16   Warwickshire County Record Office, QS0039/4 Warwick Quarter Sessions minutes 1704–21, Easter Sessions, 1716.

use of Church House as a place of work and habitation for the poor.[17] It is not possible to say how successful most of these initiatives were, or, indeed, how accurate were the reports coming from the Warwickshire parishes. The Justices were careful to stress, at least in some instances, that funding for these workhouses was to be raised locally, and that no county rate could be expected to underwrite them. This was spelt out in the order approving the Atherstone house of correction in 1725.[18] This may help to explain why, although the Justices of the Peace had powers to control these houses and demand accounts from the overseers, they are rarely mentioned again in the surviving records of the court. Lack of central support, or the failure to raise monies locally, may well have undermined parochial resolve. Six years after the dispute at Fillongley had seemingly been settled, for example, the Warwickshire Justices were informed that the house 'had not yet been put to use' and that no flax or wool had been purchased.[19]

Before moving on to examine the situation in Birmingham, it is worth reflecting upon what this evidence seems to imply. The most widely accepted narrative of Poor Law history is to see the workhouse as largely an eighteenth-century phenomenon, principally encouraged by the Poor Relief Act of 1722–3.[20] Prior to this, isolated, and, it seems, pioneering work was undertaken by the London Corporation of the Poor (1647) and the Bristol Corporation of the Poor (1696). In both these cases the London and Bristol parishes combined in order to secure local Acts to maintain the poor and build workhouses and houses of correction.[21] Indeed, it is claimed that the 1647 London Act is among the first pieces of legislation to refer to the workhouse by name.[22] As we have already seen, however, the Warwickshire Justices were employing the term as early as 1625, and continued to do so throughout the century. In the light of this and of the other evidence presented so far in this chapter, the dates for the

---

17   Ratcliff and Johnson (eds), *Warwick County Records Vol. I*, p. 223.

18   Warwickshire County Record Office, QS0039/5 Warwick Quarter Sessions minutes 1721–56, 5 October 1725.

19   S.C. Ratcliff and H.C. Johnson eds, *Warwick County Records Vol. II, Quarter Sessions Order Book 1637–50*, Warwick, 1936, p. 92.

20   *An Act for Amending the Laws relating to the Settlement, Employment, and Relief of the Poor*, 1723, 9 Geo. I, c. 7; See S. Webb and B. Webb, *English Poor Law History, Part 1: The Old Poor Law*, London, 1963, p. 243.

21   T.V. Hitchcock, 'The English Workhouse: A Study in Institutional Poor Relief in Selected Counties 1696–1750', DPhil, St. Anthony's College, University of Oxford, 1985, pp. 46–95. See also J. Innes, 'Prisons for the Poor: English Bridewells, 1555–1800' in F. Snyder and D. Hay (eds), *Labour, Law and Crime: An Historical Perspective*, Oxford, 1987, pp. 42–122.

22   *An Ordinance for the Relief and Employment of the Poor, and the Punishment of Vagrants and other disorderly Persons in the City of London etc*, London, 1647.

establishment of many parish workhouses across the country must be radically re-assessed. Either that, or we must equally radically re-define what we mean by a workhouse and that would be to fly in the face of what its seventeenth-century progenitors said it was.

What, then, can we say of the situation in Birmingham? Quite a lot, as it happens, for the records of the Warwickshire Quarter Sessions have much to report on this, in one of the largest towns within its jurisdiction. We know, for example, that early seventeenth-century Birmingham was highly susceptible to outbreaks of plague.[23] Plague was endemic in early modern England, but Birmingham appears to have been peculiarly vulnerable. The Warwickshire Justices approved a county rate in 1633 for the relief of the Birmingham poor 'in the time of the late sickness in the plague there'.[24] Further outbreaks are recorded in 1635, 1637 and 1640, though no more are recorded after this date.[25] Inevitably such visitations fell disproportionately on the poor. It is at the time of one outbreak of plague in 1635 that we get our earliest indication of poor relief in action in the town, and of concerted efforts to deal with its consequences. The petitioner to the Quarter Sessions is one Richard Taylor, constable and overseer, who

> by the inhabitants thereof hath been employed as an agent to gather money for the poor in the time of the infection and sickness of the plague, as also to take care and have the oversight of the building of the house convenient to set the poor on work.[26]

How far this building had progressed is not revealed, but it was Taylor's 'great pains in the service of the town' which had driven him to seek reimbursement, which he had evidently not yet received from Birmingham's inhabitants. This the Justices acceded to, adding the request for Taylor to submit accounts for his work thus far. Nothing more is heard of Richard Taylor, nor of the workhouse, until 1654, when Francis Vale, described as 'a man of ill life and conversation, and one who is able to work and get his living if he had a mind so to do', is transferred from the 'common gaol' at Warwick to the master of the house of correction in Birmingham.[27] Vale is the only prisoner specifically directed to the Birmingham house by the Quarter Sessions in the seventeenth century, though this does not, of course, preclude others who may

---

23 C. Gill, *History of Birmingham*, Vol. 1, Oxford, 1952, pp. 49–50.

24 Ratcliff and Johnson (eds), *Warwick County Records Vol. I*, pp. 171–3, 204–5.

25 Ratcliff and Johnson (eds), *Warwick County Records Vol. II*, pp. 13, 65–6.

26 Ratcliff and Johnson (eds), *Warwick County Records Vol. I*, pp. 220–1.

27 S.C. Ratcliff and H.C. Johnson eds, *Warwick County Records Vol. III, Quarter Sessions Order Book 1650–57*, Warwick, 1937, p. 213.

have been so confined by a local order. Whatever that house of correction consisted of in the 1650s, it was in abeyance by midsummer 1681, when the court was informed of 'a great number of poor in that town and much need of an house of correction'.[28] Birmingham was urged to progress the work, with the reminder (as with the case of Atherstone) that its ratepayers should also continue to contribute to the workhouse and house of correction at Warwick. That request was repeated in 1685, when the sum of £400 was noted as being sufficient to complete the work.[29]

By the Epiphany Sessions of 1687, the Warwickshire Justices were showing somewhat more financial flexibility than before, allowing for the transfer of funds from the county rate for a period of two years to assist the completion of the Birmingham house.[30] It is here recognised that a house of correction in Birmingham could benefit the whole Hundred of Hemlingford, and not simply the town. Such a house in Birmingham would also take some of the pressure off the one at Warwick. Furthermore, work had progressed far enough for the court to appoint five governors in the shape of John Cotterell, Henry Porter, Edward Scotton, Thomas Rogers and James Lewis. A new set of governors was appointed in the following year, only James Lewis remaining from the previous list.[31] James Lewis remained at the centre of activities throughout the 1690s. By 1692 the sum of £70 had been raised 'to set the poor on work', £10 of which was to be spent 'repairing and fitting the public workhouse there'.[32] We can only guess that these repairs were to the building which had been in partial use back in 1654. The remaining £60 was allocated to Lewis to serve 'as a stock for setting the poor on work', that is, one assumes, for buying raw materials to supply the house. Finally, in this, the most progressive order yet, the Sessions ordered that Lewis should be paid a wage for his activities. As was regularly the case in such matters, the issue then descended into internal bickering over the cost, the nature of the money expended and accounted for, and the claims and counter-claims between the various creditors and debtors. In an atmosphere of recrimination, little progress could be made. In early 1693 the court heard that 'the work lieth dead' and recommended that the building be rented out instead.[33] By 1696, however, the original scheme had been revived once more,

---

28   Ratcliff and Johnson (eds), *Warwick County Records Vol. VII*, p. 229.

29   H.C. Johnson (ed.), *Warwick County Records Vol. VIII, Quarter Sessions Order Book 1682–90*, Warwick, 1953, pp. 124–5.

30   *Ibid.*, pp. 200–1.

31   *Ibid.*, p. 228.

32   H.C. Johnson and N.J. Williams (eds), *Warwick County Records Vol. IX, Quarter Sessions Proceedings 1690–96*, Warwick, 1964, pp. 62–3.

33   *Ibid.*, p. 68.

and the court was recommending expenditure of £70 'in repairing and altering the said workhouse and adding new buildings for the poor to live in'.[34] As has already been shown, the Justices sitting in Quarter Sessions were making no distinction between a workhouse and a house of correction and, indeed, the 1696 order evidently envisaged a residential workhouse.

Any account of the progress of the Birmingham workhouse is compromised by the lack of parish evidence locally, and the fragmentary and intermittent nature of the court involvement from Warwick. In 1729 three masters 'of the workhouse att Birmingham' were appointed, followed in 1734 by an order for the building of a house of correction in the town, naming Francis Field as the master.[35] By this time, of course, as chapter 2 indicated, town meetings were being held to establish another workhouse. A final intervention was made from Warwick in 1739, when it was ordered that one Abraham Bellamy be appointed master of the Birmingham house of correction.[36] It was to be a brief appointment for Bellamy, for in April 1741 the Justices ordered

that the bridewell and house of correction in Birmingham and all other houses of correction in ye county erected by this court except Warwick be surpressed [sic].[37]

This appears to mark the end of devolved corrective justice across the county, resources instead being centred upon the sole remaining house of correction at Warwick.

The delivery and organisation of both poor relief and exemplary justice across the whole of Warwickshire was therefore characterised by discontinuity and confusion. Birmingham was certainly no exception to that pattern, though there is more evidence of a sustained attempt to create some apparatus of relief and justice in the town than elsewhere in the county. If the town did not have a fully functioning workhouse or house of correction throughout the later seventeenth and early eighteenth century, it undoubtedly did possess one or both for part of this time. This new evidence helps to explain a minute in the Birmingham Town Book for 1733, when the inhabitants were deliberating over the construction of a new town gaol in Peck Lane. This was to replace, as the minute puts it, 'the dungeon at a place commonly called Bridewell House

---

34   *Ibid.*, pp. 120–1.
35   Warwickshire County Record Office, QS0039/5 Warwick Quarter Sessions minutes 1721–56, 5 April 1729, 15 January 1734.
36   *Ibid.*, 2 October 1739.
37   *Ibid.*, 7 April 1741, 15 January 1734.

near Pinfold Street'.[38] Pinfold Street, the location of the town's animal pound or pinfold, would be the obvious place to locate a bridewell or house of correction. There is no direct indication in the Town Book of when the gaol in Peck Lane was completed, nor any stated link between Peck Lane, which functioned as a lock-up and debtors' prison, and a house of correction, though Peck Lane and Pinfold Street were close to each other. Prior to this, according to William Hutton at least, wrong-doers appear to have been secured in a dungeon below the Leather Hall, which stood at the bottom of New Street. The peremptory demolition of the Leather Hall in 1728 or thereabouts (Hutton says that it was removed overnight) meant moving the inmates to the cellar of a house opposite and they remained there until the new premises in Peck Lane were opened for business.[39] All of which allows us to re-configure, albeit tentatively, the administration of both poor relief and corrective justice within the town of Birmingham, and push back by some years the accepted commencement. What it also makes clear is that we can no longer defend a single date for the establishment of a parish workhouse at Birmingham (or, indeed, elsewhere). The court evidence suggests that both workhouses and houses of correction came and went with alarming regularity in the course of the seventeenth century. Only in the second quarter of the eighteenth century was some form of stability achieved, when the functions of a workhouse and house of correction were more carefully and consistently differentiated.

But if the situation in Birmingham remains complex and fragmented, the same cannot be said for its close neighbour, Aston, in this period usually referred to as 'Birmingham's Aston' or 'Aston juxta Birmingham'. Given the discontinuous efforts to establish workhouses or houses of correction elsewhere in the county, Aston offers a remarkably complete and simple narrative. The Warwickshire Justices approved the plan to establish a house of correction at Aston at the Epiphany Sessions of 1701, at the same time insisting

ye dischargeing to Warwick house of correction not granted, and they are to accompt to the parish and to the court at every Easter Sessions and to take up wandring persons, and £150 stocke to be raysed upon the parish.[40]

---

38 Archives and Collections, Library of Birmingham. CP B/286011 Birmingham Town Book, 19 September 1733. Cf. Gill, *History of Birmingham*, Vol. 1, p. 68; 'Political and Administrative History: Local Government and Public Services', in W.B. Stephens (ed.), *A History of the County of Warwick, Vol. 7: The City of Birmingham*, London, 1964, p. 321.

39 W. Hutton, *The History of Birmingham*, Birmingham, 1783, pp. 334–5; R.K. Dent, *The Making of Birmingham*, Birmingham, 1894, p. 75.

40 Warwickshire County Record Office, QS0039/3 Warwick Quarter Sessions minutes 1690–1704, Epiphany 1700–1701.

Suitably encouraged, a levy to raise money for a workhouse was held in the parish in June 1701.[41] Local funds must have been sufficient, for in the following year, at the Trinity Sessions of 1702, the court nominated Humfrey Birch as master of the Aston house of correction, with 'the power to set at worke ye poor their [sic] and correct them'.[42] True to their word, Aston parish officials continued to submit accounts to the Easter Quarter Sessions yearly (with a few exceptions) for the period up to 1750, the Justices taking that annual opportunity to nominate new governors (all of them Warwickshire JPs) or to approve the appointment of a master. Here too the terms 'workhouse' and 'house of correction' were used without discrimination. In 1710, for example, the Warwickshire Justices approved the continued role of Henry Holden, doctor of physic, Edward Brandwood, gentleman, and Isaac Sadler, gentleman, 'relating to the workhouse and imploying the poore', and of Stephen Colmore as master of the house of correction 'as formerly'.[43] John Noble replaced Stephen Colmore as master in 1714.[44] Nor did the order of April 1741, quoted above, which suppressed all houses of correction outside Warwick itself, apply to the parish of Aston. Workhouse accounts were approved, new governors appointed, and masters confirmed each year at the Easter Sessions long after this point.

Exceptionally here, however, there is corroborative evidence from within the parish itself. The Birmingham antiquarian and magistrate, William Hamper (1776–1831), made copies of some early Aston parish material as part of a proposed revision of Dugdale's *Antiquities of Warwickshire*, papers which later came into the hands of James Watt junior. In 1714, according to Hamper's transcripts, one 'Mr Hill' was being paid four shillings 'for making articles for the workhouse', and a master was appointed in 1723 at a salary of £10 15s per annum. Prior to erecting a purpose-built workhouse, it would appear, the Aston overseers were renting a house for that function. If the levies were insufficient to embark upon building, then this was the only solution. Payments in 1724 for 'bricks, laying bricks and lime, and a thatcher' suggest that the building was being extended at this point. In 1734, however, the Hamper papers record that £500 was borrowed from 'Mrs Sadler' to build a new workhouse for the parish,

---

41 Archives and Collections, Library of Birmingham. MS 3001/2/31 Levy made to John Thornton, churchwarden and John Chattock, overseer for Bromwich Hide, to raise money for a workhouse in Aston Parish, Deeds of Castle Bromwich, 1700. The surviving document covers only the yields of Castle Bromwich and Water Orton.

42 Warwickshire County Record Office QS0039/3 Warwick Quarter Sessions minutes, 1690–1704, Trinity 1702.

43 Warwickshire County Record Office QS0040/1/8 Warwick Quarter Sessions order book, 1709–18, Trinity Sessions 1710.

44 *Ibid.*, Easter Sessions 1714.

a loan which was still being paid off 13 years later. According to Hamper, who transcribed the plaque over the door, this new building opened at Erdington on 1 March 1735. Hamper's transcripts state that the first Aston workhouse master was Andrew Butler, appointed in February 1735 at an annual salary of £25, with an additional £4 10s for 'housekeeping'.[45] The Quarter Sessions' minutes, on the other hand, record an order for 'a house of correction in the workhouse at Aston' in July 1735, nominating William Foster as master.[46] At this point, it would appear, the two Aston institutions were finally separated.

At Aston, therefore, it is possible to assert that a workhouse and/or house of correction was firmly established in 1701; a new workhouse was built later at Erdington in 1735, which continued in use up to and beyond the establishment of the Aston Union under the Poor Law Act of 1834. Neither the local evidence nor the minutes of the Quarter Sessions give any indication as to the location of the earlier building or buildings. We know that a prison was erected in 1778 or 1779 on High Street, Bordesley, which served as a lock-up, prior to the prisoners' appearance before the magistrates. William Hamper gives the earlier date for opening;[47] an article in the *Birmingham Journal* claims the later.[48] But, as with Peck Lane, there is no clear connection between this building and any earlier house of correction. A description of the Bordesley gaol by the prison reformer James Neild in 1802 makes it highly unlikely that this building could ever have served as a house of correction:

> Two dark damp dungeons down ten steps, by which you descend by a trap door level with the court, about twelve feet by seven each, with wood bedsteads, straw and a rug. The only light or ventilation through an iron-gate aperture, about twelve inches square. The doors open into a narrow dark passage. Brick floors an inch deep in water at my visit, 5th November 1802. These dungeons are unfit for the confinement of any human being, and may be numbered amongst the very worst in the kingdom. Over them are two rooms which open into the court, each about twelve feet square one used as a day-room, the other as a sleeping room, with a wood bedstead, straw, and rugs, for petty offenders.[49]

One can conclude from this that the priority for the Birmingham magistrates and guardians in the eighteenth century was the removal of the idle poor and petty criminals from the community to a place (usually called a house

---

45 Archives and Collections, Library of Birmingham. MS 3219/6/198/47 Papers of James Watt Jr. re: Aston.

46 Warwickshire County Record Office QS0039/5 Warwick Quarter Sessions minutes 1721–56, 15 July 1735.

47 Archives and Collections, Library of Birmingham. MS 3219/6/195/2 Papers of James Watt Jr. re: Aston.

48 *Birmingham Journal*, 1 February 1840.

49 *Gentleman's Magazine*, February 1807, p. 108.

of correction) where they could be put to work or at least isolated from their peers. As Jeremy Boulton has demonstrated, this treatment existed alongside the continuation of outdoor relief and the establishment of Knatchbull's workhouses.[50] The latter were effectively an eighteenth-century re-invention of the medieval almshouse, catering for the impotent poor, chiefly the elderly, at least until the coming of the Gilbert Unions in the 1780s.[51] That the houses of correction in the West Midlands (outside Aston) were frequently repressed fits the national picture of waves of alarm caused by fears of the consequences of mass impoverishment, followed by retrenchment on the part of those paying the poor rate and faced with the costs of maintaining such expensive establishments.[52] If the poor relief system in the region was to develop in a less spasmodic fashion, there needed to be a more unified system of accountability and bureaucratic control over the operation of the poor laws among the overseers and, later, the guardians.

---

50   J. Boulton, 'Indoors or Outdoors? Welfare Priorities and Pauper Choices in the Metropolis under the Old Poor Law, 1718–1824', in C. Briggs, P.M. Kitson and S.J. Thompson (eds), *Population, Welfare and Economic Change in Britain, 1290–1834*, Woodbridge, 2014, pp. 153–99.

51   S.R. Ottaway, *The Decline of Life: Old Age in Eighteenth-Century England*, Cambridge, 2004, pp. 247–76.

52   P. Slack, *The English Poor Law, 1531–1782*, Cambridge, 1995, p. 42.

6

Managing the Poor:
The Overseers and Guardians

Birmingham's Poor Law, inside and outside the workhouse, was conducted by two distinct bodies of individuals, in many aspects reflecting the model for local (and national) government to this day. On the one hand there were the salaried office and ancillary staff, who ran the establishment and dealt with the paperwork. They, in turn, answered to a body of elected or nominated overseers and guardians, who shouldered overall responsibility for the way the system was managed and funded. While the professionals (master and mistress of the workhouse, vestry clerk and cashier) were permanent appointments and in most cases had committed themselves to the Poor Law as a long-term career, the overseers and guardians came and went in accordance with their terms of office. It has to be said that this did not prevent former guardians from intervening in debates over the management of the workhouse, long after they had left it.

The system in Birmingham was unusual, if not unique in England, combining as it did the powers of the Gilbert Act of 1782 with measures specific to the Midlands town itself. Thomas Gilbert's Act had been passed to allow parishes (largely rural) to combine together to form a union and build a workhouse.[1] The parishes of St Philip's and St Martin's had no need to adopt the Act wholesale, having worked in tandem for 60 years, and been in possession of a workhouse for half a century. Yet the Gilbert Act probably provided the momentum to reform the existing arrangements. Within a year a Local Act 'for the better management of Birmingham workhouse' was on the statute book, the chief component of which was to authorise triennial elections for 108 guardians to oversee the operation of the Poor Law in the town.[2] In using

---

1   A. Bundage, *The English Poor Laws 1700–1930*, Basingstoke, 2002, p. 21.

2   *An Act for Providing a Proper Workhouse...*, 1783, 23 Geo. III c. 54.

both overseers and elected guardians, Birmingham united elements of both the Old and the New Poor Law, more than half a century before the latter was created. The 1783 Act also stipulated that both overseers and churchwardens were included as *ex officio* members of the body of guardians.

Poor Law expenditure under the Old Poor Law was traditionally in the hands of the annually appointed parish overseers. It was they who determined the number of levies needed to cover their costs and then distributed the money collected either in outdoor or indoor relief. Key to this was applicants' weekly attendance at the workhouse, when the overseers would grant or refuse relief. For those unable to come to Lichfield Street, a parish visitor would be despatched to visit them at home and assess their needs. The Birmingham vestry clerk told the Poor Law Commission that 'call-overs' were periodically held as well, forcing all paupers to attend in person, bringing all their dependent children with them.[3] In reality, however, call-overs were few and far between. Once a relief payment was agreed, it was up to the vestry clerk to open the coffers and fill the outstretched hand. In exceptional circumstances the overseers might also be persuaded to intervene more widely in the town's economic affairs, underwriting the cost of employing claimants to work on the Birmingham roads in 1816, or, in 1810, buying potatoes in bulk to supply them more cheaply to the poor.[4] In general, however, the Poor Law officers were reluctant to interfere in a domain that they considered properly the work of charities.

The number of overseers appointed by a parish did not remain constant. In Birmingham, once the parishes of St Martin and St Philip had been united for the purposes of poor relief, the number was set at six. By the end of the eighteenth century, the rapid growth of the town meant that the overseers were dealing with more than 4,000 cases a week. This increasing workload had obliged the authorities to double the number of overseers and it remained at twelve from around 1796.[5] The overseers themselves were formally nominated by the local magistracy from a short-list drawn up by the parish. In order to avoid a hiatus (both in work and in experience) between the standing-down of one set of officials and the installation of a new group, the introduction of the twelve new overseers was staggered over a six-monthly period. Half-way through each year six overseers retired and six of the new appointees took over their duties, and there was thus considerable continuity of personnel between one year and the next. As with the guardians, however, and all other parish officers, to be elected

---

3   *Report from His Majesty's Commissioners for Inquiring into the Administration and Practical Operation of the Poor Laws*, Appendix A, Parliamentary Papers, XXIX, 1834, p. 58a.

4   *Swinney's Birmingham Chronicle*, 25 January 1810.

5   C. Durnford and E. Hyde East, *Term Reports in the Court of the King's Bench from Michaelmas Term 1794 to Trinity Term 1796*, London, 1802, p. 541.

did not necessarily reflect a willingness to serve and there were many examples of individuals dragging their feet. In 1819, for example, John Dudley appealed against his appointment as overseer, arguing that he was not 'a substantial householder' under the terms of the Poor Law Act, and the Quarter Sessions duly overturned his election.[6] As the vestry clerk, William Brynner, told the Poor Law Commission in 1834, the Birmingham overseers were 'usually principal tradesmen or shopkeepers'.[7] Finding the time to balance two jobs (one of them unpaid) would never be easy. Reluctance to serve, however, was much more evident in the body of guardians than with the overseers.

Although the Birmingham overseers remained largely in charge of the distribution of parish funds, most particularly in dealing with applications for relief every Friday, the business of collecting the levies was devolved onto waged assistant overseers, who made the obligatory door-to-door visits. From 1782 only two assistant overseers were deemed necessary.[8] In 1821, however, when the decision was taken to rate all houses valued at £6 and above, no less than twelve new assistant overseers were appointed to collect the additional sums.[9] That the vestry felt able to pay these new assistant overseers an annual wage of £75 each suggests how much the finances of the Birmingham Poor Law were expected to be transformed by the lowering of the rating threshold.[10] The salary (which amounted to 28s a week) was attractive enough to become a job for life, and by 1834 some of the assistants were said to be old men. This was seized as the moment, therefore, to reduce their number to nine.[11] Each of the new assistants was required to pay a surety of £200. Since the collection of monies necessitated considerable personal integrity, such a considerable deposit was designed to protect the parish against dishonest dealing. While the overseers were deemed respectable (and honest) enough to undertake their duties *gratis*, such unswerving honesty could not be expected of their assistants. Although the number of rating districts into which the town was divided varied over time, it was usual for each assistant overseer to be responsible for a single district. The 1831 Local Act invested the power to appoint or dismiss the assistants with the guardians; prior to that they had been nominated at a public meeting.

In addition to enabling the two parishes to erect a new workhouse, the 1783 Act empowered Birmingham ratepayers (those assessed at £10 a year and

---

6   *Swinney's Birmingham Chronicle*, 28 October 1819.

7   *Report from His Majesty's Commissioners for Inquiring into the Administration and Practical Operation of the Poor Laws*, Appendix A, Parliamentary Papers, XXIX, 1834, p. 58a.

8   *Aris's Gazette*, 6 May 1782.

9   *Aris's Gazette*, 29 January 1821.

10   *Aris's Gazette*, 26 March 1821.

11   *Birmingham Advertiser*, 16 February 1834.

Figure 6.1 The Public Office, Moor Street, where the Guardians of the Poor of Birmingham met. Library of Birmingham. Archives and Collections: MS 897 Volume 1 No. 78

above) to elect 108 guardians of the poor, who could shoulder some of the burden of the hard-pressed overseers. The Act permitted the new body 'to act as overseers in all things appertaining to the office of overseers of the poor, except with regard to the making and collecting of rates'.[12] Birmingham's version of the Gilbert Act (which only allowed for a single elected guardian per parish) reflected the town's size and ambition. Neither the overseer nor the guardian received any payment for his work, and only an abatement to his rates for his years of office recompensed him financially. While, in normal circumstances an overseer served only for a single year; for the guardians it was for a minimum of three. Under the powers of the 1783 Act, ratepayers were permitted to nominate up to 108 candidates, delivering their preferences on a sealed piece of paper before midday on the day of the election. The election was secret (as far as that was possible) and women ratepayers could vote, even if they could not yet stand as guardians. Elections of guardians took place triennially, on or close to Lady Day (25 March). This gave Birmingham secular control of poor relief to sit alongside the ecclesiastical power of the overseers. If there was a certain tension implicit in that arrangement, it was not immediately apparent. By appointing the overseers as de facto guardians as well, it was presumably hoped to prevent direct conflict between the two bodies.

---

12   *An Act for Providing a Proper Workhouse...*, 1783, 23 Geo. III c. 54.

The first public meeting to elect the guardians took place on 17 July 1783 at the Public Office, then in Dale End. The more spacious Public Office in Moor Street did not open until 1807.[13] The Dale End building was probably the only venue capable of hosting a large meeting, other than using a church, and that, given the nature of the business, was clearly out of the question. The only other premises used by the guardians at this time was Dadley's Hotel in Moor Street. A total of 108 guardians were nominated on that day in 1783 and the list contained most of the key players in eighteenth-century Birmingham society, with the added restriction that they must be renting property at more than £12 per annum, and be resident in the town. It included (to name only a handful of the better known) Henry Clay, Edward Thomason, William Withering, Samuel Galton senior and junior, George Humphries, Isaac Spooner, Sampson Lloyd, Samuel Garbett, James Pickard, John Ryland and William Hutton.[14] The ratepayers selected the most prominent citizens of the town and, in the

Figure 6.2 Henry Clay, one of the Guardians of the Poor of Birmingham. Bisset's *Magnificent Guide for Birmingham*, 1808

---

13   W.B. Stephens (ed.), *A History of the County of Warwick, Vol. 7: The City of Birmingham*, London, 1964, p. 10.

14   William Hutton (1723–1815), historian and bookseller; Henry Clay (1767–1812), 'Japanner in Ordinary to His Majesty', Sherriff of Warwickshire in 1790; Sampson Lloyd III (1699–1779), Quaker iron manufacturer and banker; William Withering (1741–1809), physician and botanist; Samuel Galton senior (1720–99) and Samuel Galton junior (1753–1832), Quaker iron manufacturers and gun-makers; Edward Thomason (c.1769–1849), buckle manufacturer; Isaac Spooner (1735–1818), banker; Samuel Garbett (1717–1803), industrialist, ironmaster and founder of the Birmingham Commercial Committee; James Pickard (d. 1814), mill-owner and steam-engine manufacturer. Withering and Galton were both members of the Lunar Society; Hutton, Lloyd, Ryland and the Galtons were all dissenters.

Figure 6.3 Manufactory of Edward Thomason, one of the Guardians of the Poor of Birmingham. Bisset's *Magnificent Guide for Birmingham*, 1808

Figure 6.4 Dr William Withering, one of the first Guardians of the Poor of Birmingham. Archives and Collections, Library of Birmingham

Figure 6.5 Samuel Galton Jr., one of the first Guardians of the Poor of Birmingham. Archives and Collections, Library of Birmingham

Figure 6.6 William Hutton, one of the first Guardians of the Poor of Birmingham, and Birmingham's first historian. Archives and Collections, Library of Birmingham: MS 4085 Box 87

absence of any form of political representation at this date (50 years before the town's representation in Parliament), they chose mostly industrialists. The list included Anglicans, Unitarians and Quakers.

Not that being elected always led to taking up office. A year after that first election it was clear that a considerable number of the nominees had not, and would not, be serving. The reasons they provided ranged widely: Mr Seager was in 'a bad state of health', Mr Dickenson 'cannot spare the time', Mr Clay was 'so much in London that he thinks he can't do his duty', Mr Russell 'may attend, but did not know he was chose [sic] guardian', Mr Lloyd 'was out three times when he was called upon'.[15] By this time around one third of those elected were dead, had moved away or had 'refused to act'. As an example of volunteerism in action, it was not impressive. This situation never really improved in the following two decades and, indeed, the choice of such a large number of guardians may have been made in the expectation that only a proportion of them would actually be willing to devote themselves to the task. One tenth of this number, 18 guardians, was said to be the quorum for general meetings,

---

15   Archives and Collections, Library of Birmingham. GP B/2/1/1 Birmingham Guardians' minutes, 9 August 1784.

though this was far from universally honoured.[16] To take another example, elections were held in April 1801 and, as usual, 108 names were set down. Of these, 36 swore an oath of office immediately afterwards: 'without favour or affection, hatred or malice, truly and impartially, according to the best of my skill and knowledge, to execute and perform...' A further 20 swore at the next guardians' meeting, 6 more a month later, 5 more in September and 4 the following year. This (around three-quarters) was the sum total of commitment. In April 1835, two years after the previous election, 28 of the 108 guardians were disqualified 'as not having attended twice in a year, or were insolvent, or not qualified'.[17] As Birmingham's net of public service spread ever wider, there was an inevitable and lucrative trade in exemptions. In April 1787, at the time of the second round of guardians' elections, *Aris's Gazette* carried a brazen advertisement that 'two certificates, exempting the bearer from all parish and ward offices' were to be auctioned at Freeth's Tavern, close to the Bull Ring.[18]

Charles Pelham Villiers, the Poor Law assistant commissioner in 1834, considered the large number of Birmingham guardians 'objectionable', and certainly no guarantee of improved management. Either the number was unwieldy, he argued, or, if the self-same few attended meetings, pointless. Villiers unfavourably contrasted the system at Birmingham with its closest neighbour at Aston, where 'the whole parish is practically under the management of the governor of the workhouse'. However, in Villiers' eyes, the size and frequency of the levies were the only true measuring-stick for success. Strictly speaking, the earliest Birmingham guardians (from 1783 onwards) were not so much elected as nominated. There is no indication of rival candidacy, and, indeed, many of the men chosen appear to have had little idea that their names were being put forward. George Edmonds, who was at least partly (no doubt solely in his mind) responsible for turning the appointment of guardians into something that could legitimately be called an election, suggested that prior to 1819 the process was little more than a formality:

> It had been the practice of the guardians in office to nominate their successors, and that there had been no check whatever offered to their proceedings, owing to the great apathy evinced in the town at the time of the election.

The sitting body might well attempt to recommend their successors after 1819 too, but with considerably less confidence in the outcome. By 1834, Edmonds

---

16   *Report from His Majesty's Commissioners for Inquiring into the Administration and Practical Operation of the Poor Laws*, Appendix A, Parliamentary Papers, XXIX, 1834, p. 55a.

17   *Birmingham Advertiser*, 16 April 1835.

18   *Aris's Gazette*, 9 April 1787.

told the assistant Poor Law commissioner, elections were conducted 'with more spirit and justice'.[19]

By 1819 we begin to see the first seriously contested election, when Birmingham factions (but not yet political parties as such) began to campaign for their own favoured candidates. Indeed, the 1819 guardians' election was the first time that what we might call a 'caucus', a political state, was evident in Birmingham's politics. According to the *Gazette*, printed lists of recommended candidates were being delivered 'almost door to door' in the run-up to polling day.[20] The conservative *Gazette* itself was aggrieved that the names of 'well-deserving gentlemen of experience' had been replaced by others with nothing like the same level of familiarity with guardianship. It is clear that a kind of limited Poor Law democracy was beginning to challenge the old continuities of parochial office. This was the self-same moment, we might add, when the first concerted campaign for Parliamentary electoral reform began. A number of these 'recommended' lists of candidates survive as broadsheets, including the list from 1819 and another from 1822.[21] As we have seen, the decision to canvass directly for nominations appears to have come from George Edmonds, whose campaigning against the current administration began with a pamphlet war in that year. Both the 1819 and 1822 lists bear his signature. Edmonds comments:

> We recommend to parishioners who are desirous to see the levies reduced, that they will (if approved) copy in writing the very respectable list below, then cut the list into tickets, wrap them up in a paper, and seal the paper and deliver it personally to the Chairman to be appointed at the meeting. We hope that ladies who are entitled to vote will not fail to be at the meeting and give their name for more efficient guardians.[22]

Cutting the rates, of course, was the manifesto pledge of practically every competing faction. It was no more likely to be achieved under Edmonds' regime than any other. But, like any political party today, no group would campaign with a promise to increase taxes.

Once this political genie had been released from the bottle in 1819, the election of Birmingham guardians became as fierce as any Parliamentary contest, and rival factions drew up their slates of recommended candidates: a blue list for the Radicals, white for the Tories, and green for the Whigs. The sitting administration of overseers and guardians drew up their own list as well. On one

---

19   *Report from His Majesty's Commissioners for Inquiring into the Administration and Practical Operation of the Poor Laws*, Appendix A, Parliamentary Papers, XXIX, 1834, p. 55a.

20   *Aris's Gazette*, 5 April 1819.

21   Archives and Collections, Library of Birmingham. MS 662/2–3 Timmins collection.

22   Archives and Collections, Library of Birmingham. MS 662/2 Timmins collection.

surviving sheet from 1828 the 108 names were printed far enough apart for them to be 'cut into strips and enclosed in a letter'.[23] They represent a blatant attempt to steer the electorate, and were probably illegal. The rival Birmingham newspapers entered the fray just as enthusiastically. In 1830 the conservative *Monthly Argus* railed at the 'artful Unitarian, holy Quaker and wretched saintly sinner', who held sway in the guardians' boardroom.[24] For the radical *Midland Representative* on the other hand, these democratically elected guardians might provide the strong local administration that Birmingham was still not yet entitled to:

> But properly elected guardians would become a local Parliament, and might advantageously be entrusted with the direction of all public funds and public business of the town – the paving and lighting etc., now under the Street Commissioners, the funds of the Grammar School, public education, the preservation and enforcement of laws, and the appointment of the police and magistrates.[25]

By the 1830s the election of Poor Law guardians had become fully politicised. The decade of reform, incorporation and Chartism showed the once lauded cohesion of Brummagem society had fractured along party lines and this was as evident in the election of guardians as it was in most other aspects of town life. If the ratepayers were now able to elect their members of Parliament and (after 1838) their town councillors too, they would elect their guardians just as ferociously, and similarly along party lines. The *Birmingham Journal* reported that a total of 1,670 ratepayers turned out to vote in 1840, of whom around 40 were women.[26] Yet the guardians' election was far from a simple reflection of the wider political battles. The outcome of the 1840 election, for example, was practically a clean sweep for the Tories, filling 99 of the 108 places, with only 6 Whigs and 3 Radicals to join them. That, at least, was how the reformist *Journal* (with some dismay) saw the outcome of the poll.[27] The Birmingham guardians' election, therefore, entirely reversed the results of both the Parliamentary and municipal elections in the town, which were (as usual) dominated by the radical voice of the Birmingham Political Union. It would be hard to determine how far this more politicised form of guardianship actually altered the policies of the board; the day-to-day stewardship of a Poor Law authority did not admit of sudden and drastic changes of direction. Nevertheless, we may note that the decision (in 1831) to admit the press to meetings of the guardians coincided with a new board, just as the

---

23   Archives and Collections, Library of Birmingham. 202322 Birmingham Miscellaneous M/1.

24   *Monthly Argus & Public Censor*, Vol. 2, July 1830, p. 20.

25   *Midland Representative & Birmingham Herald*, 25 April 1831.

26   *Birmingham Journal*, 28 March 1840.

27   *Birmingham Journal*, 4 April 1840.

Monthly Argus had hoped and that the 1834 board declared soon after its election its opposition to the Whiggish New Poor Law Act.[28]

Once elected, the guardians were sub-divided into smaller committees or groups to serve successively, with quarterly meetings of the full board to ratify or vote on important decisions. Initially, meetings of each group of twelve guardians were held weekly in the workhouse, as outlined in the 1783 Act, and their deliberations are recorded in the guardians' minute books, which begin in 1783. Yet we may question how well the new arrangement worked. There are periods of up to 18 months (between October 1786 and January 1788, for example) when no meetings are recorded at all, and many instances where only a list of attendees, and no decisions, are minuted. One meeting (in July 1786) was adjourned solely because an inmate had climbed over the workhouse wall and escaped.[29] By the 1790s this arrangement had collapsed entirely and willing guardians were simply allocated a committee such as clothing, house, asylum, provisions and so forth, which met separately and put forward proposals to be considered by the larger body.

There remained some overlapping responsibilities between the overseers and guardians, however.[30] Guardians could serve as overseers, and vice versa, and both overseers and guardians had the power to admit or eject paupers from the house. But the good conduct of the workhouse and the appointment and management of staff was the responsibility of the guardians alone. The overall division reflected, not only the difference between matters secular and sacred, but also the (by now) ancient terms of the Great Poor Law Act of 1601. It was the overseers' duty to set rates, to make weekly payments for out-relief, to put out apprentices and to investigate all matters relating to bastardy. Neither guardians nor workhouses had been envisaged in the 1601 Act and therefore most of the guardians' responsibilities had evolved since 1601: to supervise the nursing of children, choose bookkeepers and secure provisions for the workhouse.

The guardians also committed themselves in 1783 to attend the workhouse every day 'to see the family of this house breakfast, dine and sup and to preserve good order', though there is little evidence that they did so very regularly.[31] The term 'family' is here first used, and it became the standard metaphor in Birmingham to describe the workhouse community. The parental role of the governor and matron (in normal circumstances a husband and wife) was thus

---

28 *Birmingham Journal*, 16 April 1831; *Aris's Gazette*, 18 April 1831; Archives and Collections, Library of Birmingham. GP B/2/1/3 Birmingham Guardians' minutes, 12 May 1834.

29 Archives and Collections, Library of Birmingham. GP B/2/1/1 Birmingham Guardians' minutes, 5 July 1786.

30 *Ibid.*, 29 March 1784.

31 *Ibid.*, 5 January 1784.

underlined, and given the presence of 250 children under fifteen years of age already resident, the term was not inappropriate. But the family model did not simply reflect the presence of children in the house. The paupers too could be seen, and could see themselves, as children of the Poor Law, their status as autonomous adults diminished by their dependency. In 1825, when the conduct of the governess, Mrs Cheshire, was denounced in the press, one of the inmates sprang to her defence. John Banks, himself an old man, told a committee of enquiry: 'The mistress behaved to him as if he had been one of her own children.' The fact that Mrs Cheshire's own offspring shared the accommodation perhaps helped to emphasise the parental nature of the relationship.[32]

The reorganisation of Birmingham's Poor Law provision in 1783 was welcomed enthusiastically by the poet and inn-keeper, John Freeth. Freeth's 1790 poem was addressed to 'The Birmingham Overseers', but it seems likely that Freeth was not distinguishing between the overseers and guardians, and was not entirely correct about the date of reform:

> Years ago vestry-meetings unpleasant were found,
> But now the proceedings with pleasure are crown'd;
> Alteration took place in the year 'eighty-five,
> And the spirit of office is still kept alive.[33]

The moment was celebrated by the presentation of a magnificent ornamental casket in japanned ware and tortoiseshell to the six overseers in 1784. The box, currently in private hands, was both made and presented by Henry Clay, the town's leading japanner and one of the newly elected guardians. We might interpret the gift as both an acknowledgement of the work of the retiring overseers and a tacit implication that the reins of power were now in the hands of others.[34]

There is one matter left to discuss here, itself an inevitable consequence of a structure of command which was, at the top, unpaid. It concerns the perennially thorny issue of expenses. The work of an overseer or guardian was not light; there were regular meetings to attend, examinations of paupers, interviews with applicants for out-relief, sittings to arrange apprenticeships, as well as frequent inspections of the workhouse, infirmary and asylum. There were also interviews with the out-poor, within and without the parish, visits to

---

32   Archives and Collections, Library of Birmingham. GP B/2/1/2 Birmingham Guardians' minutes, 25 October 1825.

33   J. Horden, *John Freeth (1731–1808): Political Ballad-Writer and Innkeeper*, Oxford, 1993, p. 184. Freeth was perfectly willing to accept sponsorship for some of his verse. We cannot say whether his views on Poor Law reform were heart-felt or financially 'encouraged'.

34   The casket was sold at auction for £7,000 at the Hansons' autumn sale in September 2013. Cf. *Antiques Trade Gazette*, 4 November 2013.

Figure 6.7 Japanned and tortoiseshell casket presented to the retiring Overseers of the Poor in 1784 by Henry Clay, japanner, one of the newly appointed Guardians of the Poor of Birmingham as a result of the 1783 Act of Parliament. Image courtesy of Hansons Auctioneers and Valuers Ltd, London and Etwall, Derbyshire.

patients at lunatic asylums, or to children in foster homes. Although the parish overseers and guardians were compelled to labour without pay, they could hardly be expected (they would have argued) to find their expenses out of their own pockets as well. As John Freeth himself noted, in the verse preceding his paean of praise to the settlement of 1784:

Overseers the good things of the world love to taste,
Of the present to speak – not forgetting the last;
Unanimity through the whole business appears,
For why – they were all in the cause volunteers.[35]

The level of such expenses, of course, could hardly fail to provoke controversy, especially as they underpinned a system that had at its heart the good governance of the indigent and the prudent management of ratepayers' money.

The kind of individuals thrust into office by the Poor Law did not expect to share the meagre food of the workhouse inmates, or to sleep (on their journeys away from Birmingham) in the casual ward. But, as with the expenses of Members of Parliament since 1911, what may begin as the necessary overheads of public service could easily tip into the unspoken perks of office. And the more the actual cost of the Poor Law was revealed, by open meetings and the publication of annual accounts, the more sensitive did the matter of expenses become. It must be added that it was not an issue limited to parochial officials; Birmingham magistrates too were subjected to growing criticism for similar self-indulgence at their sittings, the cost of which came out of the county rate. This was in the period when radicals, such as John Wade and William Cobbett, attacked the established church, the government and the monarchy for 'elite parasitism', often termed 'old corruption', and the local authorities of Birmingham suffered similar criticisms in their turn.[36]

In the overall scheme of things, the expenses of overseers and guardians represented little more than a drop in the ocean of Poor Law expenditure. By the early 1830s, after all, the total cost of poor relief in the town (and therefore the cost to the ratepayers) amounted to some £45,000 a year.[37] A few lavish meals and comfortable hotel breakfasts did not add significantly to that. It was more a matter of principle. Noisy public meetings and newspaper editors, keen to stir up and exploit popular dissent, could quickly turn a fish supper or a complimentary glass of sherry into a public outrage. Lavish expenditure

---

35   J. Freeth, *The Political Songster or A Touch on the Times*, Birmingham, 1790, p. 165.

36   P. Harling, *The Waning of 'Old Corruption': The Politics of Economical Reform in Britain, 1779–1846*, Oxford, 1996, pp. 143–5.

37   Workhouse accounts 1833–4 in *Birmingham Advertiser*, 3 July 1834.

became the *bete noire* of the early nineteenth-century Poor Law, more so (at least in Birmingham) than ill treatment or parsimony. In 1824, for example, a correspondent to *Aris's Gazette* ('A Payer of Poor's [*sic*] Levies') protested vehemently at the cost of the food and drink supplied to the overseers out of parish funds. There was a bill of £80 for brandy drunk at call-overs and at the election of new overseers, a bill for fish that exceeded £65, and an expenses-paid trip to the lunatic asylum at Droitwich, which amounted to more than £25. That the drink was supplied by a company owned by one of the overseers himself, who could thus be seen to profit directly from the operation, only added a further whiff of corruption to the charge of prodigality:

> One cannot make an accustomed call at the Minerva for a glass of ale, or a butcher's to buy Sunday's dinner, without hearing: 'Have you heard of the overseers' extravagant proceedings at the workhouse?'[38]

The Minerva in Peck Lane, as the unofficial headquarters of the town's Tories, might be expected to attract such gossip, but mutterings of this kind were not limited to the bars and the newspapers, nor to the Tories. Ten years later, the high costs incurred by overseers making a tour of inspection of the Staffordshire County Asylum, were being raised in the guardians' boardroom itself. Henry Knight accused the overseers of 'making a holiday of it', a charge, of course, denied. It was over such issues that tensions between the increasingly politicised guardians and the parish officials became only too apparent. James Oram, an ex-guardian himself, after examination of the workhouse books, revealed to the *Birmingham Journal* a remarkably long list of luxuries consumed, we might guess, at dinners for the parish officials:

> In addition, turkeys, geese, ducks, chickens, pigeons, force-meat, tripe, fish, fish sauce, jelly, eggs, cream cheeses, anchovies, capers, mushrooms, catsup [ketchup], apricots, apples, peas, plums, raspberries, cranberries, bilberries, lemons, oranges, asparagus, cucumbers, sallad [*sic*], nutmegs, cloves, and lemon peel.[39]

But if the issue was one of accountability, it had largely been achieved by the end of the 1830s, and wining and dining at the ratepayers' expense had come to an end. When, at a guardians' meeting in April 1838, Henry Knight and George Edmonds put forward the motion to end all such practices, there was hardly a murmur of dissent.[40]

---

38 *Aris's Gazette*, 15 November 1824.

39 *Birmingham Journal*, 9 May 1835.

40 *Aris's Gazette*, 19 April 1838.

7

Thirty Acres and a Cow:
The Use of Birmingham's Parish Land

One major difficulty in meeting the ever-increasing, but always variable, demands of the poor was the fact that many parishes had little in the way of liquid assets. If one sets aside the occasional charitable legacy (and that was usually ring-fenced), in many cases the parish tended to own very little, or little that was readily disposable in financial terms. Thus it lived a hand-to-mouth existence, entirely reliant on the regular collection of rates or levies, which, in Birmingham's case, was every three weeks or so, with the assessment recorded in the 'Grand Levy Book'.[1] Even then, collecting was always patchy and the sums harvested rarely lived up to expectations.[2] What land and property a parish owned through bequests was usually scattered far and wide, and only raised moderate sums in rents from tenants. What happened in 1798, then, transformed Birmingham's parochial fortunes, and in many ways changed the way the town thought about its poor provision.

From the Middle Ages onwards the manor of Birmingham, the boundaries of which were coterminous with the parish, consisted of an urban centre, concentrated in the south-eastern corner, and what was known as the 'foreign'. The latter was the area of modern Ladywood, Rotton Park and Winson Green, stretching as far as the boundary with the neighbouring parish of Handsworth. Most of the 'foreign', at least up to the early nineteenth century, consisted of waste and heathland, thinly populated and largely ignored. To most people it was simply 'the Heath'. In 1798 the Bill for enclosing Birmingham Heath

---

1   C. Durnford and E. Hyde East, *Term Reports in the Court of the King's Bench from Michaelmas Term 1794 to Trinity Term 1796*, London, 1802, p. 541.

2   J.A. Langford, *A Century of Birmingham Life: Or, A Chronicle of Local Events, from 1741–1841*, Vol. 2, Birmingham, 1868, p. 449. Langford estimated that in 1882, despite a levy of £4,041 only £1,700 was collected.

was presented to Parliament. Wherever it was attempted, enclosure ran up against England's complicated jigsaw of land ownership; more often than not, landowners had plots of land scattered over a wide area. If enclosure was to be truly effective, it usually involved exchanging pieces here and there to make the map simpler, and ownership more unified. Given the sparse habitation on the Heath, enclosure would not spell economic disaster for many small farmers in the way it often did elsewhere. Nevertheless, the parish recognised an opportunity that would not be coming its way again. It would not oppose the enclosure of Birmingham Heath, if thirty acres of the said land were set aside for the use of the poor.[3] The landowners concerned were more than happy to see their Bill make untroubled progress through the Commons, given the costs involved, and a clause was inserted to that effect.[4] The Bill received royal assent on 26 May 1798.[5]

The land thus appropriated for parish use included Key (or Kaye) Hill, and soon after, in February 1800, Key Hill was itself enclosed with raised banks and fences by its new owners.[6] The attraction of Key Hill, and the reason the parish was so keen to secure it, was that it contained a sand mine, and industrialising Birmingham and the Black Country would pay good prices for the kind of fine sand available there. Sand outcrops exist in large quantities in this part of the city. The street name Sand Pits, leading on to the Dudley Road and the large excavations at both Key Hill and Warstone Lane cemeteries, are continuing testimony to the erstwhile importance of the material. Sand was needed both in the glass and casting industries, and as an ingredient in mortar.

The methodical way the guardians of the poor of Birmingham went about the exploitation of Key Hill was clear-sighted and designed for the long term. First they secured the site with fencing, then (in 1801) they took out a lease on another piece of land adjacent to the Birmingham Canal for use as a wharf.[7] Here the sand could be stored, prior to being loaded onto boats. Use of the Birmingham Canal, cutting through the heart of the South Staffordshire coalfields and on to Wolverhampton, ensured that factories and builders across the Black Country and beyond could be potential customers. The sand was also sold on-site, as well as being delivered (at a higher price) to clients across the

---

3   Archives and Collections, Library of Birmingham. GP B/2/1/1 Birmingham Guardians' minutes, 19 April 1798.

4   *Ibid.*, 24 April 1798.

5   *Birmingham Inclosure Act*, 1797, 38 Geo. III c. 54.

6   Archives and Collections, Library of Birmingham. GP B/2/1/1 Birmingham Guardians' minutes, 3 February 1800.

7   *Ibid.*, 24 November 1801.

town.[8] By 1805 the sand mine at Key Hill was making a profit of some £120 a year, which was invested back in stocks.[9] Demand for this sand fluctuated, of course, as the local economy (and building industry) contracted and expanded and at times the sand lying at the wharf resembled a mighty and unstable mountain. In January 1838, indeed, the hill gave way and ruined ten yards of hedge on Mr Shakespeare's land next door.[10] It was, it seems, often easier to excavate the sand than it was to off-load it. At the height of the operation the excavations at Key Hill must have resembled an open-cast mine, though one with much more unstable materials. If the collapse of the sand over at the wharf was unfortunate, it could have even more serious consequences for the men working under the cliff at Key Hill. Two of the wheelers died when the sand bank collapsed on them in April 1826.[11]

So how was the sand got up? Central to this question was Birmingham's changed policy towards its out-poor, evident from 1819 onwards. A new board of guardians, elected in March 1819, took office immediately after the internal scandal that had led to the dismissal of the previous workhouse governor (see chapter 8). Allegations of poor accounting procedures and wasteful expenditure appear to have galvanised the board into drawing up a far tighter economic regime for the workhouse itself. In addition, relief payments were to be used to employ the able-bodied men, rather than simply to sustain them whilst unemployed. In modern parlance, it was a policy of 'off welfare and into work', albeit work provided directly by the parish. The board might well also have had in mind the recent Select Vestries Acts of 1818 and 1819 (usually referred to as the Sturges Bourne Acts) which heralded a tougher stance nationally towards the able-bodied claimant.[12] Any able-bodied man applying for poor relief, therefore, was sent to the sand mine, or, as it was sometimes called, the sand 'cliff'. Here they would dig out the sand, load it onto wheelbarrows and wheel it the quarter of a mile or so from Key Hill to the canal.[13] The outward journey to the wharf was mainly uphill. The logic of this was that if an applicant

---

8   *Aris's Gazette*, 14 March 1805.

9   Archives and Collections, Library of Birmingham. GP B/2/1/1 Birmingham Guardians' minutes, 15 October 1805.

10   Archives and Collections, Library of Birmingham. CP B/660986 Birmingham Overseer's Minutes Vol. 5, 2 January 1838.

11   *Aris's Gazette*, 17 April 1826.

12   The Select Vestries Acts were promoted by William Sturges Bourne, MP for Bandon Bridge, and refers to the *Act for the Regulation of Parish Vestries*, 1818, 58 Geo. III c. 69, and the *Act to Amend the Law for the Relief of the Poor*, 1819, 59 Geo. III c. 12; W.E. Tate, *The Parish Chest: A Study of the Records of Parochial Administration in England*, 3rd edn, Cambridge, 1969, pp. 21–2.

13   Archives and Collections, Library of Birmingham. MS 2126/EB9/1829 Regulations of Birmingham Workhouse (with anonymous annotations), 1830.

felt exploited, ground down or underpaid, he would go off in search of more gainful employment. Working at Key Hill was never meant to be an attractive proposition. The working party at the sand mine was supplemented by able-bodied men from the workhouse too, albeit in much smaller numbers. Nor, as we shall see, was the use of local labour limited to the mine alone. What was going on at Key Hill represents the translation of the workhouse system to the out-poor. Just as an able-bodied man or woman accommodated in the house would be expected to work for their upkeep, so the applicant for outdoor relief was now equally expected to pay his way. It was a more than useful way of weeding out the honest from the idle.

The formation of what would later be termed a 'labour colony' was not unique to Birmingham, though relatively rare at this early date. Michelle Higgs associates such colonies principally with the New Poor Law and mainly from the 1860s onwards. Great Yarmouth Union, for example, was employing able-bodied men in this way in 1887, and many unions offered labour or stone yards as a condition of relief.[14] Heather Shore, drawing on much earlier evidence, notes the use of a labour colony by the Westminster parishes in 1722, though chiefly as means of clearing the streets of the 'loose and disorderly'.[15] What is particularly noteworthy about the Birmingham example is both its date and the long-term nature of the operation. If, as Steven King argues, the arrival of the able-bodied male was a key factor in the 'crisis of the Old Poor Law' from the 1790s onwards, the united Birmingham parishes found an imaginative, evolving and (at times) cost-effective solution to it.[16] The work at Key Hill was managed by a committee of guardians (the Key Hill committee), whose regular reports show frequent variation in the output of the mine. In 1817 the sand was making a profit of £44, which had risen in 1818 to £53.[17] In the year ending Lady Day 1822 it was said to have generated profits of £436 12s.[18] Output necessarily reflected overall employment or unemployment levels in the town. Nor is it always clear whether the figures reported to the guardians or to the press took account of running costs such as the rent of the wharf, payments to task-masters and wheelers, and the cost of tools.

By 1820 around thirty or forty men were digging and wheeling sand at Key Hill six days a week, with a paid overseer on hand to keep a tally of how

---

14   M. Higgs, *Life in the Victorian and Edwardian Workhouse*, Stroud, 2007, pp. 28–9.

15   H. Shore, 'Crime, Criminal Networks and Survival Strategies of the Poor in Early Eighteenth-Century London', in S. King and A. Tomkins (eds), *The Poor in England 1700–1850: An Economy of Makeshifts*, Manchester, 2003, pp. 144–5.

16   S. King, *Poverty and Welfare in England 1700–1850: A Regional Perspective*, Manchester, 2000, p. 166.

17   Archives and Collections, Library of Birmingham. GP B/2/1/2 Birmingham Guardians' minutes, 11 August 1818.

18   *Aris's Gazette*, 1 April 1822.

many loads each man delivered to the wharf.[19] According to the Birmingham guardians' minutes, the men themselves were paid three farthings (¾d) per barrow or one penny a barrow if the sand was wet, and therefore more compacted and heavier. A man was permitted to earn between five and seven shillings a week.[20] The arithmetic of this indicates that on average a worker must have wheeled about sixteen barrows a day, and walked eight miles to the wharf and back. The workers' well-worn shoes were repaired for them in the workhouse, at least until the guardians put a stop to this allowance in 1833.[21] How much the wheelers earned at Key Hill was probably a matter of personal choice or physical fitness. Certainly at Aston parish, which was also deploying able-bodied men in sand or gravel pits in the 1830s, and perhaps also at Key Hill, it was said that a man could earn three shillings a day.[22] It was his own decision how many days he worked, or whether he pursued other employment elsewhere to supplement his income. Nevertheless, his outdoor relief, if he continued to draw it, depended upon his presence at the sand mine.

The quantities of sand deposited at the wharf always varied, depending on how many unemployed men were ready and willing to work at the mine, but at its most productive Key Hill was yielding 400 tons of sand a month.[23] By the mid-1820s, however, when there were more jobs available in the real economy, the number of unemployed wheelers fell away. By April 1823 the workforce was down to around twenty-six, including both men from the house and out-poor.[24] And here was a strange irony, not budgeted for in the original equation. When the economy was flat, there were more men wheeling, but less customers buying. When the local economy was buoyant and the need for sand at its height, there were not enough unemployed men wheeling sand to meet demand. It was at this point, in 1824, that the guardians invested in two horses and two carts to transport the sand more quickly up to the canal. By this date it was estimated that there were around 200,000 cubic yards of sand left at Key Hill, providing enough work for another thirty or forty years. The supply was never, in fact, exhausted. The sand mine had fulfilled its main purpose, which was to find work for the unemployed; the financial gains were largely incidental and (once the wheelers and the overseer had been paid) not great. All the guardians could hope for, and in this their hopes were in large part fulfilled, was that the sand mine operation broke even.

---

19   Archives and Collections, Library of Birmingham. GP B/2/1/2 Guardians' minutes, 27 June 1820.

20   *Ibid.*, 3 October 1820.

21   Archives and Collections, Library of Birmingham. GP B/2/1/3 Guardians' minutes, 6 February 1833.

22   *Birmingham Advertiser*, 23 January 1834.

23   Archives and Collections, Library of Birmingham. GP B/2/1/2 Guardians' minutes, 15 January 1821.

24   *Ibid.*, 8 April 1823.

The annual accounts for 1832/3 (beginning and ending at Lady Day) show a profit of £918 from the sale of sand,[25] and in 1833/4 receipts amounted to £1,013.[26] Nevertheless, profit and loss in Poor Law terms were always in the eye of the beholder. What to one set of guardians might appear an ideal way to keep down costs (and thus to relieve the pressure on the ratepayers) could seem very different to another group. Poor Law accounting, for all its evident complexity, was incapable of combining all the factors that might allow for a realistic and balanced assessment of the economics. As has already been noted, alongside the price of the sand must be placed the wages of all those involved in wheeling and the cost of canal transportation; and along with that the savings accrued from payments for out-relief and (less measurable still) the deterrent effect of the wheeling upon applications for relief. The Birmingham guardians never found time to assess fully the pros and cons of the operation as activity at the Key Hill mine was being wound down by 1832, not because of the shortage of labour (in January 1833 more than 250 men were still wheeling sand to the wharf) but because of the adverse publicity it was generating. By this date Key Hill was no longer the wasteland it had once been, but an upwardly mobile neighbourhood of new houses and the new residents objected to the sight of the unemployed passing backwards and forwards in front of their houses. And on days of inclement weather, when no wheeling could take place, idle hands found even less acceptable things to do.[27] What the guardians invariably called 'depredations' (generally robberies from gardens) were taking place. Mrs Shakespeare, for one, was less than enthusiastic about the view from her window. Acting through a solicitor, she informed the Key Hill committee that 'she has been endeavouring to let her house at Birmingham Heath and is prevented from doing so solely in consequence of nuisances occasioned by the sand wheelers'.[28]

Mrs Shakespeare was not alone in recoiling at the presence of the unemployed. The activity on Key Hill made visible to all what was in normal circumstances hidden behind workhouse walls, and the unpalatable truths about parish labour were no longer simply buried in the annual accounts. In a poem printed in Joseph Allday's *Monthly Argus* ('The Devil's Second Visit to Birmingham') an anonymous writer (probably Allday himself) drew the obvious parallel between two different forms of slave labour:

---

25 *Birmingham Journal*, 29 June 1833; *Aris's Gazette*, 1 July 1833.

26 *Birmingham Journal*, 5 July 1834.

27 Archives and Collections, Library of Birmingham. GP B/2/1/3 Birmingham Guardians' minutes, 10 January 1833.

28 *Ibid.*, 2 July 1833.

At Carrs Lane he heard a sermon at night
On the 'abolition of slavery',
And the Devil he chuckled with inward delight
At the preacher's religious knavery,
For that morn he had seen a body of men,
Extending for near a mile,
Attempting to gain a morsel of bread,
Under loads of sand and soil,
And he thought of mortals' consistency
And it made the Devil smile.[29]

In Allday's opinion, the non-conformist clique who had campaigned so vociferously against slavery abroad were just as responsible for a Poor Law that used the same brutal methods at home. This was a familiar line of attack for the Tories of the time, as it had been used by Richard Oastler in his letter on 'Yorkshire slavery' sent to the *Leeds Mercury* which mocked the employment of children in mills owned by dissenters who campaigned against 'colonial slavery'.[30] The radical *Birmingham Journal* shared Allday's opinion on this form of parish labour, even if it did not share his politics:

> The necessity of the times have taught the Birmingham parishioners to be much more rigorous task-masters, and to be much more scanty in doling out their allowance of relief, than they were ten years ago; the beggared artisans are compelled more ruthlessly than ever to undergo the cruel drudgery of sand-wheeling as the condition to obtain any support ... At the present time, in the midst of the hay harvest – a period when there is usually a superabundance of demand for labour – there are more white slaves at work at the sand pits and compelled to wheel a barrow, containing one and a quarter hundredweight of sand nearly nine miles uphill and then wheel it empty back again to obtain a single shilling.[31]

The *Journal's* attack was hardly a model of accuracy, and based (perhaps) more on hearsay than investigation. Had the sand-wheelers truly been taking their loads nine miles in each direction, they might have delivered them by hand to the Black Country foundries themselves and never needed the canal. Nor is there any real evidence that the Poor Law regime in 1832 was more harsh, or the terms of relief more restrictive, than it had been ten years before. The industrialist and rising radical politician, George Frederick Muntz, who lived

---

29   *Monthly Argus & Public Censor*, Vol. III, September 1831, p. 264.

30   *Leeds Mercury*, 29 September 1830.

31   *Birmingham Journal*, 14 July 1832.

at nearby Hockley Abbey, was quick to write to the newspaper to correct the figures, if not to change the overall impression:

> The poor who apply for relief are now employed at sand-wheeling, without any distinction as to their capability. A married man is allowed to wheel a barrow, containing one and three-quarters hundredweight of sand three-quarters of a mile and the empty barrow the same distance for one penny eight times a day. A single man is only allowed to wheel ten barrows a day.[32]

There is, remarkably, an indication in the surviving records of how the able-bodied poor themselves felt about forced labour at the mine. In a case heard before the magistrates in February 1828, one individual gave his response to the prospect of sand-wheeling. William Nash had been charged by the Birmingham overseers 'with neglecting to support his wife and family'. The magistrates were informed that Nash had been employed to wheel sand and was earning 'about eight shillings a week'. The man's refusal to undertake this work had brought him to the magistrates' court, where he was sentenced to three weeks' hard labour at the house of correction in Warwick. Hard labour at Warwick meant the tread-mill. On leaving the dock William Nash commented: 'Well, that will be as easy as sand-wheeling.' For his impertinence Nash's sentence was increased to one month.[33]

Local opposition probably served to bring forward what the guardians intended to do anyway: to release the parish land for other purposes. With ambitious rebuilding plans under consideration at the workhouse, that time had now come. The final straw was when the Key Hill committee informed the vestry that the mine was now losing upwards of £1,000 a year.[34] The hole in the public finances, however, was matched by an even deeper hole in the middle of Key Hill. What was to be done with that? John Kempson, the parish surveyor, had already warned the guardians that the mine was being worked at too great a depth, if they were planning to rent the land for building.[35]

Salvation came from the most unexpected of directions. The General Cemetery Company, formed to create a new burial-ground for Birmingham's non-conformists, put in an offer for the land.[36] With the right amount of

---

32 *Birmingham Journal*, 11 August 1832.

33 *Birmingham Journal*, 8 February 1828.

34 Archives and Collections, Library of Birmingham. GP B/2/1/3 Birmingham Guardians' minutes, 7 July 1835.

35 *Ibid.*, 31 July 1832.

36 *Ibid.*, 2 April 1833.

levelling, landscaping and planting, Key Hill could make a more than passable last resting-place, and the views were still chiefly rural. The land was valued at £5,750, and while the sale was being finalised, workhouse men continued to dig the sand and began levelling off the rest for its future use. The sand mine was finally closed in July 1835, and the barrows and implements sold off.[37] In that same month, on 14 July 1835, the foundation stone of the cemetery chapel was laid, and the first interment took place in the following year. The place was described as 'tastefully and admirably laid out in walks, with ornamental lawns and shrubberies'.[38]

The sand mine at Key Hill did not represent the sum total of the guardians' exploitation of their land on Birmingham Heath, however. Setting aside the two acres taken up by the mine, there were another twenty eight acres or so, both at Key Hill and further west towards the Handsworth parish boundary, together with another eighteen acres of freehold land.[39] In the long term this land was probably most profitably exploited by leasing it for building, though this depended on the willingness of builders and industrialists to expand north-westwards from the town centre. Only Matthew Boulton had done so thus far, as well as a couple of glass manufacturers. Allowing building on the parish land, however, would require another Act of Parliament, since it was not authorised in the original Enclosure Act. In the short to medium term, however, the Key Hill Committee had more imaginative plans. The majority of the land was leased out for gardens and allotments, bringing in an annual rent of just over £81.[40] As for the remainder, by 1820 the committee had developed a comprehensive farming regime, deploying the unemployed, as well as men and women from the workhouse, as gardeners and farm labourers. Almost eight acres of land on the Heath were planted with potatoes, while the land at Key Hill not being mined was turned into a market garden to grow vegetables.[41] The first crop was plundered, apparently, by boys and girls from the Blue Coat School, but after this initial setback the garden was highly productive.[42]

The original idea of turning the Heath into farmland 'for the benefit of the poor' seems to have come from the overseers in 1817, though it took a little

---

37   *Ibid.*, 15 July 1835.

38   J. McKenna, *In the Midst of Life: A History of the Burial Grounds of Birmingham*, Birmingham, 1992, p. 12; Langford, *A Century of Birmingham Life*, Vol. 2, pp. 566–7.

39   *Birmingham Journal*, 22 March 1828.

40   Archives and Collections, Library of Birmingham. GP B/2/1/1 Birmingham Guardians' minutes, 15 October 1805.

41   Archives and Collections, Library of Birmingham. GP B/2/1/2 Birmingham Guardians' minutes, 27 June 1820.

42   Archives and Collections, Library of Birmingham. GP B/2/1/1 Birmingham Guardians' minutes, 25 June 1800.

time to disentangle the leases with its current tenants.[43] The economics of this agricultural operation were similar to that at the sand mine. The out-poor would be paid little more than a minimum wage (of one shilling a day), but this would induce them either to seek more constructive and better-paid work elsewhere, or at least to inculcate them in the values of honest toil. In May 1821, when the parish was swamped with applications for out-relief, a further piece of land on the Heath (adjoining the parish land) was rented from the Colmore family.[44] This additional land was said to amount to 30 acres.[45] Nor was digging the only form of labour. Stones were picked out of the ground by boys from the house and were then broken up by the out-poor to lay on the roads as gravel.[46] Yet the Key Hill Committee knew enough about market gardening and crop rotation to make full use of the land available. Turnips shared the same plot as early potatoes, winter (root) vegetables were planted in October, and later potatoes were grown elsewhere. What the committee was doing, step by careful step, was to turn the parish land into a parish farm, and by 1822 the farm was fully functioning. A total of thirteen acres were planted with potatoes, five with flax, seven and a half acres with wheat and two with turnips. In addition, by this date the farm also contained twenty sheep and two pigs, which were fed on the potatoes too small to be harvested.[47] In December of that year the committee gleefully reported that they had 'thirty ewe sheep in lamb and ten fine hogs nearly ready for slaughter'.[48] Such was the runaway success of the farm that by 1823 almost fifty acres were in cultivation, providing early and late potatoes, turnips, beans, flax, barley and clover.[49] Parish cows were soon to be the grateful consumers of the clover and the soil was thus enriched by their manure.

What happened to all this produce? The potatoes and vegetables went to the kitchens at the workhouse and the asylum and by 1823 there were enough left over to be supplied to the out-poor, either as part of their relief or sold to them at a reduced price.[50] A warehouse at the top of Lancaster Street, not far from the workhouse, stored the spare potatoes, and the needy

43 Archives and Collections, Library of Birmingham. CP B/660983 Birmingham Overseers' Minutes, Vol. 2, 31 October 1817.

44 Archives and Collections, Library of Birmingham. GP B/2/1/2 Birmingham Guardians' minutes, 16 May 1821.

45 *Aris's Gazette*, 1 April 1822.

46 Archives and Collections, Library of Birmingham. GP B/2/1/2 Birmingham Guardians' minutes, 1 January 1822.

47 *Ibid.*, 25 June 1822.

48 *Ibid.*, 31 December 1822.

49 *Ibid.*, 1 July 1823.

50 *Ibid.*, 8 April 1823.

were issued with tickets, permitting them to buy twenty pounds for 6d.[51] It was a form of relief which had been tried at an earlier time of hardship (such as in 1809) but not with home-grown produce.[52] Given that a rise in the price of potatoes in Birmingham was often the trigger for social unrest, it was not an entirely altruistic gesture, however. Mutton was probably sent to the house too and some of the bacon as well, though the chief advantage of having animals on the farm was to fertilise it. As for the wheat and the flax, use of these was even more ingenious. From November 1818 the guardians had introduced hand-mills into the workhouse, employing the inmates to grind corn.[53] The flour was then used in the house to bake bread. Wheat from the parish land could never fully meet the needs of the workhouse and the asylum, but it reduced the amount which had to be bought. As for the flax, this was the subject of an even more imaginative experiment, devised by the Employment Committee.

While many of the labour schemes dreamt up by the guardians might appear ad hoc and transient, the growing of flax on parish land was a more integrated and long-term concept. Detailed consultation was therefore held with a professional flax producer in the shape of James Law of Hull.[54] Flax could be grown on the parish land, rotted down on site, a process called 'dew-rotted' or 'dew-retted', and then delivered to the weaving-shop in the workhouse, where the fibre was turned into linen by (and for) the inmates. By April 1822, according to the *Gazette*, 2,394 yards of cloth had been woven by women at the workhouse.[55] The growing of flax for this purpose appears to have lasted for around five years, until the summer of 1824. This kind of vertical integration was not limited to Birmingham. A similar experiment was taking place at exactly this moment in Great Malvern, under the auspices of Apphia, Lady Lyttelton. A School of Ancient Industry 'for the spinning of wool, flax, hemp etc' was established in 1815 for females of the poorer classes, and by the early 1820s was also employing the girls to grow and harvest hemp and flax to supply the spinners.[56] The engineer Andrew Yarranton had put forward such an idea

---

51 Archives and Collections, Library of Birmingham. CP B/660984 Birmingham Overseers' Minutes, Vol. 3, 14 February 1823.

52 Archives and Collections, Library of Birmingham. CP B/660982 Birmingham Overseers' Minutes, Vol. 1, 19 January 1809.

53 Archives and Collections, Library of Birmingham. GP B/2/1/2 Birmingham Guardians' minutes, 19 January 1819.

54 *Edmonds' Weekly Recorder*, 7 October 1819.

55 *Aris's Gazette*, 1 April 1822.

56 J. Chambers, *A General History of Malvern*, Worcester, 1817, pp. 272–3; M. Southall, *A Description of Malvern and its Concomitants*, London, 1822, pp. 69–71.

as early as 1677.[57] Not that the growing of flax was universally welcomed. Birmingham's workhouse poet, George Davis, clearly believed a solution to the town's social ills lay more with bread than with linen:

> Instead of encouraging the growing of flax,
> 'Twere better the sinews of loaves to relax.
> And set them all growing to sizeable things.[58]

It is unlikely that a workhouse with over 500 inmates, many of them infirm and unproductive, could ever have been entirely self-sufficient, but the farming experiment on Birmingham Heath was still a remarkable achievement. We cannot tell if it instilled in its workers the appropriate instincts of honest endeavour and self-reliance, or encouraged any kind of 'allotment mentality', but it undoubtedly met the needs of temporary employment in difficult economic times and deployed that employment to good effect. The ratepayers and guardians could hardly have asked for more. There is no obvious indication in the guardians' minutes as to why the farm was wound up, other than the rising value of real estate, which made the sale or leasing of parish land a more tempting (and more manageable) possibility. Whilst a Bill to allow such a sale was being drafted and discussed, the farm was slowly dismantled. The last piece of imaginative recycling tried by the committee was in January 1828, when an elbow of the canal close to the farm was cleared of mud by the unemployed. The mud was carted to the farm and used instead of manure.[59] By April 1829, however, the land which had grown the workhouse potatoes and turnips had been let.[60] It was estimated that leasing the land for building would bring in some £1,600, far too good an opportunity to ignore.[61]

The annual workhouse accounts for 1824/5 are perhaps the closest we can get to a balanced assessment of how the parish land contributed to the parish economy. The sums provided here have been rounded up or down to the nearest pound. The sale of sand in that year amounted to £959, representing the only figure in the credit column. No produce from the farm was sold on the open market. Against this must be placed the cost of labour at the farm, including carts, horses and 'implements of husbandry', which totalled £485.

---

57 A. Yarranton, *England's Improvement by Sea and Land*, London, 1677, pp. 191–2.

58 Archives and Collections, Library of Birmingham. MS 3456 Poems of George Davis, 1790–1819.

59 Archives and Collections, Library of Birmingham. GP B/2/1/2 Birmingham Guardians' minutes, 1 January 1828.

60 Archives and Collections, Library of Birmingham. GP B/2/1/3 Birmingham Guardians' minutes, 28 April 1829.

61 *Aris's Gazette*, 16 March 1829.

Wages and equipment at the sand mine amounted to £523, though this has to be set against out-relief, which would have been paid anyway. In addition, the Key Hill committee was renting additional farmland at £30 a year, the canal wharf at £38, and a stable was rented at 5 guineas to store the flax and potatoes. Rent of the mill in Steelhouse Lane for the grinding of corn came to £25 per annum. Overall the cost of providing labour at the farm and sand mine reached £1,106 in that year, £147 more than the receipts from the sale of sand.[62] From the early 1830s, then, the parish land at Birmingham Heath and Key Hill became more useful as a source of revenue than as a place of labour. But its story was not quite finished yet. When, just over a decade later, the guardians came to consider the location for a new workhouse, and the borough searched for a site for its new asylum and prison, it was once more to the Heath that they both turned. The tenancy agreements were terminated, and the town grouped all of its social institutions together on the self-same land. The presence of City Hospital (the former workhouse and infirmary), Winson Green Prison and the Borough Asylum, later known as All Saints Hospital (now itself part of the prison) are the enduring legacy of that deal struck over the Birmingham Enclosure Act two hundred years earlier.

62   *Aris's Gazette*, 27 June 1825.

8

Managing the Poor:
Masters, Matrons and Clerks

It is a constant disappointment for genealogists to discover that there are rarely, if ever, complete records of the inmates of workhouses and this is as true at Birmingham as elsewhere. But the gaps in the paperwork go deeper than this. It is also impossible to produce, even if we wanted to, a full list of the staff of Birmingham workhouse, certainly not before 1783, when the guardians' minutes begin to record new appointments and changes of personnel. Nor is this simply a problem for family history. The way careers in the Poor Law were forged and furthered, the nature and expectations of office, discipline and promotion, the life experience of officers, are all far from unimportant components of the system and how, as historians, we evaluate it. Uncovering what we can of these men and women, then, is a valuable, if challenging, exercise. Despite these glaring holes in the early Poor Law records in Birmingham, we can supply a few pieces of this imperfect jigsaw. As previously noted, the first Town Book records the decision to approach Samuel Whitley, the master of the Wolverhampton workhouse, to become the first master or governor at Lichfield Street, at an annual salary not exceeding £25, though there is no confirmation that he actually took up the offer.[1] By 1739, in the period covered by a single surviving volume of eighteenth-century accounts, the master was one Mr Pye. His quarterly salary was recorded as £5.[2]

So chronologically detached is this item from all the other workhouse records that it is probably better to deal with what it contains separately. In addition to Mr Pye, whose salary is recorded up to January 1749 (shortly before the

---

1   Archives and Collections, Library of Birmingham. CP B/286011 Birmingham Town Book, 7 August 1734.

2   Archives and Collections, Library of Birmingham. CP B/380973 Accounts of the Birmingham Workhouse and Record of Out-Relief to the Poor, 1739–48.

volume ends), there are payments to a housekeeper, a Mrs Gunson, at £6 a year. This suggests that Mr Pye was, unusually for a workhouse master, unmarried. Almost all of his successors would work as husband and wife. Mrs Gunson was assisted by a servant girl, Ann Allen, who received £3 a year in wages. It seems likely that all three of them were resident in the workhouse and that their remuneration also included bed and board. This may also be true of Charles Thacker, the one other individual recorded as receiving wages, especially as he was paid only two shillings a week. We may note the vocabulary here. A salary (good in pounds, but better in guineas) was paid quarterly; wages were paid weekly and pay was at a daily rate. The choice of words distinguishes between manual and white-collar work and between a profession, a trade and a job. The evidence from the accounts suggests that Charles Thacker was employed as an 'outrider' (as he might have been termed in a medieval monastery), paid to execute removals, to apprehend vagrants and to round up single mothers. He caught seven such women in March 1748 alone; for this service he received a bonus payment. The rest of the work done in the house at this time was either bought in or performed by the inmates. The washer women, recruited from among the paupers themselves, were encouraged in their task by being given an allowance of ale, a common incentive (known as a perquisite) for manual workers. Among those who received payment for services was one William Weely, who looked after a couple of cows (probably not within the workhouse grounds), which provided the milk for the inmates' porridge. He was paid £5 per annum. A man called Bloxidge was hired to shave the men's beards and probably to cut hair as well, a regular workhouse task which must later have been performed by an inmate. Shaving, as far as we can tell, was usually done on Sundays to ensure the men were decently groomed for divine worship. Other regular work included digging the workhouse garden and planting seeds and Mr Avery's annual job of whitewashing the building. Whitewashing or lime-washing was a regular workhouse task, helping (it was believed) to combat the spread of infection and disease. In September 1743 John Harrison was paid £1 for sinking a well in the yard. Subsequently (though this is only noted in October 1747), Mr Collins received £1 a year to maintain the pump which drew up the water. Prior to sinking the well, it is likely that water had to be purchased from one of the many Birmingham water-carriers who plied their trade through the streets of the town. Finally, we may note regular payments for carriage. This meant two things: either the transporting of paupers back to their native parish, or the transfer of bodies to the churchyard for burial. The latter was no uncommon procedure; eleven people were thus carried in April 1747 alone. All this we can glean from this sole account book.

The sequencing of workhouse masters and mistresses for the middle years of the eighteenth century is complex. A lease for property in Walmer Lane from

May 1759 names William Bache as 'master of the workhouse and gunmaker', and this is the only named official we can insert in this fragmentary period.[3] In the absence of surviving Poor Law records one has to rely almost entirely on the advertisements for staff issued in the local press. In 1767 the overseers advertised for a new master[4], in 1769 for a master and mistress[5], and in 1775 for a mistress.[6] Although the preferred arrangement was for a married couple to take charge of the 'family', the overseers were reluctant, at least in the early period, to dismiss an incumbent master or mistress, if his or her spouse died. As a result, a single man or woman was, from time to time, required to fill in. The advertisement for a mistress in 1775 unusually amounts to what we might call a job description, the earliest to survive from Birmingham workhouse. The successful female candidate was expected to:

> Attend as head carver on meat days.
>
> Cut out all linen (wearing apparel and household), give out to be made and ensure its return to the store-room.
>
> Take account of linen given to the washerwomen, give out soap to the same, and ensure it returned to the poor when dry.
>
> Ensure that the poor have a change of linen once a week.
>
> Ensure that beds are sheeted once a week.
>
> Go over the house once a day to inspect the bedding.
>
> See that rooms and stairs are cleaned as often as the weather permits.
>
> Appoint menial servants of the house for washing, brewing etc.
>
> Appoint nurses for the infirmary.
>
> Keep account of all linen.[7]

Once the guardians took over the running of the house, following their first election in 1783, they wasted little time in flexing their statutory muscles over the appointment of officials. Under the new arrangements they were to choose the workhouse master and they did so swiftly, electing Samuel and Mary Craddock of Wolverhampton to serve as governor and governess.[8] It was remarkably convenient that, at the dawn of a new age for Birmingham's Poor

---

3   Archives and Collections, Library of Birmingham. MS 464/1-2. Lease and counterpart lease, 5 May 1759: Title deeds relating to property in Lancaster Street, otherwise Walmer Lane. The streets around Lichfield Street were at the centre of Birmingham's eighteeth-century gun quarter.

4   *Aris's Gazette*, 22 June 1767.

5   *Aris's Gazette*, 31 July 1769.

6   *Aris's Gazette*, 30 January 1775.

7   *Aris's Gazette*, 30 January 1775.

8   Archives and Collections, Library of Birmingham. GP B/2/1/1 Birmingham Guardians' minutes, 10 November 1783.

Law, the previous incumbent, Mr Fletcher, died at exactly the right moment to allow for a new appointment.[9] The Craddocks' initial salary seems to have been fifty guineas (£52 10s per annum), though this is not specified until 1786, when a new appointment was made.[10] The need for a new appointment on this occasion was the death of Mrs Craddock on 20 July 1786 and the guardians were now insistent upon a husband and wife team to run the house.[11] In August 1786, therefore, John and Elizabeth Spurrier of Walsall were selected and their salaries were then fixed at fifty guineas for Mr Spurrier and £20 for Mrs Spurrier.[12] The advertisement included the proviso, though it hardly needed to be said, that 'constant residence in the house will be required'.[13]

The Spurriers' association with the workhouse was to be a lengthy, if somewhat convoluted one, but it is worth untangling for the light it throws on the family connections within the Birmingham Poor Law. We know that John Spurrier died in office on 8 December 1792[14], and at the start of 1793 a general meeting of the guardians nominated John and Maria Spurrier as governor and governess on the same salaries.[15] It seems probable that this was the son and daughter-in-law of the late governor. As for Elizabeth Spurrier (John senior's widow), she was not sent packing, but was retained in residence to work in the clothing department as 'cloaths cutter-out' on an annuity of ten guineas.[16] Thus the workhouse at this time was run by the cosy family circle of a husband and wife and his mother. The death of Maria Spurrier on 14 December 1800 again deprived the workhouse of a married couple as master and matron and John Spurrier junior was obliged to step down. Maria (or Hannah Maria, as she is called on her tombstone) was buried at St Mary, Whittall Street, the closest Anglican church to the workhouse. She was 41 years old.

A new appointment was delayed until after the 1801 guardians' elections, when Mr and Mrs Hinchcliffe of Halesowen were appointed, now at a salary of £70 for the governor and £30 for the governess.[17] Clearly the family connection

---

9   *Aris's Gazette*, 28 July 1783.

10   Archives and Collections, Library of Birmingham. GP B/2/1/1 Birmingham Guardians' minutes, 21 August 1786.

11   *Aris's Gazette*, 24 July 1786.

12   Archives and Collections, Library of Birmingham. GP B/2/1/1 Birmingham Guardians' minutes, 28 August 1786.

13   *Ibid.*, 31 July 1786.

14   *Swinney's Birmingham Chronicle*, 13 December 1792.

15   Archives and Collections, Library of Birmingham. GP B/2/1/1 Birmingham Guardians' minutes, 25 January 1793.

16   *Ibid.*, 27 October 1795.

17   Archives and Collections, Library of Birmingham. GP B/2/1/1 Birmingham Guardians' minutes, 16 June 1801.

which had kept Elizabeth Spurrier in the clothes-room no longer existed, and she was awarded £19 10s 'in lieu of board', but a further ten guineas a year 'for her attendance and services in the cloathes [sic] room'.[18] Mrs Spurrier was still being paid 10s a week as superintendent of the clothing department in 1811.[19] By this date Elizabeth had been attached to Lichfield Street for twenty-five years. The sheer scale of Birmingham's workhouse meant that the wages paid to its masters dwarfed those of the surrounding parishes. When the Harborne overseers advertised for a new governor for their 'house of industry' in April 1810, the salary offered (along with board and washing) was just £30 a year and this was to cover both husband and wife.[20] The arrival of George Hinchcliffe in 1801 heralded a major change in the nature of the office of governor at Birmingham. Not only was Mr Hinchcliffe deployed (at least initially) in visiting the out-poor, for which he received an additional gratuity[21] and his wife in visiting the girls apprenticed at the mills outside the town[22], but Hinchcliffe himself put forward the proposal to 'farm out' the poor in the workhouse. This was a step which had been tried elsewhere, in Sutton Coldfield, Aston and many Black Country parishes, but was new to Birmingham. The governor would be paid a sum of money to run the workhouse, effectively as a private business, employing the paupers 'to his advantage'. He would provide all the necessary machinery, or at least be responsible for its maintenance, appoint individuals to manage and oversee the labour force, ensure good order, and draw out what profits he could.[23] In setting out his proposals, Hinchcliffe put an upper limit of six on the number of additional staff, such as nurses, he was obliged to appoint (and pay for). As for the guardians, they would not relinquish entire control, for they would continue to appoint and pay clerks and accounting staff and to keep an eye on the whole process. An agreement was thrashed out over the winter of 1803 and finalised in January 1804. The initial contract was for seven years and Mr Hinchcliffe would be paid £100 a year initially, rising by £10 each year.[24] At their next meeting the guardians declared themselves 'perfectly satisfied' with the new arrangement.[25] This radical new arrangement ran for almost two terms,

---

18 *Ibid.*, 3 November 1801.

19 *Ibid.*, 15 July 1811.

20 *Aris's Gazette*, 30 April 1810.

21 Archives and Collections, Library of Birmingham. GP B/2/1/1 Birmingham Guardians' minutes, 5 October 1802.

22 Archives and Collections, Library of Birmingham. CP B/660892 Birmingham Overseers' Minutes, Vol. 1, 26 August 1803.

23 Archives and Collections, Library of Birmingham. GP/B/2/1/1 Birmingham Guardians' minutes, 1 February 1803.

24 *Ibid.*, 3 January 1804.

25 *Ibid.*, 7 February 1804.

approaching thirteen years, by which time George Hinchcliffe's salary had risen to an astonishing £300 per annum, combining his basic salary as governor of £70 with the incremental £230 for working the paupers. By this date he was a widower, but the governor's son, Joshua, was employed as a resident clerk in the clothes department.[26] The overseers' minutes also record that Joshua was paid an additional £5 a year 'for the relief of vagrants'.[27] Mrs Hinchcliffe had passed away on 27 March 1810, and it is testimony either to her husband's powers of persuasion, or to the nature of his contract with the guardians, that George Hinchcliffe was allowed to remain in office as a single man.

George Hinchcliffe's regime ended in disgrace, legal action and suicide, however. A workhouse was never far from its next scandal, but in most recorded cases they involved the ill-treatment of paupers by over-zealous or harsh officials. The story in Birmingham in 1818 was one of lax administration, embezzlement and the wholesale squandering of resources. Such issues would always be of more than passing interest to hard-pressed ratepayers, and, of course, to journalists. The termination of the guardians' contract with George Hinchcliffe in 1817 shows how sensitive they were to outside criticism. Birmingham ratepayers, urged on by the local press, were quick to condemn anything they saw as profiteering at their expense. 'Rumours of Mr Hinchcliffe's large profits from the labour of the poor,' said the guardians in response, 'were exaggerated', but nevertheless decided that it was politic from this point on to keep the duties of the governor of the workhouse separate from any business arrangement. Hinchcliffe would, therefore, continue to superintend work in the manufactory, and continue to draw a salary of £300, but would no longer have direct responsibility for the selling of goods manufactured in the house.[28] However, it turned out that the irregularities in the system were far more extensive than the size of the master's salary alone. When the scandal broke it revealed the depth to which Hinchcliffe's business model operated, and prompted an investigation undertaken by a committee of guardians in the early months of 1818.[29] They discovered that in the kitchen department the servants had been permitted to supplement their low wages, by selling whatever bones, grease and dripping was left over from the cooking of meat. As it happened, the Protestant Dissenting Charity School in the town had been rocked by a

---

26   Archives and Collections, Library of Birmingham. GP B/2/1/2 Birmingham Guardians' minutes, 28 October 1817.

27   Archives and Collections, Library of Birmingham. CP B/660983 Birmingham Overseers' Minutes, Vol. 2, 4 July 1815.

28   Archives and Collections, Library of Birmingham. GP B/2/1/2 Birmingham Guardians' minutes, 28 October 1817.

29   *Ibid.*, 17 March 1818.

similar dispute just a few years earlier. In 1806 one of the pupils, Elizabeth Marshall, was subjected to a severe beating by the mistress, Mrs Shaw, when the girl revealed that the dripping and fat from the kitchen had likewise been sold outside the school, and the money pocketed by Mrs Shaw.[30]

The sale of kitchen by-products, and, in particular, dripping, was common practice in the commercial world. Hotels regularly did this, with no means of keeping the fat, or no inclination to do so; instead they found their way into hands of local butchers or shopkeepers. The custom is referred to by George Gissing in his novel *New Grub Street*.[31] Such items were known as 'perquisites', or 'perks', and had long been part of the workhouse system, which had always been reluctant to pay wages to inmates. Although these perquisites represented a meagre return for the servants individually, they could amount to a considerable loss to the parish. The investigating committee of guardians reported that between twenty-five and twenty-eight pounds of dripping were being sold from the workhouse kitchen every week, which at 6d a pound, amounted to a sum of perhaps 13s a week. In March 1818 the committee of guardians recommended that the practice should stop, and the servants be paid 'a fair and proper wage' instead.[32] But it was what the committee called 'depredations' in the clothing department that spelled the end, not only for the business model, but for Mr Hinchcliffe himself. The scandal also involved Ann Martin, who had worked as superintendent here, probably since the death of Elizabeth Spurrier. Since the governor's son, Joshua Hinchcliffe, had been looking after the paperwork in this section, he too was implicated. The workhouse clothes store was an extensive operation; here was stockpiled clothing for inmates and for the out-poor, the clothes in which paupers had entered the workhouse (and which were then taken from them) and the apparel of those who died in the house. Much of the clothing was made up by women in the manufactory, but the raw material was cut up here too. The annual turnover in the clothes room was vast, estimated at £4,000 per annum. It was alleged that Mrs Martin had been profiting from the sale of material, and converting the cash into shares with the Crown Copper Co.[33] The production of clothing was all part of George Hinchcliffe's contract for farming out the workhouse labour and from the outset the value of the goods probably mattered less to the guardians than the fact that the master

---

30 Archives and Collections, Library of Birmingham. MS 3629/13 [471911] Register of Children at the Protestant Dissenting Working Charity School, Vol. 1, 1798–1835, p. 16.

31 G. Gissing, *New Grub Street*, London, 1891, p. 316.

32 Archives and Collections, Library of Birmingham. GP B/2/1/2 Birmingham Guardians' minutes, 17 March 1818.

33 The head office of the company was in Cannon Street, Birmingham; the smelting works were in Neath, South Wales.

was keeping idle hands busy. Indeed, since they had no direct financial stake in it, they did not feel the need to scrutinise this aspect of his operation too closely. In his submission to Parliament in 1803/4, the workhouse clerk stated that pauper labour included 'picking of oakum, carding and spinning wool, spinning jersey and flax, making stocking yarn, weaving hurden and linseys', but added significantly that 'no particular accompt is kept of the value of the knitting, sewing, making and mending, which is very considerable.'[34] Indeed, he did not even declare that the labour was farmed out. To the guardians, what Hinchcliffe was doing was an innovative kind of 'internal farming'.

The extent of Ann Martin's black-market enterprise was revealed by the husband of the woman who had been receiving the clothes. Mrs Martin had been passing the items to an assistant, Mary Palmer, who had then taken them for sale to a house next door to the workhouse. Mr S. (his full name is not revealed) estimated that his wife had been paying between 30s and 40s a week for the cast-offs; she had, he claimed, been ignorant of their origin. The writer's defence of his wife was founded, of course, on the brazenness of the arrangement; had Mrs Martin or her assistant been more underhand, Mrs S. might have become suspicious. Mary Palmer took clothing to the shop twice a day and customers came from as far afield as Oldbury and Dudley to buy them. Much of the surplus material was snapped up by wholesale clothes-dealers.[35]

That the scam could go on for so long without being reported is not, in itself, surprising. For one thing, the activities of the Poor Law authorities were always shrouded in secrecy. Long after the guardians' meetings had been thrown open to the press, the *Monthly Argus* was still commenting that 'conccalment has been the order of the day'.[36] For another, the sheer scale of the Birmingham workhouse and its stores made micro-management well-nigh impossible. With as many as 600 inmates, and as few as half-a-dozen full-time staff, the institution was always vulnerable to malpractice and 'fencing'. Birmingham was also something of a regional centre for the cheap and second-hand clothes trade and among its many customers, ironically, were overseers of the poor from neighbouring parishes. John Allin, who ran a store in Hay Market, now the site of Birmingham Council House, specifically addressed them in an advertising jingle in April 1799:

---

34 *Abstract of answers and returns made pursuant to the Act of 43 George III relative to the expense and maintenance of the poor in England*, Parliamentary Papers, XIII, 1803–4, p. 536.

35 'H.W.S', *Plain Truth, or a Correct Statement of the Late Events Relative to the Birmingham Workhouse*, Birmingham, n.d [1818?], p. 8.

36 *Monthly Argus & Public Censor*, January 1830, p. 297.

Ye neighb'ring Overseers, who oft to Town repair,
And wish to cloathe the Poor with Prudence and with Care,
I pray you'll condescend to look into my shop,
I have no kind of Doubt your Pence you'll freely drop;
With ease I can provide with ev'ry Thing complete,
Coat, Waistcoat, Shirts and Shoes, yea, Stockings for the Feet;
Hats, Breeches, Gowns, Stays, Aprons, Cloaks,
In short, all Things to suit poor Folks –
So cheap, so good, quite strong and sound,
And all this new for one small Pound.[37]

Mrs S. was arrested in January 1818 and her conveyance to the Public Office in Moor Street (as described by her husband) together with the abuse she was subjected to en route, reflected both the survival of the ancient tradition of 'rough music' in the town, as well as the extreme sensitivity of the issue. A very motley band provided her with musical accompaniment to court:

Among the principal female performers in this vocal band was an old withered Egyptian figure, playing on a Welsh harp, the sound of which nearly rent the contaminated air of the lower part of Lichfield Street.[38]

Once the scandal came out, retribution swiftly followed. Mrs S. was prosecuted, Mary Palmer was taken into custody and Ellen Haywood, another inmate, absconded from the workhouse and fled to London. She too was arrested but acquitted for insufficient evidence. Mrs Martin herself committed suicide, and her brother-in-law (probably holding shares on her account) also attempted to take his own life. The housekeeper's death was reported in the *Gazette* on 13 April 1818, along with the inquest verdict of 'lunacy'.[39] The committee of enquiry found it impossible to believe that the governor was ignorant of what had been taking place, though they remained uncertain whether to accuse him of complicity or negligence. They felt 'much pain in coming to these resolutions against a man who has been employed by the parish for so long a period', but nevertheless recommended the governor's immediate dismissal. George Hinchcliffe endeavoured to defend himself but was forced out on 2 May and was dead by the end of the month.[40] The two deaths stopped the guardians

---

37   Langford, *A Century of Birmingham Life*, Vol. II, p. 139.

38   'H.W.S', *Plain Truth*, p. 32.

39   *Aris's Gazette*, 13 April 1818.

40   Archives and Collections, Library of Birmingham. GP B/2/1/2 Birmingham Guardian's minutes, 2 June 1818.

from fully investigating the crimes; perhaps they were reluctant to speak ill of the dead. More likely that the more raking of the dead embers that occurred, the more the charge of neglect might be levelled at them. Better by far to reach for a new broom. It should be noted that 'depredations' did not begin under the regime of Mr Hinchcliffe of course, nor (we can be sure) did they end there. As early as 1759, the governor of the workhouse, William Bache, was complaining to the press that the workhouse garden had been robbed of 'quantities of greens' and offering a reward of half a guinea for information.[41] Shortly before the 1818 scandal came officially to light, Ann Adkins, a pauper in the house, was also convicted at the Quarter Sessions for selling provisions from the workhouse to three shopkeepers in Lichfield Street. All four individuals ended up in the Warwick house of correction.[42]

We can take the story a little further, however, even if the guardians' minutes at this point fall silent. Between February and June 1819 the radical reformer George Edmonds published a barrage of criticism, directed at the guardians, in a series of eleven letters, addressed to the inhabitants of Birmingham. The last of these letters provoked the guardians into setting up yet another committee (the usual response in such situations) to investigate, and the latter set out its (mostly negative) findings several years later in 1825.

Unlike the guardians, Edmonds did not direct any of his criticism towards George Hinchcliffe; he saved it for the guardians themselves, which we have dealt with in another chapter, and for 'peculiating' workhouse staff such as Mrs Martin. She had entered the workhouse as a pauper, Edmonds claimed, but by the time of her death had £1,300 in shares in Crown Copper, and additional monies in the hands of her banker and in other companies.[43] We must, of course, be wary of testimony which is politically motivated (Edmonds compared the condition of the workhouse to 'the corruption of another house of guardians – the House of Commons'), but the guardians' earlier admission that the house had been subject to 'depredations' surely makes some of George Edmonds' evidence admissible. The following is Edmonds' list of items reputedly found in Mrs Martin's 'private store' after her death. It does, at the very least, throw light on the range of food and provisions stored in the workhouse:

Two casks of raisins, one good, the other mouldy, thirty-eight papers of mould candles, half a dozen pounds in each paper, thirty-six dozen pounds of dip candles, fourteen pounds of rush-lights, twelve pounds best coffee, four pounds nutmegs, two pounds mace, twenty-four pounds stone blue, a cart load of mops, long brushes, chair brushes,

---

41   Langford, *A Century of Birmingham Life*, Vol. I, p. 80.

42   *Aris's Gazette*, 9 September 1816.

43   G. Edmonds, *Letter III to the Inhabitants of Birmingham*, Birmingham, 1819.

seventy-six pair pig's chawls, from the pork butchers, I suppose, several dozen of dried neats' tongues, three hundredweight hung beef, three hundredweight bacon, a number of hams, some good, some lying cut and spoiled among the saw dust.[44]

Nor were the stolen articles all secreted away. 'Hand-carts loaded with flour, cheese etc. etc.' George Edmonds adds, 'were seen passing several times a week into Aston Street, and lost themselves near an old iron shop in that street.' Edmonds goes on to claim that shops were selling goods from the Birmingham workhouse as far afield as Oldbury and in Dudley, just as Mr S. had also alleged.[45] There is, of course, no record of such disappearances in the surviving records, but we may note that in January 1817 the overseers were concerned that a shift with the workhouse mark on it had been bought and sold in the town.[46]

Edmonds had another 'peculiating servant' to set alongside Mrs Martin, though not on quite the same scale, worth mentioning for the light thrown on the distribution of food in the house.[47] The individual is not named, but Edmonds claims the man had entered the house as 'a cripple' and had been subsequently employed to cut and serve the bread allowance. The inmates, it was alleged, would regularly give him a penny or two for a larger portion of bread, and, if they refused to do so, he would serve them less than their entitlement. By such means the man had laid up £300 in profits. The individual concerned, says Edmonds, had been dismissed from his job as bread-cutter, but had found other work in the house instead.

The 'system of plunder', vividly described by George Edmonds and at least partly accepted by the guardians, led directly to the sacking of George Hinchcliffe. William Cheshire, who was already employed as a clerk at the house, was temporarily appointed as Hinchcliffe's successor in April 1818 and he and his wife were officially nominated as governor and governess in June. Internal appointments were, as we have already seen, the norm in Birmingham workhouse, but the couple evidently met the criteria advertised in the press: 'a middle-aged man and wife of regular and industrious habits'.[48] The Cheshires' joint salary of £150 (with board and lodgings) was a sizeable saving on what had been paid to Mr Hinchcliffe, though this was increased to £200 three years

44   *Ibid.*

45   *Ibid.*

46   Archives and Collections, Library of Birmingham. CP B/660983 Birmingham Overseers' Minutes, Vol. 3, 21 January 1817.

47   G. Edmonds, *Letter IV to the Inhabitants of Birmingham*, Birmingham, 1819.

48   *Aris's Gazette*, 4 May 1818.

later.[49] The Cheshires' children were also accommodated in the house, and Mr Cheshire was still paying for the board of one of his daughters at the time of his death in 1829.[50]

There is no doubt that the dismissal of the elderly George Hinchcliffe and appointment of William Cheshire was designed to effect a radical revolution in the way Birmingham workhouse was being run, and the guardians admitted as such some years later:

> The lavish distribution of linen was one of the evils of the old system. One of the jobs of the Cheshires was to repress this and extricate the ratepayers from the load of debt by which it was oppressed.[51]

There's little doubt that William Cheshire had all the necessary secretarial skills for good accounting. Prior to his appointment at the workhouse, he had worked as confidential clerk and bookkeeper to Matthew Boulton at the Soho Manufactory. Such are the riches of Boulton's private and company archives that we can trace Cheshire's career in some detail, prior to his appointment as workhouse master. Born in 1762, Cheshire had sought Boulton's help in setting up in business, manufacturing black buttons 'from a composition of his own invention'.[52] When the enterprise failed in 1796, he was offered work at Soho at a salary that rose to just over 100 guineas a year; he left this employment in 1812.[53] It was in a fresh spirit of openness and transparency that the new workhouse governor began to issue (under his own name) statistics of poor relief to the press. The first such summary appeared in June 1818, detailing both the numbers in receipt of out-relief (and their respective costs), together with occupancy rates for the workhouse and asylum.[54] For the first time the Birmingham ratepayers could see exactly how their poor rates were being spent. Indeed, as early as October 1818 the *Gazette* was commending the new regime for a considerable reduction in weekly expenditure, down from as much as £1,400 a week to £870 (a figure that covers both indoor and outdoor

---

49 Archives and Collections, Library of Birmingham. GP B/2/1/2 Birmingham Guardians' minutes, 15 January 1821.

50 Archives and Collections, Library of Birmingham. GP B/2/1/3 Birmingham Guardians' minutes, 30 June 1829.

51 Archives and Collections, Library of Birmingham. GP B/2/1/2 Birmingham Guardians' minutes, 25 October 1825.

52 Archives and Collections, Library of Birmingham. MS 3782/12/59/152 Matthew Boulton Papers.

53 I am grateful to Fiona Tait of Birmingham Archives and Collections for biographical information on Cheshire.

54 *Aris's Gazette*, 6 June 1818.

relief).[55] This saving included the lowering of the master's and matron's joint salary.[56] Yet the tighter ship run by Mr and Mrs Cheshire was subject to just as heavy a bombardment as the previous regime. As early as August 1818 a petition signed by more than 450 ratepayers and businesses (the largest single petition ever to appear in the *Gazette*) requested from the overseers and guardians a statement outlining the reasons for the dismissal of Hinchcliffe and others.[57] No such statement appears to have been made. So emotive a subject was the Poor Law that it was almost impossible for any workhouse to operate a system that appeared to be both fair to the ratepayers and kind to the inmates and there were few outside the charmed circle of guardians and overseers who were ever prepared to give it the benefit of the doubt. Long before the Poor Law Amendment Act brought such opinions to the fore, the system was either extravagant or it was degrading.

In 1825, George Edmonds was once again at the vanguard of the attack, although this time there was also testimony from a number of inmates to underline his claims. Much of this criticism, and the findings of the committee set up to test its accuracy (and the reliability of the witnesses), relates to the internal conditions of the workhouse. This is dealt with in later chapters, but much too was directed personally at the Cheshires themselves and particularly at Mary Cheshire, whose hands-on dealing with inmates was said to be exactly that. The ill-treatment of which Mrs Cheshire was accused ranged from banging the head of 'Jabber, an insane woman' against a wall, to putting a mop in the face of an old pensioner and 'pouring a gaund [*sic*] of water in a hole in his trousers'. Another witness reported that 'at supper time Mary Cheshire frequently took a spoon, filled it and rammed it in the face of Dummy'.[58] Such evidence cannot, of course, be proved and the committee in most cases dismissed it, but it does reflect the stresses of an institution which was part care-home and part mental asylum and no doubt such pressures were particularly felt at meal times. For Mary Cheshire in particular, accustomed to the tranquil life of a clerk's wife, it must have been a very rude awakening indeed. If William and Mary Cheshire were largely exonerated from blame in the eyes of the committee, one head did fall in the enquiry, and the testimony which led to his downfall came from a woman by the name of Jane Simons.

---

55 *Aris's Gazette*, 5 October 1818.

56 Archives and Collections, Library of Birmingham. 89104A Birmingham Scrapbook 3, Birmingham Workhouse Accounts 1819–20, p. 360.

57 *Aris's Gazette*, 10 August 1818.

58 Archives and Collections, Library of Birmingham. GP B/2/1/2 Birmingham Guardians' Minutes, Report of the Committee appointed to enquire into certain charges made by Ann Lichfield against the Superintendence of the Workhouse, 25 October 1825.

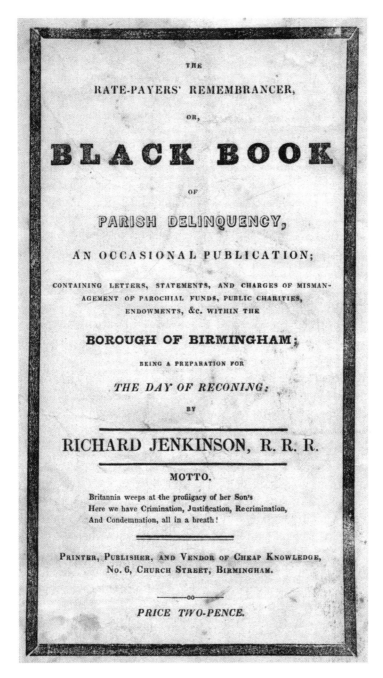

Figure 8.1 Frontispiece of *The rate payers' remembrance, or The Black Book of parish delinquency* by Richard Jenkinson, 1835. This contained letters reprinted from the *Birmingham Journal* concerning the mismanagement of parish funds and public charities in Birmingham. Archives and Collections, Library of Birmingham: LP41.11 [663383]

Simons had worked as a nurse in the infirmary for five years, but finally left on account of ill-treatment by Mrs Cheshire and by Mr Horton, 'the keeper of the insane ward', and because 'she did not have enough coals'. Simons' allegation was that, after Mrs Cheshire's arrival, the linen 'became indifferent', and in her time 'no more than five shirts were given to paupers'. George Hinchcliffe had faced a similar allegation back in 1818. Male inmates were supposed to be supplied with a fresh shirt on Sundays (in time, no doubt, for church), but were found to be wearing an old one again by Monday.[59] As a parting-shot the embittered nurse added that Horton's wife had slept with him in the insane ward for three or four weeks. The clothing books, which were now in a somewhat better state of repair than in Hinchcliffe's day, contradicted part of this. A total of 111 shirts, they showed, had been distributed to the infirmary and insane wards over this period. The committee accepted that the allegation that Horton and his wife had slept in the insane ward might well be true, but this needed to come from a more morally upright source than Jane Simons, 'having herself had so little delicacy as to sleep for some time in a ward where twenty to thirty men slept and no other woman was present'. In the absence of stronger evidence an argument *ad hominem* was always useful. Nevertheless, Mr Horton's presence could be dispensed with, and his place taken by 'a man of sufficient capability, of better principle and more humanity'.[60]

Having sacked one governor in 1818, the guardians were clearly not about to dismiss another in 1825, especially if he had been doing little more than obeying orders by reducing overheads. Indeed, the committee felt that general confidence and trust in the Cheshires was increased by the whole affair, not diminished. Governing a workhouse was a hard job at the best of times without unlooked for elements such as 'insubordination, delinquency, passion, outrage, accident or exigencies'.[61] And in this they were probably perfectly correct. William Cheshire continued in the post of governor for a further four years, dying in office (at the age of 66, on 9 June 1829), and once more the house clerk, Thomas Alcock, stepped into his shoes.[62] The latter was then thirty-nine years old. Alcock had commenced his Poor Law career eight years earlier in 1821 as one of the newly appointed assistant overseers.[63] From here it was but two short steps up the career ladder to governorship. Here again the system proved to be

59   Archives and Collections, Library of Birmingham. 64374 Birmingham Institutions B/1; 'H.W.S.', *Plain Truth*, p. 16.

60   Archives and Collections, Library of Birmingham. GP B/2/1/2 Birmingham Guardians' minutes, 25 October 1825.

61   *Ibid.*

62   Archives and Collections, Library of Birmingham. CP B/660985 Birmingham Overseers' Minutes, Vol. 4, 9 June 1829.

63   *Aris's Gazette*, 26 May 1821.

remarkably flexible in dealing with a complicated family situation. Mr Alcock likewise boarded his children in the workhouse,[64] while Mrs Cheshire stayed on as governess on a salary of £80 a year, the cost of boarding her daughter being waived.[65] The arrangement was only a temporary one. Mary Cheshire survived her husband by less than a year, dying on 30 January 1830. She was buried beside him in St Martin's churchyard. The assumption is that Thomas Alcock was at this point a widower. By the time his salary was revised upwards to £250 in 1831 he had remarried and the parish could once more revert to the preferred model of a married couple.[66] If running the workhouse was not testing enough, the Alcocks (in this case Mr Alcock and his daughter, Mary) also acted as master and matron of the Asylum for the Infant Poor for two years. This cosy shuffling of staff did not go entirely unnoticed or unchallenged, at least in the conservative *Monthly Argus*. Its editor, Joseph Allday, denounced 'Governor Alcock' as not worth £200 a year, let alone £250, and proposed replacing him 'with some honest young man at £100'.[67] Allday's suggestion was, of course, not to be taken seriously. Young men might find employment in the Poor Law system, as Alcock himself had, but it would not be as workhouse master. Nevertheless, Allday's underlying point, that the wages paid to higher officials under the Birmingham system had an irresistible upward momentum, appears true enough.

Thomas Alcock died, after eleven years in office (aged forty-nine), on 1 October 1840,[68] and his widow asked to be relieved of her duties as soon as was possible after this time.[69] Thomas Alcock's gravestone at St Philip's (now removed) described him as 'a most affectionate husband, a kind and indulgent father and a sincere friend'. It did not refer to his profession. However, around ninety of the guardians and a considerable number of inmates 'decently habited in mourning', attended the funeral.[70] Yet even here scandal followed this least controversial of all the workhouse masters to his grave. The *Journal* saw cause to complain of the presence of forty police-officers in the procession to St Philip's.[71] Extravagant policing had now replaced workhouse expenditure as the *cause celebre*. Alcock's death gave the guardians the opportunity to lower

---

64   Archives and Collections, Library of Birmingham. GP B/2/1/3 Birmingham Guardians' minutes, 27 April 1830.

65   *Ibid.*, 30 June 1829.

66   *Ibid.*, 16 November 1831.

67   *Monthly Argus & Public Censor*, Vol. 2, July 1830, p. 7.

68   *Aris's Gazette*, 19 October 1840.

69   Archives and Collections, Library of Birmingham. GP B/2/1/4 Birmingham Guardians' minutes, 13 October 1840.

70   *Birmingham Journal*, 10 October 1840.

71   *Ibid.*

the master's salary again to £150 per annum, £100 below what the Alcocks had received and half the salary of George Hinchcliffe. Nevertheless, there were twenty-seven applications for the post, of which seven were thought suitably qualified.[72] Of those interviewed and named, Mr and Mrs West were in their late thirties and had four children; Mr and Mrs Clarke were aged fifty-five and fifty-eight, and their children were 'out of hand'. If this was not already reason enough to appoint them, the Clarkes' earlier 'parochial experience of sixteen years' as governor and matron in London and Oxford probably tipped the balance in their favour. F.H. West was by profession a police superintendent.[73]

The complete list of the Birmingham workhouse governors (such as we have it) therefore looks like this:

1735	Samuel Whitley (?)
1739	Mr Pye
1759	William Bache (died 1768)
1768	Mr Fletcher (died 1783)
1783	Samuel and Mary Craddock
1786	John Spurrier Snr and Elizabeth Spurrier
1793	John Spurrier Jnr and Hannah Maria Spurrier
1801	George Hinchcliffe and wife
1818	William and Mary Cheshire
1829	Thomas Alcock and wife
1840	Mr & Mrs Clarke

The various masters and mistresses listed above do not represent the sum total of those employed in the workhouse, however. By November 1831 the parish was also employing six individuals to handle the growing mountain of paperwork, bills and receipts and to make visits to the out-poor. Two were based in the cashier's office, and four in the vestry clerk's office.[74] Such secretarial assistance was not inexpensive, however. William Warner Brynner, the vestry clerk, was by this date receiving an annual salary of £200, as was the cashier, Joseph Welch. Like many, at this time, in the workhouse hierarchy and the public services of Britain as a whole, Joseph Welch had benefited from an ingrained tradition of nepotism and patronage. He first appears in the

---

72   Archives and Collections, Library of Birmingham. GP B/2/1/4 Birmingham Guardians' minutes, 23 November 1840.

73   *Aris's Gazette*, 23 November 1840.

74   Archives and Collections, Library of Birmingham. GP B/2/1/3 Birmingham Guardians' minutes, 16 November 1831.

records in 1828 as an apprentice clerk to his father (on 5s a week),[75] though by October 1828 Joseph's salary had grown considerably to £39 per annum.[76] After the death of James Welch in 1829 Joseph took his father's place.[77] James Welch himself had been a cashier in the workhouse at least since 1795. In the following year, on his marriage, he asked permission to live outside the house. This was probably the last time any of the clerks lived in and Welch was granted 15s a week to cover the loss of his bed and board allowance.[78] James Welch's salary progression over this time illustrates the marked inflation in professional wages in the early nineteenth century, though, no doubt he would have argued that it also reflected the growing importance of his job and the rising tide of Poor Law bureaucracy. In May 1802 the cashier's annual salary was £70,[79] yet by 1817 had reached a mighty £250.[80] Only when son succeeded father was there an opportunity to rein it back. The salary of the vestry clerk had likewise risen from £90 per annum in 1818 to £200 ten years later. In addition, James Welch conducted divine service in the asylum, for which he received an additional five guineas a year.

One justification for the increase in wages was the accumulation of additional duties and responsibilities, a growth which meant that the guardians had sub-divided the work of the officials over the previous half-century. In 1818 the vestry clerk handled apprenticeships and indentures, settlement cases and removals, and any matters which had to go before the magistrates. Minutes of the meetings of the overseers and guardians were taken by an assistant in this office. William Brynner's duties included examining house-bound paupers as to their settlement and presenting such evidence to the magistrates. The cashier supervised and recorded all cash transactions, and acted as treasurer to the guardians.[81] All these duties had once been performed by a single clerk, with junior assistance. Only on the resignation of Jeremiah Wright in March 1802 had they been divided into two clerks' jobs 'at moderate salaries'.[82] They

---

75   *Ibid.*, 20 May 1828.

76   Archives and Collections, Library of Birmingham. GP B/1/3/1/2 Birmingham Poor Law Union Cash Books, 4 October 1828.

77   Archives and Collections, Library of Birmingham. GP B/2/1/3 Birmingham Guardians' minutes, 30 June 1829.

78   Archives and Collections, Library of Birmingham. GP B/2/1/1 Birmingham Guardians' minutes, 11 May 1796.

79   *Ibid.*, 11 May 1802.

80   *Ibid.*, 28 October 1817.

81   Archives and Collections, Library of Birmingham. GP B/2/1/2 Birmingham Guardians' minutes, 27 October 1818.

82   Archives and Collections, Library of Birmingham. GP B/2/1/1 Birmingham Guardians' minutes, 30 March 1802.

did not remain 'moderate' for long, however. The salaries paid by Birmingham were noticeably higher than those of the neighbouring Poor Law Unions. At Kings Norton in 1841 the clerk (Ralph Docker) was paid £100 a year, while the governor and matron (Mr and Mrs Phillips) received an annual salary of £60, plus board and lodgings.[83] At Aston the master and matron together received £63 a year, plus provisions, though the number of inmates was half that of Birmingham.[84] This was increased to £75 in December 1838.[85] In April 1838 the clerk's annual salary at Aston was also increased to £50.[86] In addition to these desk jobs, Birmingham employed a number of officials whose duties lay principally outside the house. As mentioned in chapter 6, twelve assistant overseers were appointed in 1821 to collect levies.[87] The annual wage bill for this group amounted to £900 a year. In 1818 Mr Coleman was paid 20s a week to remove paupers to the parish which was responsible for them and to carry out liaison work with other parishes.[88] The parish also employed visitors, probably to accompany the overseer when examining applications for outdoor relief. In 1795 one man was employed as visitor to the poor.[89] By 1818 this had been increased to one man and an assistant, then to two visitors, and finally to two visitors and an assistant.[90] Over this period the visitor's salary had grown from 12s per week (just over £31 a year) to £50 in 1818 and to £105 in 1828. By this point the total wage bill for visiting had risen to £265 a year. By 1831 the wages bill alone, if we include those of the governor and governess, amounted to almost £1,000 a year. At Kings Norton the total wage bill (covering the Union clerk, receiving officer, governor and matron, porter and cook and schoolmistress) came to £309.[91] Such was the costly bureaucracy of the nineteenth-century Poor Law in Birmingham.

By no means does this cover all the paid labour in the house, however. Many other servants, some drawn from the body of inmates as the 1818 scandal

---

83   Archives and Collections, Library of Birmingham. GP KN/2/1/1 King's Norton Guardians' minutes, 7 May 1841.

84   Archives and Collections, Library of Birmingham. GP AS/2/1/1 Aston Guardians' minutes, 3 October 1838.

85   *Ibid.*, 12 December 1838.

86   *Ibid.*, 3 April 1838.

87   *Aris's Gazette*, 26 May 1821.

88   Archives and Collections, Library of Birmingham. CP B/660983 Birmingham Overseers' Minutes, Vol. 2, 8 September 1818.

89   Archives and Collections, Library of Birmingham. GP B/2/1/1 Birmingham Guardian's minutes, 27 October 1795.

90   Archives and Collections, Library of Birmingham. GP B/2/1/2 Birmingham Guardians' minutes, 27 October 1818.

91   Archives and Collections, Library of Birmingham. GP KN/2/1/2 King's Norton Guardians' minutes, 7 May 1841.

indicated, were needed to cook and serve food, to brew the beer and bake the bread, to act as porters and carriers, to supervise employment and to manage the clothing and bedwear. It is also likely that the gate-keeper or porter, whose job was to monitor inward and outward traffic from the house, was in fact an inmate. But since such servants were paid weekly, or (in the case of inmates) not at all, the surviving records rarely refer to them or quantify the costs. In 1818 the wage bill for sundry servants came to £1 16s 6d a week, and the wages of nurses to £3 18s.[92] Under this bureaucratic army of professional clerks, amateur guardians, and unpaid ancillary staff the Birmingham Poor Law navigated the choppy waters of Birmingham's needs in the eighteenth and early nineteenth century. It was an expensive ship to maintain, undoubtedly, though no contemporary could say for certain why, when and how it had become so. A more detailed investigation of the operations of certain vital aspects of the relief system, such as the Asylum for the Infant Poor, the infirmary, the mortuary and the insane ward will, however, illustrate how the demands of the poor law had required increasingly specialist functions and led to the expansion of the staff required to administer these.

---

92 Archives and Collections, Library of Birmingham. GP B/2/1/2 Birmingham Guardians' minutes, 27 October 1818.

9

Birmingham's First Hospital:
The Workhouse Infirmary

The story of medical treatment in Birmingham is almost always said to have begun with the opening of the General Hospital in Summer Lane in October 1779. Certainly that major institution, well supported by subscribers and from the receipts of the Triennial Music Festival, was a key development in Birmingham's medical history. It attracted the best doctors and the most funding.[1] Yet Birmingham's first hospital had actually been open for close to forty years already by that time, tucked away at the rear of the workhouse. Moreover, the workhouse infirmary was the one institution in the town where treatment was free at the point of use, since the General Hospital required a letter of recommendation or sponsorship from a subscriber. The earliest indication that the inhabitants of the town were considering the need for some kind of hospital or infirmary is in 1735, at exactly the moment when the first workhouse was being constructed. The first Town Book reports:

> Whereas great inconvenienceys have happend to publick houses by soldiers having divers diseases ... it is thought proper to hire a convenient house to serve for the use of an infirmary for the use of such soldiers.[2]

Whether such a temporary measure was actually adopted at this time is difficult to confirm, but by 1740 a further town's meeting had declared that: 'an

---

1   J. Reinarz, *Health Care in Birmingham: The Birmingham Teaching Hospitals 1779–1939*, Woodbridge, 2009, pp. 12–29.

2   Archives and Collections, Library of Birmingham. CP B/286011 Birmingham Town Book, 10 June 1735. The precise meaning of the reference to 'soldiers' and 'publick houses' in this context remains unclear.

infirmary shall be built, not to exceed £140'.[3] No more was said of this proposal in the Town Book, though this does not mean that it did not happen. As we have seen, William Hutton's date (1766) for the addition of an infirmary wing to the workhouse, accepted by all historians since that time (most notably D.G. Watts in the *Victoria County History*) is clearly wrong.[4] The workhouse already had both of its adjoining wings by 1750. It is perfectly possible, then, that an infirmary block was indeed erected early in the 1740s, shortly after the town decided it needed one. In which case, Hutton's figure for the cost of the infirmary, £400, can probably be revised downwards. The cost allotted in the Town Book is likely to be closer to the truth.

That an infirmary was open by 1745 is attested by a letter to *Aris's Gazette* in September of that year, arguing against the need for a general or charity hospital:

> it being evident that there is no place where there is better provision made for the poor, and I am well informed that the inhabitants, out of their great regard to the sick and lame people, have erected an infirmary for that purpose, and allow two surgeons an annual salary for attending them and supplying them with proper medicines.[5]

Both Samuel Bradford's town plan of 1750 and Thomas Hanson's map of 1778 show a rectangular building, marked 'infirmary', occupying the north-east corner of the workhouse site, to the rear of the main building and close to Steelhouse Lane. Hanson's plan suggests that the infirmary was free-standing, and that a narrow passageway separated it from the workhouse.[6] Given contemporary fears over the transmission of fever, some separation from the workhouse wards would have been desirable and, at this early point, attainable. It was inevitable that the parish infirmary would be intimately linked to the parish workhouse, however. Even after the major changes to the Poor Law in the nineteenth century, workhouses and workhouse infirmaries continued to be built on the same site and that was as true nationally as it was in Birmingham.[7] But inevitable did not mean ideal. The stigma attached to the workhouse, and to poor relief in general,

---

3   *Ibid.*, 8 April 1740.

4   W.B. Stephens (ed.), *A History of the County of Warwick: Volume 7: The City of Birmingham*, London, 1964, p. 339. The wrong date is most recently given in an article by Jonathan Reinarz and Alistair Ritch: J. Reinarz and A. Ritch, 'Exploring Medical Care in the Nineteenth-Century Provincial Workhouse: A View from Birmingham', in J. Reinarz and L. Schwarz (eds), *Medicine and the Workhouse*, Woodbridge, 2013, p. 142.

5   *Aris's Gazette*, 23 September 1745.

6   P.L. Line, *Birmingham: A History in Maps*, Stroud, 2009, pp. 34–43.

7   K. Siena, 'Contagion, Exclusion and the Unique Medical World of the Eighteenth-Century Workhouse: London Infirmaries in their Widest Relief', in Reinarz and Schwarz (eds), *Medicine and the Workhouse*, pp. 19–39.

inevitably rubbed off on the institution next door. In 1824 John Birt Davies drew attention to the unwillingness of the poor to go to the infirmary for medical relief, and 'the repugnance of masters to send their servants thither'.[8] The Self-Supporting Dispensary, to which citizens paid what they could afford, claimed in its first annual report that a little money saved with them released the poor from 'the humiliating act of asking for relief at the workhouse'.[9] The poor either paid for or 'contrived credit' to seek help elsewhere, perhaps from the General Dispensary in Union Street, the General Hospital, or from a general practitioner, if he was willing to reduce or waive his fee. Membership of a sick club, such as the Self-Supporting Dispensary, might also serve to keep them from the dreaded infirmary. If, argued Davies, infectious diseases were more prevalent among the poor, then an infirmary which repelled, rather than attracted them, was the perfect way to disperse fever through the town.

The lack of any other records before the guardians' minutes begin in 1783 leaves a considerable hole in our knowledge of medical provision for the poor prior to the 1780s. The single volume of accounts which does exist, covering 1739 to 1748, does not refer to an infirmary by name. When the newly elected guardians of the poor were drawing up a revised set of regulations for the workhouse in 1784, however, the infirmary was well established.[10] By this date the infirmary had a pharmacy or dispensary attached to it, run by the house apothecary. It was his responsibility to make up prescriptions both for those in the infirmary and for the out-poor, and, as the rules put it, 'keep necessary assortments of drugs and galenical and chymical medicines'. 'Galenical' medicine, named after the Ancient Greek physician, Galen, consisted mostly of herbs and vegetable matter. 'Chymical' medicines, associated with the Swiss philosopher Paracelsus, consisted of combinations of sulphur, mercury and salt. The guardians' rules also refer to a 'head nurse', what might today be called a matron, who answered to the apothecary, ensured that all the infirmary wards were kept clean, and made sure that the nurses under her were 'properly employed at their leisure hours'.[11] There are no later references to a head nurse, and it is unlikely that the post survived very long. Her work would have been taken up by what the guardians would actually have called a matron, that is, the wife of the workhouse master.

Although the records themselves are lost, a useful shaft of light is afforded by an enquiry – in all likelihood undertaken by one of the parish surgeons – into

8   *Aris's Gazette*, 1 November 1824.

9   *Aris's Gazette*, 6 June 1831.

10   Archives and Collections, Library of Birmingham. 49736 BCOL 41.11 Vol. 2 *Orders and Rules to be Observed in the Birmingham Workhouse*, Birmingham, 1784, no pagination.

11   *Ibid.*

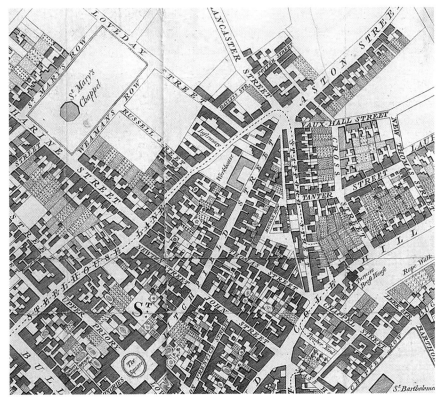

Figure 9.1 Part of map of Birmingham surveyed by Thomas Hanson, 1778, showing the Workhouse on Lichfield Street and the increasing development of that area of the town. Archives and Collections, Library of Birmingham: MAL 14004

the running of the infirmary in 1766. The deliberations of the overseers in the light of this report are recorded by *Aris*.[12] At this point there were said to be 48 beds in the workhouse infirmary, of which 12 were currently empty. In the six months to April 1766 a total of 285 cases had been admitted, and a further 350 treated as out-patients. Care was, at this time, provided by three nurses 'chose of the paupers'. But, if the wage bill was thus kept to a minimum, the cost of drugs (at £85 per annum) was high, 'amounting to more than any comparable hospital', and it was this expenditure that led to the overseers' concern. The problem with this cost analysis was that there *was* no comparable hospital. The overlap between the workhouse and its infirmary made the latter very unlike a medical institution such as the Birmingham General Hospital or a county infirmary. For one thing, as the survey pointed out, 'although many admitted

---

12   *Aris's Gazette*, 19 May 1766.

to the workhouse infirmary are aged people, still they need medicines'. Equally, the rate of discharge of patients was considerably lower than might be anticipated at a dedicated hospital. The report goes on:

> Seventeen patients are fit to be discharged, but on account of their old age or constitutional infirmity are incapable of maintaining themselves. Therefore, there not being sufficient room in the well part of the workhouse, they are maintained in the infirmary.[13]

These cases aside, every effort was made to maintain the distinction between a centre for medical care and the institution to which it was joined at the hip:

> To prevent imposition by paupers lurking in the workhouse after having been cured in the infirmary, a list is given every week to the overseers of patients admitted and cured, so that the infirmary is a receptacle for the accommodation and cure of the paupers, not a place of concealment to harbour and indulge idleness.[14]

Such was the challenge to provide professional medical care in an environment that could hardly be called conducive to it. In the eighteenth century professional expertise, surgery and prescriptions would have been provided by one of the two or three parish surgeons, and it was the obligation of one of them to visit the workhouse daily. Their role will be examined further below. By the late 1820s, however, the apothecary had effectively become the resident doctor, with a greatly extended list of responsibilities. With them came a considerable increase in his salary, to £70 a year, together with board and lodging.[15] The annual salary was still £70 when a new apothecary was sought in 1837, one reason, perhaps, for there being only two applicants.[16] The new job description drawn up for him in 1828 began to reflect the kind of practices we would expect to see in a modern hospital. The apothecary was to fix a ticket to the head of each bed, indicating 'the name of the patient, the name of the parochial surgeon, the patient's diet and date of admission'.[17] He was to visit each ward twice a day, and ensure cleanliness, discipline and proper ventilation, and he was to examine every pauper on admission to the house. The idea was to identify any potential infection before a new patient could spread it through

---

13   *Ibid.*

14   *Ibid.*

15   Archives and Collections, Library of Birmingham. GP B/2/1/3 Birmingham Guardians' minutes, 16 November 1831.

16   *Birmingham Advertiser*, 23 February 1837.

17   Archives and Collections, Library of Birmingham. GP B/2/1/3 Birmingham Guardians' minutes, 3 June 1828.

the building.[18] Such screening of inmates in some kind of 'probationary ward' was common across the Poor Law nationally, but it did depend upon a constant medical presence. In 1851 at Kings Norton Union workhouse, which did not have a resident physician, one woman, Ann Moseley, was locked in the receiving ward for forty-eight hours (with only a chamber-pot for company), because no surgeon turned up to examine her.[19] The apothecary was also to keep 'the belts for the insane'; he was not permitted to absent himself from the infirmary without leaving a note at the workhouse lodge and he was not allowed to vacate the workhouse overnight, 'without the consent of the overseers'.[20] These were onerous duties and it is hardly surprising that the infirmary saw four house surgeons come and go between 1826 and 1831. Nevertheless, Birmingham's commitment to a resident workhouse surgeon contrasts starkly with neighbouring Kings Norton Union, which remained content with daily visits by a medical officer until at least the 1870s.[21] In December 1833 Yardley parish vestry also voted on whether to employ a resident surgeon, and rejected the proposal by twelve votes to four.[22]

Purchases by the workhouse surgery and payments to suppliers of drugs and medical equipment feature regularly in the Birmingham Poor Law accounts, which begin in 1799. In May 1799, for example, the surgery was being supplied with mercury from a number of sources, including Richard Cadbury.[23] There are also regular purchases of oil, on one occasion specified as Neatsfoot oil, needed in the preparation of medicines.[24] Mortars, pestles, grinding lancets and plasters also frequently appear. Skins (probably sheepskin) were bought to combat bedsores and ulcers. In July 1814, as well as purchasing oil, the surgery also bought foxgloves. William Withering's pioneering treatise on the use of digitalis, extracted from the foxglove, in the treatment of heart disease, had been published

---

18   Archives and Collections, Library of Birmingham. 64250 BCOL 41.11 Vol. 2 *Rules and Regulations of the Guardians of the Poor of the Parish of Birmingham*, Birmingham, 1841, pp. 16–17.

19   Archives and Collections, Library of Birmingham. GP KN/2/1/5 Kings Norton Guardians' minutes, 12 February 1851.

20   Archives and Collections, Library of Birmingham. GP B/2/1/3 Birmingham Guardians' minutes, 3 June 1828.

21   Archives and Collections, Library of Birmingham. GP KN/2/1/5 Kings Norton Guardians' minutes, passim.

22   Archives and Collections, Library of Birmingham. CP Y/661613 Box 7, Yardley Parish Vestry Minutes, 1833–51.

23   Archives and Collections, Library of Birmingham. GP B/3/1/1 Birmingham Guardians' minutes, 4 May 1799.

24   Archives and Collections, Library of Birmingham. GP B/3/1/2 Birmingham Guardians' minutes, 2 July 1814.

twenty-nine years earlier.[25] In addition to the ingredients and equipment needed in the preparation of medicines, surgical appliances were equally necessary. Reference to the purchase and provision of trusses are legion throughout all Poor Law records, too numerous to need specific citation. A hernia was one of the chief medical reasons cited by claimants for their inability to work. Leeches, too, often occur, along with syringes and corks (presumably to stop up bottles of liquid medicine). Wooden legs (and wooden thighs) were also supplied to the overseers, the unit cost of one such leg in the 1810s being between 10s or 12s.[26] As in all areas of parish expenditure, the overseers dealt with a variety of contractors, even for artificial legs. The idea was both to keep the pricing competitive, and to spread their custom widely among the town's traders.

Shortly after the 1784 regulations were printed, the guardians' minutes provide an update on the size of the Birmingham workhouse infirmary. In June 1785 there were 36 patients in the sick wards (23 women and 13 men) and one resident nurse.[27] This number is remarkably low, but this was probably not due to the healthy state of the workhouse and the town, but to the number of beds which could be squeezed into the rooms at this time. It is not long after this that the guardians began to discuss ways of expanding the infirmary, a conversation which continued, off and on, for six years. In 1789 they were already admitting that accommodation for the sick was 'very inadequate', but they were equally reluctant to expand it, because enlarging the infirmary would only 'increase the evil by increasing the numbers', demonstrating, once again, the ambiguity between the responsibility of the guardians towards the public and towards the ratepayers.[28] As with the problem of overcrowding in the workhouse proper, there were only three possible solutions. One was to acquire adjacent property and expand into it, another was to rebuild on the existing site and the third was to move elsewhere. True to their nature, the guardians methodically considered all three of these options. A general meeting of guardians in March 1789, which discussed the idea of a new build out of town, is the earliest indication in the records of what would become a reality sixty years later.[29] Coincidentally, it was exactly a hundred years after this meeting that a new purpose-built infirmary was erected at Western Road, adjacent to the then union workhouse in Winson Green. For a month (until they rescinded the proposal) the guardians also considered taking the roof off the workhouse (the centre block and two wings)

---

25 *Ibid.*, 30 July 1814.

26 *Ibid.*, 30 January 1812 and 28 August 1813.

27 Archives and Collections, Library of Birmingham. GP B/2/1/1 Birmingham Guardians' minutes, 6 June 1785.

28 *Ibid.*, 23 March 1789.

29 *Ibid.*

and adding a third storey 'and cover with Westmoreland slate'.[30] Only in 1793 was the bullet irrevocably bitten, and a new infirmary block went up that summer, detached from the main workhouse buildings. John Dower's map of the town (1834) suggests that the new block was built onto the old infirmary, parallel to the eastern wing of the workhouse and occupying the whole of the eastern side of the workhouse grounds as far as Lichfield Street.[31] The building cost £1,475 and was built by William and George Jones. It was erected between July 1793 and July 1794 when the basement and fittings were completed.[32] Sadly, there is no indication at this time as to how the infirmary was organised internally, but later references suggest that the basement contained a mortuary, called variously the 'dead room' or the 'dead vaults', over which was later added an operating theatre.[33] The parish accounts record the table in the operating theatre being painted in 1812.[34] This was a fully fledged theatre, for an amputation (of a leg) took place there in 1823.[35]

What workhouse records rarely provide is a detailed picture of how the space inside was allocated, and this is equally true of workhouse infirmaries. We may not have an exact plan, but there is, however, a remarkably detailed walk-through of the infirmary and workhouse from December 1816, created as a result of a visit by a body of 'medical gentlemen', who subsequently reported to the overseers.[36] At this point the infirmary contained 83 beds and 83 patients, 6 of whom were children. The inventory also includes a room 'in the lodge passage', which could accommodate one nurse overnight. The infirmary itself was divided into nine separate rooms:

Men's ward	13 beds	11 men
Men's ward	13 beds	12 men
Upper small ward	3 beds	2 men
Belonging to surgery	1 bed	2 men
Operation room	2 beds	3 men

---

30   *Ibid.*, 28 March 1789.

31   Line, *Birmingham. A History in Maps*, p. 71.

32   Archives and Collections, Library of Birmingham. GP B/2/1/1 Birmingham Guardians' minutes, 3 June 1793.

33   Archives and Collections, Library of Birmingham. CP B/660982 Birmingham Overseers' Minutes, Vol. 1, 8 May 1809.

34   Archives and Collections, Library of Birmingham. GP B/3/1/2 Birmingham Guardians' minutes, 11 November 1812.

35   Archives and Collections, Library of Birmingham. CP B/660984 Birmingham Overseers' Minutes, Vol. 3, 26 September 1823.

36   Archives and Collections, Library of Birmingham. CP B/660983 Birmingham Overseers' Minutes, Vol. 2, 24 December 1816.

Women's insane ward	11 beds	11 women, 4 children
Salivation room	14 beds	11 women, 2 children
Middle ward	12 beds	12 women
Middle ward	13 beds	12 women

The maternity or lying-in ward is listed in the workhouse section of the report, suggesting that it was not within the infirmary block. At the time of the inspection there were 12 beds in the lying-in ward, occupied by a daunting 29 women and 8 children. It is likely that one or more beds were set aside for giving birth, after which the women returned to another (shared) bed in the ward. Yet in spite of the numbers occupying it, the visiting doctors declared the lying-in room to be 'clean and airy', lacking only 'an additional bar and curtain as a screen for the women when in labour'. This 1816 medical report shows that, at this point, no distinction could be made between those with physical and mental-health problems, though the division of males and females was clearly enforced. Only with the erection of a purpose-built insane ward in 1833 would this issue be addressed. The term 'salivation ward' probably refers to a room where the patients were undergoing some kind of treatment for venereal disease, no doubt involving mercury. We can also see that, under pressure of numbers, beds had been squeezed into the surgery and operating ward. These nine wards were under the supervision of three named nurses. Two further wards were added in 1826, when the overseers became aware of how easily infections could spread through the house.[37] Men's and women's fever wards were incorporated at this time on the top floor of the infirmary, moving the venereal ward into part of the old long room, which had begun life as the paupers' dining hall. The addition of fever wards in 1826 appears to represent the guardians' response to calls for a dedicated hospital to treat fever cases, voiced by Dr John Birt Davies, physician to the General Dispensary, two years earlier.[38] Arrangements in the infirmary had clearly not altered markedly by 1837, when the guardians were worrying about the size of the workhouse fuel bill.[39] Their survey of the apartments at this date confirmed nine rooms in the infirmary, if we include the surgery, each lit by a single fire. The lying-in room, insane wards and venereal ward are listed separately. This being the case, we can imagine that there was, by now, serious pressure on space and resultant overcrowding. In April 1833 there were 113 patients in the infirmary, rising to

---

37   Archives and Collections, Library of Birmingham. CP B/660984 Birmingham Overseers' Minutes, Vol. 3, 3 March 1826.

38   Aris's Gazette, 1 November 1824. Davies wrote the letter pseudonymously as 'Medicus'.

39   Archives and Collections, Library of Birmingham. GP B/2/1/3 Birmingham Guardians' minutes, 19 July 1837.

126 (June 1834), 141 (January 1835), 155 (January 1838) and eventually 233 (April 1847).[40]

Those admitted with venereal complaints were separately housed and their afflictions (deemed to be self-inflicted) were considered a matter of censure, not of sympathy. Not only were these patients treated differently, they looked so too. At least until 1809, when the overseers expressed disapproval of the practice, their heads were shaved upon admission.[41] It was always the overseers, generally more driven to moral and religious sentiment than their fellow guardians, who directed their attention to these patients. The number of such cases was normally not high; there were 13 venereal patients in August 1818, and only 3 in November 1834.[42] The numbers were low enough for the workhouse visitors to suggest that the best way of dealing with such patients was isolation from each other, since 'the absence of evil company, or solitude, is conducive of penitence'.[43] A sudden rise in venereal admissions in 1838, however, triggered the kind of righteous indignation never far below the surface. Having broken out of their one room, there were now patients with sexually transmitted diseases mingling freely with more deserving cases. The two workhouse visitors, Messrs Swinden and Hill, exclaimed:

> They do not consider the legitimate use to make of those wards, as it not only keeps more deserving objects out of them, but is also exceedingly offensive and disgusting to those other patients by whom they are surrounded.[44]

By the following month the sinners had been duly removed.[45] It is possible to conjecture that there had not been some sudden, dramatic rise in sexually transmitted diseases in the town at this time, but that one or more of the parish surgeons had become freer with tickets of admission for such individuals than had previously been the case.

Once the numbers of patients rose well above one hundred, there was clearly need for additional staff and this was demonstrated in the *Ninth Annual Report of the Poor Law Commissioners* (1843). Here the assistant commissioners covering the West Midlands, Alfred Power and Robert Weale, submitted a

---

40   *Ibid.*, April 1833, June 1834, January 1835, January 1838; GP/B/2/1/5 Birmingham Guardians' minutes, April 1847.

41   Archives and Collections, Library of Birmingham. CP B/660982 Birmingham Overseers' Minutes, Vol. 1, 19 December 1809.

42   Archives and Collections, Library of Birmingham. CP B/660986 Birmingham Overseers' Minutes, Vol. 5, 11 November 1834.

43   *Ibid.*, 6 June 1837.

44   *Ibid.*, 6 March 1838.

45   *Ibid.*, 17 April 1838.

complete list of all employees within the Birmingham workhouse, along with their salaries. The list for the infirmary was still headed by the house surgeon, with two assistants, each paid £1 10s a week. Their salaries were actually larger than those of the other surgeons, who were still receiving £70 a year, but the latter did not include board and lodging and were not employed full-time. In addition to these three, Power and Weale listed the following:

Ann Howlett	Nurse in men's infirmary	£10 pa
Elizabeth Vincent	Nurse in women's infirmary	£10 pa
M.A. Raven	Nurse in women's bedridden ward	£8 pa
Elizabeth Line	Nurse in women's venereal ward	£8 pa
Ann Titley	Nurse in women's insane ward	£10 pa
Ann Rose	Nurse in aged and infirm women's ward	£8 pa
Thomas Lamb	Assistant keeper in men's insane ward	£8 pa

The schedule shows a continued blurring between care for the elderly and medical treatment and between mental and physical illness. In terms of staffing by salaried individuals there had been little advance by 1843, but in addition Power and Weale listed inmates who were paid to assist in the wards. Some received a weekly 'gratuity' (never referred to as 'pay') and others an annual sum. The table included wards not to be considered as part of the infirmary, but they are included here for completeness.

Joseph Gregory	Attendant in men's venereal ward	1s pw
George Galey	Night attendant in men's sick ward	1s 9d pw
George Baker	Attendant in men's fever ward	1s 6d pw
Isabella Taylor	Nurse in women's fever ward	£6 pa
Elizabeth Higgs	Nurse in lying-in ward	£5 pa
William Ware	Keeper in men's insane ward	4s 6d pw
Catharine Tipton	Nurse in children's ward	1s pw
Mary Johnson	Nurse in women's insane attic	£5 10s pa
Elizabeth Atherley	Nurse in women's day room	1s pw
Maria Horton	Nurse in infirm men and boys' rooms	£5 pa
William Percival	Wardsman to able-bodied men	1s pw
Joshua Haywood	Wardsman to partially disabled men	1s pw
Maria Knight	Nurse in women and children's ward	1s pw[46]

46　*Ninth Annual Report of the Poor Law Commissioners, Appendix A: Reports of Assistant commissioners, No. 2, Mr Power and Mr Weale's Report on Birmingham*, London, 1843, pp. 139–40.

Since 1816, the pauper nurses had been rewarded 'for good behaviour',[47] but in 1819 this consisted, not of money, but of tea, sugar and butter, luxuries they would not otherwise have enjoyed.[48]

Maternity care and midwifery for the poor had been a central feature of the Poor Law since its creation, long before there had been a workhouse or a lying-in ward. Even the little volume of eighteenth-century workhouse accounts for Birmingham demonstrates such concerns. For example, in April 1743 the overseers paid Widow Ball 3s 6d for seven days work 'subsisting a big bellyd vagrant'. She may be the same as the 'big bellyd travelling woman', Mary Willnott, who was paid 2s out-relief three days later. [49] Nor was illegitimate birth the sole concern of the overseers; if the woman was deemed a vagrant or traveller, then the parish constable might become involved too. A single surviving volume of constables' accounts, also from the 1740s, similarly shows the parish constable supporting the expectant mother financially. Here too it is at the Balls' house that care is provided.

> 6 May 1749. Paid Charles Thacker's wife for ye woman at Ball's for a blanket and other necessaries in lying in, drink etc. 2s 6d.

And later in the same month

> 18 May. Charles Thacker and wife and Thomas Ball for a vagrant lying in, and several necessary expenses attending of it. Her name is Mary Gillet.[50]

Charles Thacker was already in the pay of the parish constable, paid a weekly wage to transport prisoners to the gaol at Warwick, clean the dungeon and the Old Cross chamber, along with a variety of other official duties. Here, as elsewhere, we can see how issues of poverty and law and order regularly intersected in the eighteenth century, and the responsibilities of parish constable and overseer show no clear demarcation line between them. These fragmentary references also suggest that the parish was using a private house as a destination for pregnant women, rather than sending them always to the workhouse. Perhaps we should consider Widow Ball as the earliest named example of the parish midwives.

---

47   Archives and Collections, Library of Birmingham. CP B/660983 Birmingham Overseers' Minutes, Vol. 2, 24 December 1816.

48   *Ibid.*, 10 August 1819.

49   Archives and Collections, Library of Birmingham. CP B/380973 Accounts of the Birmingham Workhouse and Record of Out-relief to the Poor, 1 April 1743.

50   Archives and Collections, Library of Birmingham. MS 3069/13/3/31 (Collections and manuscript notes of W.B. Bickley) Constables' disbursements in the parish of Birmingham, 1748–9.

Advanced pregnancy (that is, a month before birth) was always accepted as a legitimate reason for relief, at least if the woman had no husband or family to support her, but in many cases this would inevitably lead directly to the workhouse. Part of the workhouse had certainly been set aside as a lying-in ward by 1748, when the overseers paid 4s 6d 'for lighting three women in the house'.[51] Since all the candles in the house were snuffed out at night, providing lights in the ward in the early hours incurred an expense, which had to be accounted for. From this point onwards, the workhouse would serve as a maternity hospital, as well as its numerous other functions, and the lying-in ward remained constantly in use. As previously noted, in 1816 the lying-in ward was accommodating no less than 20 women and 8 children.[52] Workhouses were well used to more than one person sharing a bed, but in a maternity ward this seems particularly challenging. A successful childbirth, however, was never the end of parish responsibility. The new mother would not be in a position to support herself or her family for many months after that. Nor would the overseers consider separating her from her baby until the child was at least two or three years old. The arrangement, then, was to move mother and child a month or so after birth into another ward for women and children. In 1834, when there were 4 women and children there, the room was described as 'more comfortless than even the tramp room', the brick floor allowing damp to seep in.[53] It was evidently on the ground floor of the workhouse. Since the women in question were almost always single mothers, the authorities signified their moral disapproval by the poor quality of the accommodation and it undoubtedly took its toll on the health of the infants. This system of post-natal care self-evidently had its problems in a place as unsettled and confined as a parish workhouse. In the eyes of the parish surgeons young children were especially vulnerable 'in a small space, amidst the noise and in the vitiated atmosphere of an institution'.[54] The best solution, in their opinion, was to whisk the child away as soon as was possible 'into the family', by which they meant the Asylum for the Infant Poor in Summer Lane. From the 1830s onwards very young children begin to be sent to the Asylum. Whether they were any less vulnerable in Summer Lane than Lichfield Street is open to question.

The authoritarian actions of the surgeons here were more understandable in the context of serious infant mortality in the workhouse at this time. No

---

51   Archives and Collections, Library of Birmingham. CP B/380973 Accounts of the Birmingham Workhouse and Record of Out-relief to the Poor, 15 July 1748.

52   Archives and Collections, Library of Birmingham. CP B/660983 Birmingham Overseers' Minutes, Vol. 2, 24 December 1816.

53   Archives and Collections, Library of Birmingham. CP B/660986 Birmingham Overseers' Minutes, Vol. 5, 11 November 1834.

54   Archives and Collections, Library of Birmingham. CP B/660985 Birmingham Overseers' Minutes, Vol. 4, 19 March 1833.

statistics of mortality are given, but it was worrying enough for the overseers to seek expert medical opinion. In the opinion of the surgeons consulted, the children were dying from severe malnutrition, what they referred to as 'marasmus'.[55] This, they argued, could partly be combated by restricting breast-feeding to a period of eight or nine months, 'instead of [weaning] being delayed, as is commonly the case, to the end of a year, a year and a half, and even of two years'. There is by no means complete medical agreement on this issue even today, but it seems likely that the pauper mothers were continuing to practice what they would have done at home: to extend the period of breast-feeding to avoid another pregnancy. The sooner this practice was terminated, thought the surgeons, the quicker the child could be taken across to the healthier surroundings of the asylum instead. However, whilst doctors wanted to discourage extended breast-feeding, neither did they want to encourage the opposite extreme of very early weaning, thus depriving infants of their 'natural and only proper nourishment'.[56] The surgeons, decreeing that breast-feeding for the first nine months of life was vital, therefore recommended that the practice of giving the mother bread and milk (which could be used to feed the new baby) just a month after delivery be discontinued. 'This custom we believe to be injurious both as interfering with the natural food of the child, and as directly sanctioning the giving of artificial food by the mother.'[57]

It was not, of course, only in the workhouse that women gave birth. A lying-in hospital was not established in Birmingham until 1842 and prior to that care was necessarily in the community. It was a characteristic of most villages, from the Middle Ages onwards, to have a woman, more often than not a widow, who acted as a midwife, welcoming new arrivals into the world with a mixture of hands-on experience and herbal remedies. Such unofficial medical care was recognised by the parish with occasional payments. In about 1760 the Birmingham overseers formalised such an arrangement by paying the woman half-a-crown (2s 6d) for each case she attended. These payments could amount to considerable sums. In a two-month spell between April and June 1799 the parish midwife – Sarah Bradney – received a total of £5, reflecting her attendance at 40 births.[58] It was in 1820, at a time of increasing professionalism in medical practice, that this system was placed on a more formal footing. The reason put forward by the overseers for elbowing aside tradition was:

---

55   *Ibid.*

56   *Ibid.*

57   *Ibid.*

58   Archives and Collections, Library of Birmingham. GP B/2/1/1 Birmingham Guardians' minutes, 20 April 1799–22 June 1799.

...because of the great dangers and even fatal consequences to which the poor women in this town are exposed from the circumstance of their being attended in labour by women altogether incompetent to the management of midwifery cases.[59]

From this point onwards the parish employed a total of four trained midwives, conveniently located in the four districts into which the town was medically divided: Mrs Bradney in Price Street, Mrs Rooker in Lichfield Street, Mrs Lane in Alcester Street and Mrs Davis in Cherry Street. The missionary, Thomas Finigan, describes a visit by one of the parish midwives to an expectant mother in Silver Street in October 1837:

Elizabeth Best ... had no food of any kind, nor any bed covering, [and] scarce body covering. In this state she was put to bed and delivered by the parish midwife of a female child. Her husband and son are in fever in the same room and all in a perishing state from want.[60]

Finigan gave the family money to pay for 'coals, bread, grits and candle', but the case highlights the difficulties of a home birth, and the serious challenges faced by mother and child in such circumstances. Although Mrs Best had the assistance of the parish midwife, her 'lying-in linen' was provided by another charity. The mother, in fact, died a week later and the child was taken into the workhouse. Under the new arrangement each midwife would be appointed and trained by one of the parish surgeons, and paid 2s 6d or 4s (the reason for two different fees is not explained) for each birth. Ann Rooker, for one, had been performing this task for many years already and probably knew more about it than the doctor who now offered her training. She continued to do so until 1835, when the parish surgeons declared that, after more than thirty years' service, she was 'by age and illness altogether incapacitated'.[61] Ann Rooker was by now seventy-seven years old, and her husband, Samuel, seventy-five – 'and both very infirm'. The overseers' response to this was twofold, and evidence that parochial attitudes had not been entirely swept aside by professionalism. Ann Rooker's daughter, Mrs Edge, took over from her mother as midwife, as was often the case in village communities, and Mrs Rooker and her husband were awarded an allowance of 7s per week, lifting their income a little above the paupers she had so often attended.

---

59 Archives and Collections, Library of Birmingham. CP B/660983 Birmingham Overseers' Minutes, Vol. 2, 4 January 1820.

60 Archives and Collections, Library of Birmingham. MS 3255 Journal of the Rev T.A. Finigan, 21 October 1837, p. 147.

61 Archives and Collections, Library of Birmingham. CP B/660986 Birmingham Overseers' Minutes, Vol. 5, 10 November 1835.

By the nineteenth century, in addition to the generalist treatment provided by the workhouse infirmary, a number of more specialist hospitals had opened their doors, all funded chiefly by subscribers. The Orthopaedic Hospital was created in 1817, the Eye Hospital 'for the relief of the poor afflicted with diseases of the eye' in 1823 and a Lying-in Hospital opened in 1842. In addition to these, a 'house of recovery' or fever hospital was set up on Bishopgate Street in 1828. The object of the latter institution, declared the governors in June 1828:

> ... is to provide and maintain a place of daily reception for persons labouring under acute diseases, and more especially for the immediate removal of domestic servants when attacked by febrile affections of a contagious or uncertain nature.[62]

Specialist treatment was therefore in place, but was it possible for the poor to take advantage of it? Most institutions operated a ticketing system, supplying notes of recommendation to their subscribers, who in turn passed them on to deserving cases. This was equally true of the General Hospital, and a number of the suburban Birmingham parishes, including Northfield and Edgbaston, as well as Birmingham itself, took the precaution of paying an annual subscription. Deserving cases, however, faced another problem after admission, one highlighted by Thomas Finigan. Finigan and his wife rescued a young woman, Jane Osbourne, from a brothel in Smallbrook Street in August 1837. The woman was, in Finigan's opinion, in 'decline' and he applied successfully, first to a governor of the General Hospital, and then to the secretary, to have her admitted.[63] When the missionary visited Jane in the ward a week later, he found several of her former co-workers also there. 'There was no washing done in the hospital for any of the patients,' writes Finigan. 'These girls came to her and offered to wash her things.' Suspecting an attempt to lure her back to the house in Smallbrook Street, Finigan took home the washing himself.[64] Any surcharges, whether for food or cleaning, made a long stay in the General Hospital problematic for any patient who had no other form of financial support.

Charitable though their institution might be in status, the committee and surgeons of the General Hospital were far from seeing its role as supplementing that of the workhouse infirmary, or as being as 'general' as the title might imply. It contained no dedicated fever ward, no lying-in ward, and no facilities for the treatment of mental illness. A bequest of thirty guineas by Edward Hiccox (and

---

62   *Birmingham Journal*, 14 June 1828.

63   Archives and Collections, Library of Birmingham. MS 3255 Journal of the Rev T.A. Finigan, 24 August 1837, p. 75.

64   *Ibid.*, 2 September 1837, pp. 91–2.

a subscription of ten guineas for seven years) 'if the General Hospital includes a ward for lunatics' was politely turned down.[65] A fever ward was only opened in 1834, *after* the 1832 cholera epidemic had died down.[66] The kind of territorial disputes regularly seen among medical practitioners in the early nineteenth century are only too evident in the tetchy relationship between the surgeons of the infirmary and those of the General Hospital. There is no better example of this social and medical divide than in 1782, when the surgeons of the General Hospital complained of the transfer of patients from the workhouse infirmary. They come, said the annual report, 'without change of linen, and with vermin and the itch'.[67] Additionally, they 'often behaved in an ungrateful, disorderly manner'. Evidently the hospital authorities did not take kindly to the introduction of 'workhouse behaviour' into their institution. Not all the pauper patients came from Lichfield Street, it has to be said, though a large proportion probably did. Nor was it easy to release the beds after treatment was completed. 'They have remained a burden on the charity,' the report went on, 'despite applications to parishes to remove them.'

Overall responsibility for the medical care, both of the inmates of the workhouse and of the out-poor, lay with the parish surgeons, and as the town grew, so their numbers, responsibilities (and salaries) rose. In 1795 each of the three surgeons was paid 20 guineas a year, and shared a further £10, set aside for the purchase and prescription of drugs.[68] In 1803 a fourth surgeon was added, and the salaries were increased to £25 per annum.[69] The doctors were then on three-year contracts, and appointments tended to be made (or renewed) shortly after a new set of guardians took office. In 1829 the total number of parish surgeons was raised to six.[70] The surgeons' salaries could not be called lavish, although we must remember that their main income would have come from private patients outside the Poor Law. Indeed, a correspondent to the *Birmingham Journal* in 1836 saw these two income streams as diametrically opposed. 'Either the surgeon neglects his private practice,' writes the pseudonymous contributor, 'or he neglects the paupers. The result is that the paupers are generally left to apprentices.'[71] Yet the parish doctors undoubtedly worked hard for such modest returns, as the statistics of medical relief amply

---

65   *Aris's Gazette*, 6 January 1766.

66   *Birmingham Advertiser*, 29 January 1835.

67   *Aris's Gazette*, 1 July 1782.

68   Archives and Collections, Library of Birmingham. GP B/2/1/1 Birmingham Guardians' minutes, 27 October 1795.

69   *Ibid.*, 27 September 1803.

70   *Birmingham Journal*, 28 November 1829.

71   *Birmingham Journal*, 2 April 1836.

demonstrate. One quarterly report for the workhouse surgeons, released in October 1819, shows a total of 85 patients being treated in the infirmary (57 women and 28 men), though this figure conceals the actual number of new admissions, which totalled 177. In addition to examining and treating these, the surgeons made a total of 1,740 home visits over these three months, and inoculated 435 poor children.[72]

By the mid-1830s each of the six doctors did the rounds for a week by rotation, largely freeing him from parish duties for the next five weeks. In response to increased public interest and scrutiny, the *Birmingham Advertiser* began to publish a weekly itemised list of the work of each 'surgeon of the week'. During one week in August 1834, for example, Mr Green admitted 14 patients into the infirmary and discharged 6, leaving a total of 134 occupying the wards. In addition he (or his locum) visited 85 out-patients and undertook 6 midwifery cases.[73] By 1825 the medical salaries had risen to £30 a year, but the appointment of an in-house apothecary at this time meant that the surgeons had less direct contact with the infirmary wards.[74] The apothecary or house surgeon, who had no opportunity for private work, was paid £70, with board and lodging. The annual salary of a surgeon was also expected, by this date, to cover the cost of medicines, as well as the remuneration of any assistant they chose to employ. Not a particular hardship, this, since the assistant was more often than not the surgeon's own son. Most famously, this was true of Edward Townsend Cox, whose son, William Sands Cox, followed him both into private practice and into service as a parish surgeon.[75] Sands Cox was permitted by the guardians to share his father's duties as parish surgeon in January 1827.[76] Such blatant nepotism did not go unnoticed or uncriticised. A letter to the *Birmingham Journal* in June 1827, signed by 'a member of the Royal College of Surgeons', complained of Cox's appointment, 'with no other right than having been permitted by the guardians to act as assistant to his father'.[77] Medical rivalry within the practice remained intense and competitive. This kind of arrangement was common practice within the medical profession; only when it fell under the umbrella of the Poor Law would it be seen as questionable. The steady rise in pay reflects the growing importance of medical treatment

72   *Edmonds' Weekly Recorder*, 9 October 1819.

73   *Birmingham Advertiser*, 14 August 1834.

74   Archives and Collections, Library of Birmingham. GP B/2/1/2 Birmingham Guardians' minutes, 26 April 1825.

75   J.T.J. Morrison, *William Sands Cox and the Birmingham Medical School*, Birmingham, 1926, pp. 5–9.

76   Archives and Collections, Library of Birmingham. GP B/2/1/3 Birmingham Guardians' minutes, 30 January 1827.

77   *Birmingham Journal*, 16 June 1827.

within the Poor Law, but also an increasing respect for the medical profession itself. On the positive side this meant that medical advice was regularly taken, and taken seriously, on all aspects of workhouse life, from the condition of the privies to the ventilation of the dormitories. On the negative side, it also meant that the overseers, in a difference of opinion between a pauper and a medical officer in particular, were reluctant to question the surgeons' judgement and behaviour. A revealing instance of this is the wording of a minute from 1831, when two of the overseers, making their weekly visit to the Asylum for the Infant Poor, complained that one of the medical gentlemen 'does not attend there so often as we think his official duties require'. The overseers as a group replied that 'they are fully aware of the remissness, but ... it is rather delicate to interfere [and] to censure any professional gentleman'.[78]

We may guess that most surgical procedures performed by the parish surgeons occurred in the workhouse infirmary. Nevertheless, the diaries of the Congregationalist missionaries show that operations were sometimes performed in the home as well. In February 1838 Edwin Derrington records a visit to a house in Lower Trinity Street, where a girl had been bled with leeches:

> and such was the wretched state of poverty they were in that they had no change, and the poor girl remained in the clotted blood ... I obtained an under garment for her from her own good friend, Mrs Goodson.[79]

Far more challenging was the laryngotomy performed on a young man in Cecil Street and described by Peter Sibree in January 1839:

> An inflammation of the windpipe approaching to suffocation had obliged the medical gentlemen to open his larynx and insert a pipe, from which he was breathing and not through his mouth.[80]

No doubt both of these patients might have fared better had they been in the infirmary. Here are the consequences of overcrowding in the infirmary, which we would otherwise not see. The man in Cecil Street died the following day. Such was the medical provision for those who could not afford professional medical attention. Birmingham was, as it happened, full of talented doctors,

---

78   Archives and Collections, Library of Birmingham. CP B/660985 Birmingham Overseers' Minutes, Vol. 4, 18 October 1831.

79   Archives and Collections, Library of Birmingham. CC1/82 Congregational Town Mission, 21 February 1838.

80   Archives and Collections, Library of Birmingham. CC1/71 Congregational Town Mission, 13 January 1839.

and many of them, like William Sands Cox, William Withering and William Small, to name only three, were willing to devote some of their time to the poor, and to offer their advice more widely on matters of health, sanitation and diet. Without that, a bad situation might have been made much worse.

10

The Doings of Death

As long as we have a man's body, we play our Vanities upon it, surrounding it in state, and packing it up in gilt nails and velvet; and we finish our duty by placing over it a stone, and written all over with lies.

William Makepeace Thackeray, *Vanity Fair*

A revealing story was circulating around Birmingham in the 1790s, at a time when England was at war with France, the town's foreign markets were out of reach and huge numbers were out of work. Many individuals, pressed low by poverty, bankruptcy and bleak prospects, headed down to 'Vaughton's Hole' and ended their troubles in its muddy waters. The hole itself was a deep pool on a bend on the river Rea, which marked the boundary between the parishes of Aston and Birmingham. It was said that the parish overseers, seeing rather too many bodies being washed up on the banks of the river, would go down with long poles and push the victims back into the stream, hoping that they would end up on the opposite bank of the river. The point of the tale, apart from indicating the low reputation of overseers (alongside journalists and politicians) was that the responsibility for the burial of those who died in poverty lay with the parish. In difficult financial times the overseers of Aston and Birmingham were simply endeavouring to offload the cost onto each other.

The issues surrounding death and its aftermath were an ever-present and significant part of poor relief. The earliest surviving accounts from Birmingham workhouse show this all too clearly. Indeed, the very first page, dated August 1739, contains a payment of 1s 6d to Sarah Short 'towards burying her child, her husband runn [sic].' Two months later the Price family appear no less than seven times in the space of five weeks:

19 October	John Price and five children, woman sick	1s 6d
22 October	John Price, child dead	1s

26 October	Price child burying fees	2s 4d
2 November	John Price, wife ill	1s
8 November	Price wife, four children	2s
16 November	Price wife, he run, four children	2s
23 November	Price wife, four children, he a soldier	2s

This sequence of payments makes an interesting family saga in itself, but also serves to highlight how expensive the cost of death was to a family on a meagre, or non-existent, income. At 2s 4d it cost more to inter a small child than it did to support this family of six for a week. Incidentally, we might add that over the following months Mrs Price's explanation for her husband's continuing absence and therefore her need for relief, regularly alternated between 'he run' and 'he a soldier'. The overseers seemed to have been perfectly happy to accept either account. The payments to Sarah Short and the Price family were as out-relief; this early volume of accounts also records the expenses resulting from death in the workhouse too, though the individuals concerned were never mentioned by name. Even by 1740 the overseers were combining the payments together to save time and space: 'Church fees at St Philip's for burying paupers' (25 June 1740) and 'burying ffees at new church' (23 January 1741). The latter interments were also at St Philip's, completed only sixteen years earlier and they amounted to a considerable £1 10s 4d. In April 1747, in addition to the burial fees at St Philip's, the overseers were also paying one shilling each 'for carrying eleven people to church'.[1]

Such expenses continued for a long time thereafter. Seventy years later, the workhouse accounts for 1818/19 were showing a little under £400 spent on coffins and burial fees in the course of one year alone, almost as much as was spent on fuel to heat the place.[2] By 1832 the annual cost of coffins had dropped a little to £324 15s 3d.[3] The annual accounts for 1835/6 record a total of £66 spent on coffins for inmates, and £164 on those for the out-poor.[4] Death was expensive, or rather, the cost of a 'decent' interment was. And the stillborn children who were secretly (and illegally) concealed in a corner of St Phillip's churchyard cruelly demonstrated that even the cheapest of interments was beyond the reach of some. The body of one such stillborn female, interred in a box, was uncovered at St Philip's in January 1840, a humble piece of

---

1 Archives and Collections, Library of Birmingham. CP B/9380973 Accounts of the Birmingham Workhouse and Record of Out-Relief to the Poor, 1739–48.

2 *Edmonds' Weekly Recorder*, July 1819.

3 *Birmingham Journal*, 7 July 1832.

4 *Aris's Gazette*, 4 July 1836.

wood marking the place of burial.[5] These kinds of makeshift, yet semi-formal, interments by families were not uncommon. There were the fees payable to the church and officials, the cost of the burial place, along with the full panoply of mourning: hearse, coffin, coffin furniture, mourning wear, gloves for the pall-bearers and a wake for neighbours and friends. Behind the personal tragedies a whole Birmingham industry grew up. As J. Allin, who ran a clothes' warehouse known as The Flag at the top of New Street, put it:

> With hatbands, favours, gloves and pall
> Most cheerfully I'll serve you all.[6]

If a family was not in receipt of poor relief already, the £3 or so cost of an average funeral could easily drive it to the workhouse. Mr Allin, helpful as always, provided one way to keep costs down:

> And then to prove myself your friend,
> As mourning days will have their end,
> I'll buy the very things I sold,
> And sell them all again for old.[7]

Death was ever-present in the back streets of Birmingham, but it took place silently, as far as surviving official records go. Only the parish registers bleakly record its passage. The town missionaries saw it, however, and the rituals which accompanied it, long-established customs among the town's poorest citizens. They saw the half-closed shutters, which signified a death in the house; they saw the arrival of the women to lay out the dead; they saw too how public and crowded was the death-bed scene itself. The Congregationalist missionary, Edwin Derrington, describes the death of an infant from what he refers to as 'black fever' (by which he probably meant typhus):

> I had scarcely entered the house, when one woman after another followed me, until I had, I suppose, all the neighbours in the house, about eight in number. This gave me an opportunity of saying a word for my Master. I did so, gave each of them a tract, prayed and left.[8]

---

5   *Birmingham Journal*, 25 January 1840.

6   *Aris's Gazette*, 23 December 1799.

7   *Ibid.*

8   Archives and Collections, Library of Birmingham. CC1/64 Congregational Town Mission, 22 June 1840.

In the tight-knit communities of the Birmingham courts, a front door was no guarantee of private space. Indeed, the division between public and private space, if it was observed at all, was rarely maintained at all in times of affliction. As another of the missionaries, Thomas Finigan, noted:

> There is no new occurrence in my district. The people have a habit of going into each other's houses when they see anyone enter having the appearance of a doctor or a minister.[9]

Edwin Derrington also saw, with some horror, how even death could not be allowed to interrupt the search for money and sustenance:

> Died a woman of advanced age ... On the Sunday his mother lay dead in the house [the son] was fitting up a cart to go to some market town, I think to the Wolverhampton races, and this was done with the utmost indifference.[10]

We might note that Mr Derrington was as much (if not more) concerned with Sabbath-breaking as he was with what he saw as the absence of proper mourning. Two years earlier Derrington describes as grim a scene as any in his diaries, and one where poverty and death were inextricably joined:

> Next I visited a scene of extream [sic] wretchedness in Meriden Street, a family whom the neighbours say brought a good house of furniture with them into the court when they came, but through want of work they had parted with, or pawned all, even their bed. The poor woman had been confined a week or two ago and only had a bed of rags or straw. I found the man, his wife, and three children, all living in the room, and the baby there dead, which they had endeavoured to get buried as a still-born infant, but could not succeed. It had already lain to [sic] long, yet they must wait three days longer ... I left two shillings.[11]

The parish, clearly, had as much to do with the dead as it had with the living.

It was one of the ancient responsibilities of the parish overseers to meet the cost of death and the expenses which followed from it. They had to consider where paupers could most decently be buried, how they were to be conveyed there and what they would be buried in. And they struck deals and compared prices, just as energetically with coffin makers and church beadles as they did

---

9   Archives and Collections, Library of Birmingham. MS 3255 Journal of the Rev T.A. Finigan, 10 October 1837, p. 136.

10   Archives and Collections, Library of Birmingham. CC1/64 Congregational Town Mission, 12 August 1840.

11   Archives and Collections, Library of Birmingham. CC1/61 Congregational Town Mission, 16 January 1838.

with the butchers and bakers. Nor did the overseers have to deal solely with death and burial. The demise of a family member, particularly the bread-winner, might have an immediate effect on the bereaved in terms of their ability to survive independently. In December 1840 Derrington noted in passing how many widows filled his pews:

> The situation of Town Missionary is one that is likely to gather around him the semblances of mourning and desertion in those creatures of distress, whom death has deprived of a partner, in some cases a support and a guide. Widows are to be seen making up a part, and that not a very small one, of those who meet to hear from his lips the words of eternal life. I think I have numbered nine at the Sabbath evening service. The sable group appeared before me, presenting the doings of death, as though situated among the mourning women.[12]

If Derrington's observations here are impressionistic, one of the Birmingham guardians sought to give them a more statistical basis. In 1837 Edward Knight undertook a survey of the casual poor receiving out-relief, to back up his proposals for a reorganisation of the system of payment then in place. Of the casuals receiving out-relief (with tickets) in a given week in December 1837 Knight counted 651 widows, out of an overall total of 884 persons. The male equivalent – widowers with or without children – stood at just 17. Of the 943 persons who applied without tickets, Knight counted a much lower total of 201 widows, though again this was far higher than the 36 widowers. Edward Knight questioned why so many widows were receiving permanent relief, given that their condition was 'hardly because of the state of trade'.[13] We can add to these figures those whose relief was paid weekly (as pensioners) without application. These were the poor of the 'first class', described as 'those whose wants appear to be of a more permanent kind'. In December 1837 they numbered 859 cases, of whom 661 were single or widowed women. However we look at these figures and explain the causes of such high male mortality, it appears that Birmingham was full of poor widows, comprising around half of all those receiving out-relief.

Although early parish records show the overseers bearing the full range of funeral costs for the poor – laying-out, supply of a coffin, burial fees and wake – by the nineteenth century they were generally only willing to pay for the coffin, unless the individual had died in the workhouse itself. A family might expect to receive a one-off payment of five shillings, which would cover the cost of a simple coffin. Yet in an organisation that scrutinised its costs so intently, it

---

12 *Ibid.*, 15 December 1840.

13 Archives and Collections, Library of Birmingham. GP B/2/1/3 Birmingham Guardians' minutes, 13 February 1838: E. Knight, *Observations on the Relief of Cases of Out Poor in Birmingham*, Birmingham 1838.

was remarkably easy to abuse the system. The fraudster had only to convince a ratepayer to write him or her a letter of recommendation, take the note to the workhouse clerk and the price of a coffin would be handed over. The tale of a dead relative at home and no money to bury him, was rarely questioned. One such tale of 'imposition' came before the Public Office in March 1835, when Mary Mitchell was sentenced to three months in the house of correction for falsely claiming burial costs for her father-in-law.[14] The heavy sentence, the maximum a magistrate could hand out without recourse to a higher court, was meant as a warning to others. Yet in a system which still accepted the 'note of recommendation' as proof of need, abuse was clearly an ever-present risk. In another case from 1834, selected for notice in the press for its hopeless naivety, Sarah Higgins was sentenced to six weeks in the house of correction for presenting an obviously fabricated letter of recommendation, purportedly to come from a respected ratepayer. The note read: 'I certifie that Sarah Higins as a child ded, and is an objecet of Releef.'[15] Poor English was the downfall of many a fraudulent claim. The regular warnings made to the public in the local press about notes of recommendation for shoes and other small articles, without personally verifying the need, underlined a perennial problem.

The Birmingham overseers negotiated for the supply of coffins in bulk. In 1809 the parish contract was with two suppliers, Henry Biggs and Thomas Jackson, who were selling coffins to the house for between 4s and 7s each, the prices having lately been raised. Three prices are quoted, based on the age (and therefore the size) of the occupant. A price of 7s was for an adult, 4s for a child under twelve years and 3s for a child under six years.[16] As can be seen, this was already a considerable hike on the costs of seventy years earlier. Henry Biggs is listed in *Chapman's Birmingham Directory* of 1801 as 'Henry Biggs, joiner and coffin maker, Castle Street', and the Biggs family, Henry, then James, then Mary, continued to supply the parish with coffins until at least 1820.[17] Even in a town as populous and unhealthy as Birmingham, making coffins was probably not a viable trade on its own and most coffin makers undertook related work as required. Biggs was 'joiner and coffin maker', and another later supplier, Thomas Lawrence, appears simply as 'carpenter and joiner, Hill Street' in *Wrightson & Webb's Birmingham Directory* of 1833.[18] Coffin maker is never listed as a separate profession in the directories or the early censuses;

14 *Aris's Gazette*, 9 March 1835.

15 *Birmingham Advertiser*, 23 January 1834.

16 Archives and Collections, Library of Birmingham. CP B/660982 Birmingham Overseers' Minutes, Vol. 1, 8 August 1809.

17 *Chapman's Birmingham Directory*, Birmingham, 1801, p. 9.

18 *Wrightson and Webb's Birmingham Directory*, Birmingham, 1833, p. 52.

the making of coffin furniture, however, was considered an independent trade, although only two individuals gave their profession as 'coffin furniture maker' in the 1831 census.[19] In contrast, the *New Triennial Directory* of 1808 details eight coffin furniture makers in the town and *Chapman's Directory* lists no less than nineteen.[20] The curious term 'coffin furniture' perhaps needs some explanation. It refers to the metal decoration or embellishment of the coffin with a name-plate, handles and 'lace' ornament. As such it was an archetypal Birmingham industry, the stamping of metal toys and ornaments echoing down so many back streets, though particularly in the Hockley area. A report on the industry appears as the final chapter in Samuel Timmins' magisterial *Birmingham and the Midland Hardware District*, published in 1866, by which date there were estimated to be twelve firms and 150 people employed in the making of coffin furniture. Their work was especially in rolled lead, but also in black tin, Britannia metal and brass. Aitken writes:

> The most economical of companies in 'the black business', whose advertisements appear immediately after the announcements of deaths in our newspapers, find it necessary to nail a groat's worth of pathetic sham-finery even on a pauper's coffin.[21]

Augustus Pugin was equally dismissive of the trade:

> Nothing can be more hideous, than the raised metal work, called coffin furniture, that is so generally used at the present time; heathen emblems, posturing angels, trumpets, death's heads and cross bones, are mingled together in a glorious confusion, and many of them partake of a ludicrous character.[22]

The relevance of Aitken's comment will become clear later. The overseers had no direct dealings with the coffin furniture manufacturers until the late 1830s, but felt their presence all the same. As with many items supplied to the workhouse, the overseers endeavoured to drive down costs by engaging a number of different traders, who could then be played off against each other. In 1829 Mr Caswell had recently taken over the Biggs' business and was supplying coffins at 6s 3d for adults and 3s 3d for children. Another supplier, Thomas Lawrence, was allowed a share of the workhouse business, 'if he offers the same

---

19 *Birmingham Journal*, 16 July 1831.

20 *Thomson and Wrightson's New Triennial Directory of Birmingham*, Birmingham, 1808, p. 123; *Chapman's Birmingham Directory*, p. 9.

21 S. Timmins, *Birmingham and the Midland Hardware District*, London, 1866, p. 704.

22 A.W. Pugin, *Glossary of Ecclesiastical Ornament and Costume*, London, 1844, p. 77.

price'.[23] This price also included delivery and, in the case of a death outside the workhouse, 'screwing up at the house of the deceased'.[24] Messrs Caswell and Lawrence were still furnishing the overseers with coffins in 1832[25] and Lawrence was also awarded the contract for supplying coffins to Aston Union.[26] A contract with the workhouse was not something to be given up lightly and with rumours of cholera in the air, Mr Caswell and Mr Lawrence must have been rubbing their hands with expectations of busy times ahead.

The general account books, which begin in 1799, contain regular payments to the coffin makers and allow us to see how costs escalated. In the month of January 1812, for example, Birmingham spent £8 4s 6d on coffins, rising to £13 9s in January 1813. By the following year (January 1814) the payments were up to £23 19s 6d. By January 1817 Mary Biggs and her son were supplying coffins to the value of £20 5s, and by January 1834 the overall bill had risen to a hefty £51 16s. Of this sum only £7 10s was needed for the interment of workhouse inmates; the rest was spent on the out-poor. Whatever corners the overseers and guardians cut in the years that followed must be seen in the context of ever-growing demand. The role of the overseers was not limited to the supply of coffins to the poor. They also had choices to make as to a place of burial, there being no obligation to use a single churchyard for Poor Law interments. By the nineteenth century there were already four Anglican graveyards near the centre of Birmingham at St Martin's and St Philip's (1715), at St Bartholomew's in Masshouse Lane (1752) and at St Mary's (1774), very close to the workhouse, in Whittall Street. The questions to be considered by the paupers' pay-masters were always the same: how much did they charge and how deep did they bury? In 1812 the overseers had decided that St Martin's, the final resting-place of Birmingham folk since the Middle Ages, was no longer a viable burial-ground and they shifted interments to the relatively spacious surroundings of St Bartholomew's, 'a portion of which shall be marked out'.[27] They specified, though this turned out to be an entirely unrealistic demand, that each burial should be ten feet deep. In theory, at least, this was to be for every individual interment; doubling up was only permitted if more than one

---

23   Archives and Collections, Library of Birmingham. CP B/660985 Birmingham Overseers' Minutes, Vol. 4, 14 April 1829.

24   Archives and Collections, Library of Birmingham. CP B/660983 Birmingham Overseers' Minutes, Vol. 2, 21 December 1819.

25   Archives and Collections, Library of Birmingham. CP B/660985 Birmingham Overseers' Minutes, Vol. 4, 10 January 1832.

26   Archives and Collections, Library of Birmingham. GP AS/2/1/1 Aston Guardians' minutes, 21 March 1837.

27   Archives and Collections, Library of Birmingham. CP B/660982 Birmingham Overseers' Minutes, Vol. 1, 7 April 1812.

funeral was to be held on the same day. Nevertheless, the sheer depth of the plots must imply that the overseers intended to use them for a succession of burials. Given the quantity of earth which had to be removed, the fee of 4s for digging does not seem unreasonable, though there was also 1s to be paid to the rector and clerk, and another 1s to the sexton.

Two years later, the kind of mass graves we associate with pauper burials were specified in more detail. By then the overseers were requesting that 'graves be three feet depth of earth on the top, and of sufficient depth to hold five coffins.'[28] Workhouse funerals must have been desultory affairs; almost by definition there were unlikely to be family members to follow the coffin and any friends made in the workhouse were likely to be close to the grave themselves. A correspondent (JA) to the *Birmingham Local Notes & Queries* recalled the funeral of George Davis, the Birmingham poet, who died in the workhouse in the winter of 1819:

> He was borne to his last resting-place, at St Philip's, by poor, tottering, old men from the workhouse, who seemed to have a firm belief that their turn was not far distant.[29]

However, the overseers did try to ensure something of a send-off by asking that staff of the house, or at least such as could be spared, should attend interments. In November 1814 a minute lamented 'the very great neglect in the attending of the people of this house [at] the funerals at St Bartholomew's', and requested staff to be at the church by 2.30 pm.[30] Such staff, we might surmise, were unlikely to be the master and the clerk, but those who were also inmates of the house. It was not only the pauper inmates who were given an official send-off, backed by official money. It seems to have been an accepted responsibility of the parish to pay the funeral expenses of its more important and usually residential, staff. For an organisation which counted and accounted for every penny, this kind of casual expenditure might appear curiously out of place, yet such was the case. A kind of cosy camaraderie was enshrined within the Old Poor Law, and consistency was not one of its strong points. In July 1830, for example, the overseers paid for the funeral of Mrs Brueton, who had been matron of the Asylum for the Infant Poor for sixteen years.[31] Clearly it was the length of her

28   Archives and Collections, Library of Birmingham. CP B/660983 Birmingham Overseers' Minutes, Vol. 2, 3 May 1814.

29   Archives and Collections, Library of Birmingham. MS 3456 Album of poems by George Davis with newscutting from *Birmingham Local Notes & Queries*, p. 1.

30   Archives and Collections, Library of Birmingham. CP B/660983 Birmingham Overseers' Minutes, Vol. 2, 29 November 1814.

31   Archives and Collections, Library of Birmingham. CP B/660985 Birmingham Overseers' Minutes, Vol. 4, 5 July 1830.

service in particular which motivated the gesture on this occasion. Nor were such acts of kindness restricted to the officers themselves. In 1800 the board of guardians authorised a payment of £3 3s 4d to their clerk, James Welch, 'for the burial of his wife and child'.[32] The funeral of James Welch himself, twenty-nine years later, must have been a much grander affair. Here the guardians dipped into their pocket to the tune of £34 3s 6d.[33] A month later they lavished more than £50 on the funeral (at St Martin's) of the late master of the workhouse, William Cheshire, who had died in office.[34] It would be difficult to account for such a huge sum unless the inmates themselves attended the funeral, or at least partook of the 'funeral supper'. But in both cases we can also say that the Cheshires and the Welches remained part of 'the family'. James Welch was succeeded as clerk by his son, and Mrs Cheshire stayed on as governess.

Those who died in the workhouse or workhouse infirmary were placed in the mortuary or 'dead vault' prior to their interment. Unless there was a need for an inquest (there rarely was), they would not have remained there for long. In an institution so full of the elderly and the infirm, the turnover was fast and furious. The death rate in the house we can only guess at, since the mortuary book, often referred to in the minutes, no longer survives, and the guardians, for reasons we can well understand, did not care to publish statistics of mortality in the house. Only in the figures supplied to Frederick Eden for his survey do we have any indication of the death rate in the house, and this is only for the years 1791–5, and the first eight months of 1796.

Year	Average in house	Deaths
1791	350	128
1792	400	136
1793	470	93
1794	640	162
1795	500	121
1796 (to Sept)	464	82[35]

The markedly higher figure for 1794 is almost entirely accounted for, not by the overall rise in occupancy, but from the number of children who died. In total 40 boys and 24 girls died in the house that year, while the adult mortality rate altered little. This was three years before the opening of the Asylum for

---

32 Archives and Collections, Library of Birmingham. GP B/3/1/1 Birmingham Guardians' cash books, 25 March 1800.

33 *Ibid.*, 22 May 1829.

34 *Ibid.*, 25 June 1829.

35 F.M. Eden, *The State of the Poor*, Vol. III, London, 1797, p. 740.

the Infant Poor, and provided a strong reason for its creation. An occasional incident or scandal, however, can sometimes supply us with more information than the authorities were usually prepared to divulge. In February 1837, for example, a man named Collins from the Inkleys was buried before his wife had even been informed of her husband's death. The explanation offered for this oversight was that there had been no less than eighteen bodies in the mortuary at this point and some confusion as to their identities.[36] The mistake took place in the midst of an influenza epidemic in the town, which no doubt had also taken its toll in the workhouse.

The workhouse had its own beadle, whose duties included making arrangements for funerals and ensuring that the coffin reached the right burial place at the right time. However, the behaviour of the beadle in 1819, one Thomas Dalton, showed that even this most delicate part of workhouse life (and death) could be subject to pecuniary sleight-of-hand. Dalton was found to have been accepting 'perquisites' from the grave-digger at St Philip's for arranging burials there instead of at St Bartholomew's. There was no evidence that the clergy themselves were involved in the scam, but Dalton was criticised for being 'under the influence of the sexton of St Philip's'.[37] For the grave-digger, of course, more funerals meant more fees. The beadle was not dismissed, however. It took an even more heinous offence in the following year for Thomas Dalton to be shown the door. He was found guilty of 'a criminal connection with Sarah Taylor in the chapel ... obstinately persisting in the denial of the fact, although admitted by the girl and proved by the evidence of eye-witnesses'.[38] Dalton was sent to prison for his indiscretion; this was not what the chapel was meant to be used for. For the grave-digger at St Philip's, bribing the workhouse beadle was almost the only way to get work, for the churchyard here was rapidly reaching full capacity. Over the course of a century or so, around 60,000 burials had taken place there, and by September of 1819 the overseers were declaring it too full 'to bury with decency'.[39] Luckily for the dead, as Birmingham grew apace, new churches were appearing and new parishes being carved out of the old ones, which allowed the overseers to spread the load, at least for the burial of the out-poor. By 1839, for example, the overseers were paying for funerals at St George's, All Saints', St Thomas's, St Paul's and even in one instance at St Peter's Catholic Church, off Broad Street.

36 *Birmingham Journal*, 4 February 1837.
37 Archives and Collections, Library of Birmingham. CP B/660983 Birmingham Overseers' Minutes, Vol. 2, 27 October 1818.
38 *Ibid.*, Vol. 2, 18 May 1819.
39 *Ibid.*, Vol. 2, 28 September 1819.

Nevertheless, St Martin's and St Philip's remained the graveyards of choice for the overseers, long after they were considered to be overcrowded. The burial register from St Martin's for 1832 records the interment of 108 individuals whose address is given as the workhouse, a further 116 inmates were buried in 1833 and 104 more in 1834. The equivalent figures for St Philip's were 49 interments in 1832, 49 in 1833 and 39 in 1834. With such numbers involved one can well understand why the sextons were so keen to keep their contracts. The respective numbers for St Mary's were 1 in 1832, 14 in 1833 and 20 in 1834. The latter was also the last resting place of children from the Asylum for the Infant Poor in Summer Lane. We might add that, in the absence of any surviving internal record of deaths, the statistics gleaned from the burial registers represents our only sure way of assessing the overall death-rate in Lichfield Street before 1831. During that year, in a new spirit of cooperation with the local press, a fresh body of guardians opened their meetings to reporters and began to release detailed medical statistics for the first time. In the quarter ending September 1830, they reported 32 deaths had occurred in the workhouse infirmary.[40] The figure does not include any who died elsewhere in the workhouse. In all likelihood, the figure simply records those who passed through the mortuary. It seems, taking into account the evidence of the burial registers and the guardians' own figures, that someone died in Birmingham workhouse, on average, every couple of days.

The obvious choice of burial, once it was open for business, was St Mary's in Whittall Street, being the closest parish church to Lichfield Street. But by the 1830s the minister here was driving a particularly hard bargain. In 1838 he raised his burial fees to a devilishly high 8s (6s 6d for the interment and 1s 6d for the sexton), double what was being charged at St Philip's or St Martin's.[41] Requested to investigate the legality of this, the workhouse clerk declared that there was nothing in the Act which set up the church to prevent the minister from so doing. The overseers would simply have to take their custom elsewhere.

We might imagine, with the numbers of both living and dead growing so fast, that Birmingham's coffin makers would be enjoying the fruits of their labour. Not so, or at least not so in their dealings with the overseers. It has always been the practice of large corporations (the united parishes of Birmingham could be considered so) to squeeze their suppliers, both in terms of unit cost and the deadline of payment. The price the overseers paid for coffins took no account of inflation or the steadily rising cost of materials. An early indication of the trouble to come appears in March 1832, when John Weston of Ladywell Walk put in a remarkably low tender for a share of the coffin contract at 5s for adults and 2s

40   *Birmingham Journal*, 19 February 1831.

41   Archives and Collections, Library of Birmingham. GP B/2/1/3 Birmingham Guardians' minutes, 9 May 1838.

3d for children. But Weston was able to supply so cheaply by using rope handles instead of iron ones, a bargain the overseers felt duty-bound to turn down.[42] In 1834 Messrs Edmonds and Reynolds were selling their coffins to the parish at just 2s 6d for a child and 7s for an adult, which represents a price reduction in real terms from 1809.[43] Even in a period of relatively low inflation, the carpenters must have been feeling the pinch. The matter came to a head in 1838, when a Mr Crowley explained to the overseers the difference between the cost of coffins to him in terms of materials and what he was paid by the parish. This is probably the Thomas Crowley who is listed in *Wrightson & Webb's Birmingham Directory* of 1839 as 'timber merchant, cooper, box and case maker, Cheapside & Worcester Wharf'.[44] In the previous three months Crowley had supplied a total of 158 coffins, 33 for the workhouse and 125 to the out-poor. Crowley estimated that each adult coffin had cost him between 7s and 9s to make, yet he received only 4s per item from the overseers, a situation which, even with his wide range of products, he could not stand for long.[45] What was true for Thomas Crowley was undoubtedly the case for the other coffin makers as well. But they had found a cunning way around the short-fall, by means of what was called 'embellishment'. The trick relied on the idea of the 'respectable funeral'. So deeply ingrained was the notion of public respectability in Victorian England, even (perhaps especially) among the poor, that families were prepared to drive themselves deep into debt to make sure that their loved one received a 'decent' send-off. A combination of peer pressure, slick advertising and family solidarity meant that the Victorian funeral was as much a matter of preserving standards as it was of showing grief. The funeral was a public act, not a private one, and a cheap funeral 'on the parish' was no way to present one's family face to the world. And, as funerals for the wealthy classes became ever more elaborate and expensive, so many of the lower classes aspired upwards and paid considerable sums for their aspirations.

The coffin makers were not slow to recognise this. The coffin itself, on arrival at the home of the deceased, was as plain as any wooden box. But that need not be the case; with the aid of a few embellishments such as a name plate, polished handles, coloured beading, perhaps an angel or two, cheap could be made to look respectable. And, as we have already seen, there was no shortage of Birmingham workshops ready to supply such decoration. The overseers

---

42 Archives and Collections, Library of Birmingham. CP B/660985 Birmingham Overseers' Minutes, Vol. 4, 27 March 1832.

43 Archives and Collections, Library of Birmingham. CP B/660986 Birmingham Overseers' Minutes, Vol. 5, 5 April 1834.

44 *Wrightson and Webb's Directory of Birmingham*, Birmingham, 1839, p. 22.

45 Archives and Collections, Library of Birmingham. CP B/660986 Birmingham Overseers' Minutes, Vol. 5, 5 May 1837.

were told: 'coffin makers are driven to means the most disgraceful to induce the poor to consent to such embellishments'.[46] Of those 158 coffins sold by Thomas Crowley, 85 had been so 'embellished', allowing him to charge an additional 9s 3d, and thus more than breaking even. An example reported to the guardians took the tale of extortion further still. Edwin Smith, one of the overseers, had given a particular family a note to cover the cost of a coffin for 'Widow Powell' as was usual practice. Having measured the corpse, the coffin maker told the grieving relatives that an embellished coffin would cost them 16s, and would be ready by the middle of the next day. If they wanted only a plain coffin, the type covered by the overseer's note, it could not be delivered before the evening. Given the deteriorating state of the body, the family felt obliged to pay the extra.[47] If we take nine shillings as an average cost for 'value adding' to the coffin, this was easily the equivalent of three week's rent in the late 1830s, and families often struggled to afford even it. They paid for the additional cost, learnt the overseers, 'by appeals to the benevolent'.[48] In this aspect of the Poor Law, it seemed, charity had reasserted its traditional role.

The vestry had an ingenious solution to this problem, but before they embarked upon it they felt obliged to assess the cost to the town if embellishments were to be deemed an integral part of the pauper funeral. Estimates were taken first from Thomas Crowley and then from a number of other coffin makers, including John Reynolds and Thomas Cole. Cole advertised in the 1839 directory as 'Thomas Cole, builder and coffin maker, 6 Court, Cox Street'.[49] John Reynolds does not appear in contemporary trade directories, but he offered a helpful and detailed sliding-scale to his potential customers:

These are the different alterations and charges for coffins for persons seven years of age and upwards with six handles and handle plates, angel and flower breast plate with name, lace up corners, bottom ribs and top ribs beaded, coloured and polished from 12s to 14s

With extra lace around top	14s to 16s
With extra lace around bottom	16s to 18s
Lined with flannel and padded and one pair [of] locks	18s to 20s[50]

---

46 *Ibid.*, Vol. 5, 19 September 1837.

47 Archives and Collections, Library of Birmingham. GP B/2/1/3 Birmingham Guardians' minutes, 3 October 1837.

48 Archives and Collections, Library of Birmingham. CP B/660986 Birmingham Overseers' Minutes, Vol. 5, 19 September 1837.

49 *Wrightson and Webb's Directory of Birmingham*, Birmingham, 1839, p. 48.

50 Archives and Collections, Library of Birmingham. CP B/660986 Birmingham Overseers' Minutes, Vol. 5, 23 May 1837.

Even without the extra lace and padding, these prices were beyond the pale for an authority sworn to austerity and value for money. Faced with such unacceptable expenses, the overseers drew instead upon the human resources of the workhouse itself. There was, as it happened, an inmate who had formerly made all the coffins for the workhouse in Manchester. Paid a gratuity, he would make the paupers' coffins at just 5s 3d for pine and 6s 2½d for elm.[51] An architect, Mr Cartwright, gave his services for free in fitting out the new coffin shop, and the new arrangement went ahead.[52] The wage paid to the carpenter was clearly too low and by 1838 he was receiving a much more reasonable 24s a week. It had become, for him, an unexpected career opportunity, but he had to work hard for it. By the middle of April the unnamed man had made no less than 182 coffins in three months, an average of almost four a day.[53] We should add that close to half of these coffins, 83 to be exact, were for children, a vivid indication of the level of infant mortality among Birmingham's poor. In the following quarter the man made a staggering 340 coffins, 162 being for children.[54] The employment committee would certainly have indicated if the coffin shop was employing inmates from the house, so we must assume that the carpenter was working alone. The number of coffins he was assembling, and the figure does not drop below 300 per quarter, is the one reliable indicator of just how many deaths the overseers dealt with in an average year. For all the efforts to reduce expenditure, the annual guardians' accounts continue to show the escalating cost of death to the Birmingham parishes. For the year ending Lady Day 1839 expenditure on coffins and burials for inmates and the out-poor stood at £472 14s 4d.[55] The figure for 1836/7, only three years earlier, had been just £262.[56] We cannot say exactly how long the arrangement was in place, but a coffin-maker by the name of James Robertson was still on the workhouse pay-roll in 1842 on a salary of £1 7s a week.[57] In spite of the presence of a resident coffin-maker there were still bills to be paid of course – to the timber merchant and to the Chunk Nail Co. who supplied the coffin nails – but the overall reduction in costs was considerable. As for the much sought-after embellishments, the overseers informed the guardians that 'those

51   Archives and Collections, Library of Birmingham. GP B/2/1/3 Birmingham Guardians' minutes, 19 September 1837.

52   *Ibid.*, 9 January 1838.

53   *Ibid.*, 18 April 1838.

54   Archives and Collections, Library of Birmingham. GP B/2/1/3 Birmingham Guardians' minutes, 18 July 1838.

55   *Birmingham Journal*, 29 June 1839.

56   *Birmingham Journal*, 24 June 1837.

57   *Ninth Annual Report of the Poor Law Commissioners for England and Wales*, London, 1843, p. 235.

who wish them decorated, purchase their own furniture and our man affixes it on the coffins before they leave the house'. The middle man was thus cut out of the equation and everyone (except the bereaved, of course) was happy.

11

The Asylum for the Infant Poor

Towards the end of the nineteenth century most Poor Law unions had embarked upon a policy to remove pauper children from the workhouse and to accommodate them independently in 'colonies' which came to be known euphemistically as 'cottage homes'. In the West Midlands such a step was taken as part of a unique joint venture by the unions of West Bromwich and Walsall in 1872, by Wolverhampton in 1890 and by Aston Union in 1898. Reflecting its innovative approach in so many aspects of poor relief, Birmingham had pioneered such a move almost a century earlier as the Birmingham Asylum for the Infant Poor had opened its doors on Summer Lane in 1797. Contemporary maps from 1808 to the early 1850s indicate the building's location, close to where Summer Lane turned east to join Walmer Lane, the latter being a semi-rural extension of New Town Row. The earliest indicative map (Kempson's plan of 1808) shows the Asylum at the furthest extremity of the town, and it was indeed as far from the town as one could possibly travel without crossing the parish boundary.[1] Two later maps, one from October 1838 and the second, undated, from the early 1850s, show something more than a square mark on the paper. Most helpful is that from 1838 where the Asylum buildings are shown surrounding an inner courtyard on three sides, with a retaining wall on the fourth. According to Langford, the building was still standing in 1868, some years after the children had been reincorporated into the new workhouse on Western Road.[2] Only one illustration of the Asylum exists, dating from 1 July 1828 and this confirms the impression from the maps that the institution had expanded far beyond its original frontage on Summer Lane.

New buildings, designed by Joseph Plevins, were added in 1819, at a cost of just over £600.[3] The original building had by this date been extended to

---

1   J. Kempson, *Map of the Town and Parish of Birmingham*, Birmingham, 1808.

2   J.A. Langford, *A Century of Birmingham Life*, Vol. II, Birmingham, 1868 p. 81.

3   *Edmonds' Weekly Recorder*, 10 July 1819.

Figure 11.1 The Asylum for the Infant Poor, 1 July 1828. Archives and Collections, Library of Birmingham: MS 897 Volume 1 No. 85

the left and right, with additional walled areas on each side. The cupola on the rear extension would probably have contained a bell, as was the case at the workhouse. The whole site, including the Asylum buildings, garden and 'drying ground' occupied just over an acre. William West's Directory of 1830 describes the Asylum as 'pleasantly situated, with gardens in front and rear of the building'.[4] The adjoining land (of eight acres), also owned by the parish, was rented out as gardens.[5] The Asylum for the Infant Poor could hardly have been more rural and secluded.

The choice of location had two things to recommend it. Firstly, the asylum stood on land already owned by the parish, a key financial consideration to the cash-strapped guardians of the poor. As we have already seen, land on Birmingham Heath had been acquired by the parish as part of the negotiations over the bill to enclose the Heath, presented to Parliament in 1798. Secondly, the location of the Asylum allowed the children who were sent there to be separated as far as possible from the workhouse itself (their previous abode) and from the town. Since the latter was regarded, more often than not, as a source of contamination and moral corruption, a policy of 'separate development' drove Poor Law policy in Birmingham at this time, as it would

---

4   W. West, *The History, Topography and Directory of Warwickshire*, Birmingham, 1830, p. 248.

5   Archives and Collections, Library of Birmingham. GP B/2/9/1/1 Birmingham Guardians' Estates Committee minutes, schedule of lands.

many later unions. That such segregation also took the children some distance from their parents was an inevitable (and perhaps desirable) consequence of this. Critics of Birmingham's Poor Law administration, however, were not so sanguine about the location. Joseph Allday, journalist and Peelite proprietor of the conservative *Monthly Argus & Public Censor*, was one such critic:

> The institution is so far removed from immediate view that we had nearly fallen into the same error which we fear most of its community [that is, Birmingham] have completely and totally done, viz. forgotten that such an establishment existed[6]

To Allday and his supporters quiet seclusion permitted exactly the kind of lavish expenditure and lack of public scrutiny – what Allday regularly refers to as 'hole and corner work' – that they associated with the Birmingham Poor Law administration in general. In 1830 it was the replacement of the asylum's 'humble candle and frugal lamp' with 'the splendid and brilliant gas of the Staffordshire Company' that irritated Allday.[7] It was alleged (and indeed it was the case) that the chairman of the Asylum committee was also a leading light in the local gas company.[8] This, along with the erection of an Asylum chapel and the purchase of town bread, instead of home-made workhouse loaves, fitted the expected pattern of profligate parish expenditure.

No dedicated asylum records survive, though we would expect admission and discharge registers and records of mortality to have once been kept, together with a diary or journal by the Asylum master. The Asylum committee, a sub-committee of the Poor Law guardians, would also have minuted their meetings separately and perhaps written up their regular visits to the Asylum. What survives of this significant institution is little more than summary reports of the sub-committee to the full body of guardians, along with details of specific enquiries into its running, in the weekly minutes of the Birmingham guardians and overseers. These fragmentary records can be supplemented by occasional references in the Birmingham newspapers, which refer to debates and reports not preserved elsewhere. It is, at best, an imperfect jigsaw, but one well worth piecing together. The inevitable result, however, of fragmented and discontinuous records is that any account of the Asylum is also discontinuous. What may be true of conditions and activity in the institution at one point may well change swiftly. To say that the Asylum was overcrowded or unhealthy or tightly disciplined or loosely run remains

---

6   *Monthly Argus & Public Censor*, May 1830, p. 355.

7   *Monthly Argus & Public Censor*, May 1830, p. 355.

8   *Monthly Argus & Public Censor*, December 1830, p. 295.

true only in the eyes of one visitor, under one asylum governor or at a single given moment.[9]

An early indication that the Asylum was up-and-running can be gleaned from the statistics of relief provided by the overseers to the *Birmingham Gazette*. This was not information they were especially keen to divulge, but they did so weekly from December 1795 to May 1798. A change in attitude to the release of what was seen as sensitive information usually coincided with the (triennial) election of a new body of guardians, who frequently came into office with promises of reform and transparency. One such reformist group was in power between 1795 and 1798. According to the statistics, in the early months of 1797 an average of 150 children were in the workhouse on Lichfield Street, most of whom would still have been nursed by their mothers. In addition, an average of 250 children were described as 'at nurse in the country', reflecting a long-established practice of placing children with foster mothers outside the town. However, the numbers 'at nurse' began to fall dramatically. On 10 July 1797 only 226 children were still 'at nurse' and 146 were in the workhouse;[10] by 4 September 1797 the sum total of children at nurse had dropped to thirty-four, and the number in the workhouse stood at 130.[11] The figures for 2 October 1797 describe 250 children now domiciled in the Asylum, and none at nurse.[12] The new Asylum for the Infant Poor had taken all of the children previously fostered out, together with a handful of older infants from the workhouse itself.

The way the authorities viewed the Asylum for the Infant Poor and what went on there did not remain constant. It is also true that an institution initially designed to hold 270 children might not look quite so attractive and commodious once its intake had risen to 350. As such the Asylum was subject to continuous reassessment and frequent rebuilding. The earliest alterations, just three years after opening, followed the acquisition of additional land to house the pin manufactory in 1800. By 1819 it was the conditions within the domestic part of the Asylum which were causing concern, at least to the medical officers.[13] The bedrooms were being described as 'totally unfit for human respiration', an early indication that the Victorian obsession with fresh air and the dangers of effluvia was beginning to surface:

---

9   See, for example, the Overseers' debate on discipline in April 1847. Archives and Collections, Library of Birmingham. CP B/660982 Birmingham Overseers' Minutes, Vol. 1, 7 April 1812.

10 *Aris's Gazette*, 10 July 1797.

11 *Aris's Gazette*, 2 October 1797.

12 *Aris's Gazette*, 2 October 1797.

13 Archives and Collections, Library of Birmingham. GP B/2/1/2 Birmingham Guardians' minutes, 29 June 1819.

The room in which 160 girls are confined for nine hours contains a space of 13,960 square feet, which allows 87 square feet of air to each individual. Dr Blaney in his essay on the construction of military hospitals has proved that not less than 600 square feet of air are necessary for each individual.[14]

A similar situation, they believed, prevailed in the sick room and day room:

which … is so crowded that any attempt in its present state to carry on at regular periods this important work of instruction must for the most part be abortive.[15]

Additional building work took place immediately after this, completed by October 1819. But by 1822 the Asylum was again beginning to feel cramped. This time concern centred upon the schoolroom, which had a ceiling only ten feet high, but which accommodated no less than 300 children.[16] As luck would have it, the break up and sale of the Aston Hall estate was then in progress and a five-acre site opposite the Asylum became available. The first stone of the new extension, which was to include a new schoolroom, was laid in August 1822 and the work completed the following year.[17] Yet another negative report on the poor state of accommodation in the Asylum arrived in 1836, when, for the first time, the guardians began seriously to consider moving it elsewhere.[18] In the meantime, further alterations were made in 1837, and, as we have seen, a new playground was laid in 1839. Yet, for all the additional space, the dreaded effluvia were still pervading the bedrooms:

Though the bedrooms are spacious, effluvia from the bodies of so many persons in one room are sufficient to taint the air very considerably during the night, and render it highly disagreeable and probably noxious.[19]

Birmingham's Asylum for the Infant Poor stood in an ambiguous position in relation to the workhouse. It was, as it were, a child of the Poor Law, supervised by a sub-committee of guardians and governed by staff appointed by the same body. Yet it was considerably more public in its interaction with

14   *Ibid.*

15   *Ibid.*

16   *Ibid.*, 10 July 1822

17   Archives and Collections, Library of Birmingham. CP B/660984 Birmingham Overseers' Minutes, Vol. 3, 2 August 1822.

18   *Birmingham Journal*, 8 October 1836.

19   Archives and Collections, Library of Birmingham. GP B/2/1/4 Birmingham Guardians' minutes 13 February 1838.

the town and far more conscious of public approval or disapproval than the workhouse ever was or needed to be. The fate of Birmingham's pauper children was always likely to be more newsworthy and subject to scrutiny than that of their adult counterparts. In 1795, for example, shortly before the opening of the Asylum, the guardians moved swiftly to scotch rumours of the death of a workhouse child from neglect, declaring that the story had been spread 'to injure the governor'.[20] The magistrates too were more inclined to intervene to protect children at the Asylum, something they would almost never do in the workhouse itself. In 1811, for example, they strongly reprimanded the master and mistress for 'excessively beating a girl' at Summer Lane and threatened to refer any further such case to the Quarter Sessions.[21]

The new institution would, of course, need to be separately staffed. Initially the guardians thought in terms of a matron (as a home for children the expectation was that the staff would be female), together with two female servants and a schoolmistress, recruited from among the workhouse inmates 'if such a person can be found eligible'.[22] As such, the parish would then only have to pay the wages of one woman. In addition, an Asylum committee was added to the list of Poor Law committees to scrutinise the conditions in the new institution, and it is their reports which give us most of our information about the place. The committee reported regularly to the board of guardians, but also (uniquely) issued an annual report to the press, much as any charitable institution might have done. Although William West asserted in 1830 that the Asylum was 'an excellent and well-constructed charity' in 1830,[23] Francis White, composing a similar gazetteer for Warwickshire in 1848, made no such mistake, explaining that the Asylum

is under management of a committee of guardians and overseers, supported from the Poor's rate; it will accommodate 343 children, boys and girls, averaging upwards of 300.[24]

While the Asylum was being built, a maximum capacity of 270 children was envisaged, though it did not take long to exceed capacity.[25] The average number of children in the Asylum in its first three months of existence was 217, but

20   *Aris's Gazette*, 26 January 1795.

21   *Swinney's Birmingham Chronicle*, 28 February 1811.

22   Archives and Collections, Library of Birmingham. GP B/2/1/1 Birmingham Guardians' Minutes, 5 June 1797.

23   West, *The History*, p. 248. William Hutton makes no such claim.

24   F. White, *History, Gazetteer and Directory of Warwickshire*, Sheffield, 1850, p. 28.

25   Archives and Collections, Library of Birmingham. GP B/2/1/1 Birmingham Guardians' Minutes, 9 May 1797.

within the year this had risen to 296.[26] By the second annual report, however, the average was 290 children.[27] Numbers were lower still in the years that followed. Over its first seven years the asylum maintained an average of 252 children.[28] Nevertheless, at an average cost of two shillings per child per week, the Asylum was soon saving the guardians more than £550 a year, compared with the cost of lodging them with outside nurses which was at least three shillings per child per week. Reporting at the end of the seventh year of its existence, the Asylum committee claimed total savings of £3,009 over the seven-year period, not including the profits from the children's labour.[29] Whether such savings could be maintained, once facilities needed upgrading, or the staffing budget grew, was, of course, another matter.

What kind of children were sent to Summer Lane? Although never specifically stated as such, we can deduce that admission to the Asylum was dependent firstly upon eligibility to poor relief. Children whose families were in the workhouse were the most obvious candidates and they had little choice in the matter, but those whose parents were in receipt of out-relief were also included. In the latter category the union could not compel children to be admitted and parents had the freedom to take in or take back their offspring. A parent's willingness to place a child in the hands of the Asylum matron may explain the high take-up in the second year. Nevertheless, it needs to be underlined that many of the children at Summer Lane were placed there by their parents as a deliberate act. It was left to later centuries to adopt powers of compulsion.

A report by the Asylum committee from 1818, twenty years after the institution had opened, helpfully breaks down the numbers into smaller categories. At this point there were 386 children at Summer Lane, 205 boys and 183 girls. Numbers of boys in the house almost always exceeded girls, since the latter were far easier to place in domestic employment as servants. This was more than counter-balanced by the higher death-rate among the young boys, which was most likely due to their employment. Of this total number, 137 were orphans, 92 were fatherless, 43 were motherless and, in the case of 116 children, both parents were still alive.[30] Thus the Asylum for the Infant Poor was far from being an orphanage alone and, indeed, the wildly fluctuating numbers of inmates were usually the result of parents taking the children

---

26 *Ibid.*, 27 August 1798.

27 *Aris's Gazette*, 16 September 1799.

28 *Aris's Gazette*, 19 November 1804.

29 *Aris's Gazette*, 19 November 1804.

30 Archives and Collections, Library of Birmingham. GP B/2/1/2 Birmingham Guardians' Minutes, 27 October 1818.

home, or bringing them in. The relatively loose definition of eligibility, which stated that the Asylum was for 'orphan and destitute children', was, from time to time, a bone of contention between the overseers and guardians, but it was never fundamentally altered.[31]

There is a further, even more detailed, analysis of the children's background and ages from October 1840, when there were 341 inmates in the Asylum. Of this total just 2 children were under two years of age, 198 were aged between two and nine years, and 136 aged between nine and sixteen. There were a further 5 girls resident over the age of sixteen, but they were retained in the house principally to act as nursing assistants.[32]

Of the total number of 341 children at Summer Lane, only 74 (around 22%) were therefore orphans, a much smaller percentage than in 1818 and a much smaller proportion than in the North of England.[33] A proportion of the remainder could also be considered temporarily so because of the imprisonment of their parents. Of the rest, as many had a father who was unable to support them as had a single or widowed mother. In practical terms this meant that there was continual communication with family members outside the institution and that there was constant coming and going between home and the Asylum. In addition, more children were entering and leaving the asylum than in a comparative Poor Law or charitable institution. In its second full year of operation, for example, 85 children were admitted and 83 left, which, if these numbers are added together, meant that the arrivals and departures accounted for roughly one third of the total.[34]

The relatively liberal attitude towards visitors made the Asylum unusual among Poor Law institutions, where contact with the outside world was discouraged or prevented. At Summer Lane parental visits to the children were common. One such visit was taking place in October 1837, when committee members happened to call in:

> At the time of our visit many of the parents and friends of the children were visiting them, and they seemed well pleased with the state of the children, and the children did not show any signs of regret at being left behind.[35]

---

31 *Edmonds' Weekly Recorder*, 10 July 1819.

32 Archives and Collections, Library of Birmingham. GP B/2/1/4 Birmingham Guardians' Minutes, 13 October 1825.

33 S. King, *Poverty and Welfare in England 1700–1850: A Regional Perspective*, Manchester, 2000, pp. 206–7.

34 *Aris's Gazette*, 16 September 1799.

35 Archives and Collections, Library of Birmingham. CP B/660986 Birmingham Overseers' Minutes, Vol. 5, 3 October 1837.

The Asylum for the Infant Poor did not, however, operate an entirely open-door policy. An entry in the overseers' minutes for 1839 shows that visits by parents and friends were limited to the first Monday in every month. Nor was this traffic only in one direction. In 1812 the committee discovered that the asylum boys had been slipping out of the place in the evening to visit public houses 'to obtain money by singing and other practices'.[36] The resourceful lads had been taking advantage of the moment when the yard gate was opened to take a delivery of bread in. All of this cannot have been an easy situation to manage. Institutions such as the Asylum for the Infant Poor (and the workhouse itself) probably worked best in isolation, and those who came in from the outside world introduced kinds of behaviour, attitudes and infections which challenged (and potentially undermined) the regime. In 1812 the overseers had cause to complain that 'the women in the workhouse who visited the children in the Asylum behave very disorderly'.[37] What clearer proof could there be that the children had been separated from their mothers for their own good?

The constant traffic between the outside world and the Asylum was no doubt one of the reasons behind its poor record of infection and its relatively high death-rate. Nor is there evidence in the surviving records to suggest that the parish surgeons or officers screened new inmates for infection in the careful way that the charity schools did. They had, after all, no right to refuse them entry. Regular contact between the Asylum children and outside parties was certainly believed to have compromised its medical security. In 1805, for example, the parish surgeons attributed the prevalence of diseases such as 'the itch' (which could either be scabies or impetigo) to this situation. It could be more effectively combatted, 'if means could be adopted to restrain an improper indulgence of parents in keeping their children to sleep at their houses, when permitted to go to see them'.[38] More effective still would have been some kind of receiving ward; but the Asylum did not have one. Even in its first year the Asylum committee had to report the presence of both smallpox and measles in the institution 'and other diseases to which children are incident'. But there had been, they said, no more than seven deaths.[39] In the following twelve months only three deaths are reported in the guardians' minutes.[40] In July 1831 the *Midland Representative* newspaper reported figures quoted at a guardians' meeting (significantly not recorded in the minutes themselves) that

---

36 Archives and Collections, Library of Birmingham. CP B/660982 Birmingham Overseers' Minutes, Vol. 1, 7 April 1812.

37 *Ibid.*, 30 June 1812.

38 *Ibid.*, 8 March 1805.

39 *Aris's Gazette*, 24 September 1798.

40 *Aris's Gazette*, 16 September 1799.

14 children had died in the preceding quarter, 6 of consumption, 4 of fever, 3 from smallpox and 1 from 'fits'. Ironically, the press reported that the overall health of the institution was 'very favourable'.[41]

By 1837 the Asylum committee had become more forthcoming on the subject of mortality. In that year alone the number of deaths in the Asylum was 46, falling to 26 in 1838 and 12 in 1839, though this is partly explained by a drop in admissions.[42] A number of explanations were offered for this, in addition to the free contact with the outside world. Reports by the Asylum committee comprise a veritable dictionary of diseases and epidemics which came and went: smallpox (February 1831), measles (January 1833), whooping-cough (February 1836), scald head (October 1836), smallpox (December 1838), scarlet fever (April 1840) and smallpox once more in November 1840. Over the course of just five months in 1837 the committee reported outbreaks of measles, typhus and smallpox. The attack of measles in August and September 1837 was one reason for the high mortality in that year: at least sixteen children died in this outbreak alone.[43] A second reason for the spread of infection was the lack of an isolation ward, something which John Cadbury, a member of the committee at the time, had been keen to point out in 1831:

> Otherwise they have to be removed to the fever ward at the town infirmary at the workhouse, which is occupied by adult patients, and must expose the children to additional infection and other very objectionable circumstances.[44]

As early as 1819 George Edmonds, at that time chairman of the inspecting committee, had observed 'with much regret that the children infected with measles were in the same ward as the healthy children'.[45] A dedicated sick bay was finally in place by March 1836, when it currently held 10 cases of whooping-cough, 5 of opthalmia and 'a few scrofula'.[46] The third reason for the high death toll, which the Asylum committee fell back on as an excuse, when all else failed, was the children's genetic background. 'They are,' lamented

41   *Midland Representative & Birmingham Herald*, 30 July 1831.

42   Archives and Collections, Library of Birmingham. GP B/2/1/4 Birmingham Guardians' Minutes, 7 April 1840.

43   Archives and Collections, Library of Birmingham. CP B/660986 Birmingham Overseers' Minutes, Vol. 5, 12 September 1837.

44   Archives and Collections, Library of Birmingham. CP B/660985 Birmingham Overseers' Minutes, Vol. 4, 20 December 1831.

45   *Edmonds' Weekly Recorder*, 26 June 1819.

46   Archives and Collections, Library of Birmingham. CP B/660986 Birmingham Overseers' Minutes, Vol. 5, 1 March 1836.

the committee, 'the children of poverty and frequently of disease'.[47] This partly explained, they thought, the deaths of seventeen children in the asylum in the previous two years. By 1839 the explanation for high mortality had moved forward somewhat. 'The children,' claimed the committee, 'are frequently the most unhealthy and weakly members of a family, less able to contribute by their labour, and at times of difficulty first got rid of'.[48]

If mortality was the most serious issue faced by the medical officers, there was a host of lesser infections too, which, at the very least, did not look good when presented to the guardians. In early 1831, when the asylum was described as 'not as clean and orderly as it ought to be', almost fifty of the children were suffering from some medical complaint. Seven were described as 'sick', 9 more as 'bad', 10 as having 'bad fingers' and 6 with 'bad feet'. A further 16 were suffering from scald head (ring-worm), 'a highly infectious disorder amongst the children of the poorer classes'.[49] Shared beds, and the inability to separate the infected from the healthy children would only serve to spread the infection. Nineteenth-century medical opinion held that many of the less serious infections among children (and especially skin complaints) could be combatted by diet. Ring-worm was thought to be one such preventable disease, and contemporary medical textbooks haplessly recommended the avoidance of 'salt-meat, pickles, bacon, pork and even fish'.[50]

A new dietary system was therefore introduced into the Asylum early in 1838, shifting the emphasis from 'adult' foods towards more milk-based products (though the reduced expense may also have contributed to this decision).[51] On five days a week breakfast would now consist of milk porridge and bread, with rice milk on Mondays and Thursdays. Rice pudding appeared twice on the dinner menu too, with suet pudding on Mondays and Fridays. Boiled mutton and potatoes was Tuesday's fare; roast beef and potatoes were served on Thursdays and boiled beef and potatoes on Saturdays. For supper the children ate bread and dripping, milk and water three days a week, with broth and bread on another three days, and bread and treacle, milk and water on Mondays. Most of the meals were washed down with beer.

As we have seen, the guardians initially planned to pay a single female to

---

47 Archives and Collections, Library of Birmingham. GP B/2/1/2 Birmingham Guardians' Minutes, 27 October 1818.

48 Archives and Collections, Library of Birmingham. GP B/2/1/4 Birmingham Guardians' Minutes, 13 February 1839.

49 Archives and Collections, Library of Birmingham. CP B/660985 Birmingham Overseers' Minutes, Vol. 4, 5 April 1831.

50 A.F.M. Willich, *Domestic Encyclopaedia*, London, 1802, p. 28.

51 Archives and Collections, Library of Birmingham. GP B/2/1/3 Birmingham Guardians' minutes, 8 January 1838.

take charge of the new children's home, and such a person, variously called matron or governess, was still in charge in 1804, supported by a schoolmaster and schoolmistress.[52] In 1814, however, the union appointed a married couple, Samuel Brueton and his wife, to run the Asylum, much as its sister institution was then being managed. In 1828 the Bruetons were paid a joint salary of £80 per annum, plus board and lodging, compared to the joint salary of £200 paid to the governor and governess of the workhouse.[53] By 1831 this sum had risen to £90 a year.[54] The regime under the Bruetons coincided with a relatively relaxed attitude towards staffing. Profits from the labour of children, outlined below, additionally allowed the institution to employ two cooks, two laundresses and a gardener, and a further five women were paid as chambermaids. The gardener, Joseph Birch, was the only adult male on the pay-roll, other than Mr Brueton himself, and his salary (£10 a year) was the highest. In addition, Catherine Walker was paid six guineas a year to look after the sick rooms, and three women were paid for work in the school. Two more women, paid 'for instructing of the girls in school', were probably teaching them to make lace or to plait straw.[55] Mrs Brueton died in July 1830,[56] but her husband swiftly re-married.[57] His job probably depended on it: at the Asylum a female presence was more important than a male one. Adopting his characteristic tone, Joseph Allday speculated that the first Mrs Brueton had died from being unable to swallow the *Monthly Argus* 'or from an overdose of Double X brandy'.[58] Curiously, given his interest in unwarranted parish expenditure, Allday did not criticise the fact that her funeral expenses were paid out of official funds, as was usual with workhouse managers.[59] Perhaps he was unaware of the fact.

The Bruetons finally resigned at Christmas 1836 after Mr Brueton had spent more than twenty years in post. That they left somewhat under a cloud seems

52   Archives and Collections, Library of Birmingham. GP B/2/1/1 Birmingham Guardians' minutes, 9 October 1804.

53   Archives and Collections, Library of Birmingham. GP B/2/1/3 Birmingham Guardians' minutes, 20 May 1828.

54   *Ibid.*, 16 November 1831.

55   Archives and Collections, Library of Birmingham. GP B/2/1/2 Birmingham Guardians' minutes, 27 October 1818.

56   Archives and Collections, Library of Birmingham. CP B/6609855 Birmingham Overseers' Minutes, Vol. 4, July 1830; *Index of Obituaries from Aris' Birmingham Gazette, 1830*, BCOL 78.1.

57   Archives and Collections, Library of Birmingham. CP B/660985 Birmingham Overseers' Minutes, Vol. 4, 5 July 1830.

58   *Monthly Argus & Public Censor*, August 1830, p. 95.

59   Archives and Collections, Library of Birmingham. CP B/660985 Birmingham Overseers' Minutes, Vol. 4, 5 July 1830.

clear, though the guardians' and overseers' minutes are (as is often the case) silent on the matter. The press, and in particular the radical *Philanthropist* newspaper, were less reticent. The allegations made there were that corporal punishment in the Asylum was widespread and that, to supplement their salaries, the Bruetons had outside commercial interests. The guardians (as was also usually the case) sprang to their own and the Bruetons' defence, whilst admitting that 'occasionally unnecessary force had been used, but not generally'.[60] It was always more convenient for the guardians to formulate new policy in an interregnum than to intervene whilst a master and mistress were still in post, especially if they had been so for some years. The minutes are similarly silent on what was evidently an intense argument in framing new policy for the Asylum after the departure of the Bruetons. To reformers among the guardians, the departure of the Bruetons allowed for a radical shake-up in the management of the Asylum. Their chief spokesman (James James) went public on his call for an increased salary for the master and mistress and considerable modernisation of the buildings.[61] The conservatives were, at this point, however, the majority party, elected in 1830 on a policy of reining in parish expenditure.[62] Far from increasing the cost of the institution, the departure of Mr and Mrs Brueton was seen as an opportunity to scale it back. The argument for staff cuts was made all the more compelling by the low occupancy rate by the mid-1830s. From a high point in January 1830, when there had been 362 children in the Asylum,[63] there were now just 183.[64] Nevertheless, the job descriptions issued for the vacant posts show a tightening up in the responsibilities of the two positions:

> The governor must have no other occupation, will be required to be an intelligent man of unexceptional moral character, active and industrial habits and fully sensible of the charge that will devolve upon him.

> The matron must be of unexceptional moral character, with a competent knowledge of domestic management, and can devote the whole of her time to the welfare of the children and the interests of the establishment.[65]

---

60 *The Philanthropist and Warwickshire, Worcestershire and Staffordshire Gazette*, 6 October 1836; *Aris's Gazette*, 6 October 1836.

61 *The Philanthropist and Warwickshire, Worcestershire and Staffordshire Gazette*, 6 October 1836; *Aris's Gazette*, 6 October 1836

62 *Monthly Argus & Public Censor*, Vol. 2, July 1830, p. 20.

63 *Birmingham Journal*, 12 January 1830.

64 *Birmingham Journal*, 10 December 1836.

65 *The Philanthropist and Warwickshire, Worcestershire and Staffordshire Gazette*, 27 October 1836.

These standards were exacting, especially in an age when public office was still regarded as private property, but the guardians may already have had in mind exactly the man and woman they wanted. They made the decision (clearly a money-saving one) to appoint Thomas Alcock, the governor of the Birmingham workhouse, as head of the Asylum as well.[66] At a stroke, this removed an annual £50 (the Asylum governor's salary) from the budget. Thomas Alcock's new role must have been more titular than practical, and the everyday running of the Asylum fell to Miss Alcock, the governor's daughter, who was paid £40 a year. This was probably intended only as a temporary measure, for in 1838 Mr and Mrs Edwards were appointed at £90 a year.[67] Mr Edwards' role also included teaching the boys, and he is specifically referred to as 'schoolmaster' when his personal share of the joint salary was increased to £70 in March 1840.[68] If the Asylum, like the workhouse, was thought of as a family, then the people who ran it needed ideally to reflect this parental model. On the death of Mrs Edwards in July 1840 the guardians moved to appoint the governor's mother-in-law, Sarah Webb, as the new matron.[69] As for Mr Edwards, in October of the same year he found himself in temporary charge of the workhouse as well, after the death of Thomas Alcock.[70] The attempt to keep the two institutions separate evidently did not apply to staffing.

The surviving records are far from helpful in understanding how and by whom the children were taught prior to the 1830s. A schoolmistress had recently been appointed, when the asylum committee reported to the guardians in 1804, though her teaching must have been squeezed into an already busy schedule of manual labour:

> Their education, tho' slender, produces moral order and useful subordination, to which they, while under hireling nurses, were entire strangers.[71]

As has been suggested previously, hireling labour most likely meant adult women temporarily moved across from the workhouse. In 1822 the Asylum committee was advertising for a 'respectable' man and woman to assist in the

---

66   Archives and Collections, Library of Birmingham. GP B/2/1/3 Birmingham Guardians' minutes, 7 December 1836.

67   *Ibid.*, 20 June 1838.

68   Archives and Collections, Library of Birmingham. GP B/2/1/4 Birmingham Guardians' minutes, 19 March 1840.

69   *Ibid.*, 19 August 1840.

70   *Ibid.*, 13 October 1840.

71   Archives and Collections, Library of Birmingham. GP B/2/1/1 Birmingham Guardians' minutes, 9 October 1804.

education of the children for two hours each weekday afternoon and two hours on Sunday afternoon.[72]

We may assume, though the records are imprecise on this matter, that the older and younger children were taught separately. The success (and influence) of the Birmingham Infant School in Ann Street, founded in 1826, may have led to this separation, and it was certainly in place by 1838.[73] The children in the Asylum's infant school were taught 'reading, elements of useful knowledge, morals and religious instruction.'[74] A schoolmistress familiar with the 'Infant School System' was appointed to the Asylum in that year.[75] Children then moved from the infant to the senior school at the age of seven. It is therefore likely that the infants were taught by the salaried teacher, while the older boys were under the direction of the Asylum governor. When a new governor was appointed in 1838, the requirement was that he taught the boys 'on the National School System'.[76] The older girls, whose education included sewing and knitting, would have been instructed by the matron, as part of her other domestic duties. Whatever its physical isolation, the Asylum was not deaf to the 'improvements' of educational theorists such as Samuel Wilderspin, Joseph Lancaster and Andrew Bell.[77] But the Asylum was by no means primarily a school. Even as late as 1831 only an hour's schooling a day was being provided, from 5.30 pm until 6.30 pm, in between the working day ending and supper being served.[78] This had increased a little to one and a half hours by 1836.[79] For the infants considered too young for manual work (that is, under seven years of age), there was schooling for two hours in the morning and two more in the afternoon.[80] If the timetable here reflected general practice in Sunday Schools, the form of this schooling was probably monitorial, based upon the model provided by the National or British Schools. That is, one teacher would teach a

---

72 *Aris's Gazette*, 16 September 1822.

73 Archives and Collections, Library of Birmingham. MS 1683/1 Birmingham Statistical Society for Education, 1838 Report: Supporting Evidence, p. 33.

74 *Ibid.*

75 *Birmingham Journal*, 12 May 1838.

76 *Ibid.*

77 P. McCann and F.A. Young, *Samuel Wilderspin and the Infant School Movement*, London, 1982; T.A. Markus, *Buildings and Power: Freedom and Control in the Origin of Modern Building Types*, London, 1993, pp. 48–69.

78 Archives and Collections, Library of Birmingham. CP B/660985 Birmingham Overseers' Minutes, Vol. 4, 6 December 1831.

79 Archives and Collections, Library of Birmingham. GP B/2/1/3 Birmingham Guardians' minutes, 5 October 1836.

80 Archives and Collections, Library of Birmingham. CP B/660985 Birmingham Overseers' Minutes, Vol. 4, 6 December 1831.

large hall of children by employing the older children to instruct the younger. The overseers approved the proposal to establish such a school in the Asylum in 1809, a remarkably responsive move at this date.[81] Birmingham's first school on the Lancasterian model (in Severn Street) opened only in this year.[82] This is not to say, however, that formal schooling was the sum total of the children's educational experience. On one evening visit to the Asylum in January 1832, the committee visitors noted with pleasure that the boys were being instructed in reading, while the governess was reading to the girls in the chapel. As for the younger children, they had 'gone to bed, and all appeared fast asleep and very comfortable.'[83]

The first named schoolmistress, Miss Smith, was appointed to teach in the infant school in March or April 1828.[84] Her duties were also exacting:

> She must be a person of strictly moral character, and fully competent to instruct the boys and girls in the ordinary branches of education and, as she will reside in the house, to make herself generally useful.[85]

On Miss Smith's resignation in 1835, Ann Wakefield replaced her.[86] Ann Wakefield resigned in June 1837,[87] to be replaced by Miss Lilley at an annual salary of £20.[88] The latter's stay turned out to be even shorter than her predecessor's: Miss Lilley resigned after less than a year, in March 1838.[89] Her successor, Miss Bakewell, was appointed at a much increased salary of 40 guineas, but without board.[90] By this date the Asylum committee was

---

81   Archives and Collections, Library of Birmingham. CP B/660982 Birmingham Overseers' Minutes, Vol. 1, 3 January 1809.

82   W. White, *Our Jubilee Year 1895: The Story of the Severn Street and Priory first day-schools, Birmingham*, London, 1895.

83   Archives and Collections, Library of Birmingham. CP B/660985 Birmingham Overseers' Minutes, Vol. 4, 10 January 1832.

84   Archives and Collections, Library of Birmingham. GP B/2/1/3 Birmingham Guardians' minutes, 13 October 1835.

85   *Aris's Gazette*, 10 March 1828.

86   Archives and Collections, Library of Birmingham. CP B/660985 Birmingham Overseers' Minutes, Vol. 5, 15 September 1835.

87   Archives and Collections, Library of Birmingham. GP B/2/1/3 Birmingham Guardians' minutes, 14 June 1837.

88   *Ibid.*, 3 August 1837.

89   Archives and Collections, Library of Birmingham. CP B/660986 Birmingham Overseers' Minutes, Vol. 5, 20 March 1838.

90   Archives and Collections, Library of Birmingham. GP/B/2/1/3 Birmingham Guardians' minutes, 3 July 1838.

appointing tried-and-tested teachers for the infant school, as professional as any teaching was at this early date. Miss Bakewell herself had formerly been a paid Sunday School teacher at the Unitarian Old Meeting, leaving in 1818.[91] She had thus been teaching for well over two decades. But Miss Bakewell left the Asylum in 1840, and her successor was selected in December of that year.[92] The Asylum had thus had four schoolmistresses in the space of just five years. This rapid turnover of staff within a Poor Law institution should not be considered untypical, and neighbouring Kings Norton Union saw fourteen female teachers come and go in the twenty-five years between 1847 and 1872.[93] Teaching in a workhouse or equivalent was undoubtedly a lonely and demanding profession. In most cases 'bed and board' meant permanent residence and supervision of the children did not end at the door of the schoolroom. The Asylum for the Infant Poor had, like many smaller workhouses, only three resident adults – the master, matron and teacher – who were in each other's company for most of the day. In such circumstances, friction was highly likely. There was certainly a personality clash of sorts between Miss Bakewell and the Asylum master and the guardians launched an enquiry into the reasons behind it in October 1840.[94] The experience of Miss Lilley throws a little more light on the underlying tensions. Upon her resignation from the Asylum, she applied for (and gained) the post of schoolmistress at Aston Union workhouse at Erdington. At £20 per annum, her salary here was exactly the same as at Summer Lane.[95] Evidently she had not left Summer Lane simply for more money. Miss Lilley lasted no longer at Aston than at Birmingham, and resigned in April 1839.[96] Here too, enquiries were made by the Aston guardians, who, like their colleagues at Birmingham, had been impressed by the woman's teaching skills. Miss Lilley had, it transpired, been distressed by 'the irritating and often dictatorial language and manner of the governor and matron to her'.[97] This concerned not only her

---

91 Archives and Collections, Library of Birmingham. MS 252/5 Account of teachers' salaries, Old Meeting Sunday School, 1813; Archives and Collections, Library of Birmingham. UC1 /11/2/1 Old Meeting Sunday School minutes, 1787–1818, 25 January 1818.

92 Archives and Collections, Library of Birmingham. GP B/2/1/4 Birmingham Guardians' minutes, 28 December 1840.

93 Archives and Collections, Library of Birmingham. GP KN/1/2/4–13 Kings Norton Guardians' minutes, 1847–72.

94 Archives and Collections, Library of Birmingham. GP B/2/1/4 Birmingham Guardians' minutes, 27 October 1840.

95 Archives and Collections, Library of Birmingham. GP AS/2/1/1 Aston Guardians' minutes, 1 May 1838.

96 Ibid., 23 April 1839.

97 Ibid., 22 January 1839.

teaching duties but even whether she was allowed to have a fire in her room after a certain hour. The Aston guardian who made the report was remarkably perceptive about what lay behind all this. 'Allowance must be made,' he wrote, 'for a sensitive, well-educated mind and for minds uninfluenced by education. Time will correct the evil.'[98] Time did not correct the evil, of course. The workhouse as an institution drew on the services of a wide variety of people, but only in the case of the schoolteacher and house surgeon was education a prerequisite.

Pursuing Miss Lilley and Miss Bakewell between schools and unions has allowed us to reconstruct some aspects of their careers, but this is unusual. In most cases, when the guardians made an appointment to the Asylum, they say nothing of other candidates, nor do they give details about the successful applicant's earlier career. In December 1840, however, they were much more open. There were six applicants to succeed Miss Bakewell, of whom three were interviewed.[99] All three applicants were Anglicans. This was not a requirement, however, as Miss Bakewell had come from a Unitarian background, but it probably obviated awkward alternative arrangements on Sundays. The children were generally led across to St George's church in Tower Street for services. It is clear from the description of the interviewees that the guardians expected either experience of the National School system or of what they called 'the Infant System' of Samuel Wilderspin (1792–1866). Ideally they wanted both. When she applied for the post at Summer Lane in December 1840, Matilda Fosbrooke was twenty years old, and had fifteen months' experience teaching in a National School in Sherbourne. Her claim to have 'studied the Infant System for the last fortnight' suggests no more than preparation for the interview. Her application, the committee noted, was 'in her own handwriting'. Mary Ann Nelson was twenty-three and had been an assistant at the recently opened St George's National School nearby. She was not, she confessed, acquainted with the Infant System. The successful applicant, however, was June Adeline Edwards. She understood, she said in her application, both systems 'and has passed her whole life in school duties under the superintendence of her father'. She had been an assistant in the National School system for eight years and in the Infant System for five years. More than that, she had already been working in the Asylum for three months. The guardians, as so often before, were appointing the close relation of an employee. Miss Edwards was none other than the daughter of the Asylum governor who had been implicated in the resignation of the previous schoolteacher. Within the New Poor Law, as

---

98   *Ibid.*, 23 April 1839.

99   Archives and Collections, Library of Birmingham. GP B/2/1/4 Birmingham Guardians' minutes, 28 December 1840.

in so many other aspects of public service in mid-nineteenth-century Britain, nepotism knew no limits.[100]

Almost from the point when pauper children were considered as a discrete group, with different problems from adults, the need to find appropriate occupation for them had been of paramount concern. While they were still in the workhouse, the guardians had been employing children to make lace from at least 1795. Other temporary measures were introduced to occupy the women and children in the years that followed. Once 200 children and more were housed under one roof in Summer Lane, however, employment on a much more industrial scale could be contemplated. It was no accident that the emblem over the institution's door was a beehive: busy and productive bees were what the authorities wanted to nurture.[101] The Asylum was indeed busy from the outset. In its first annual report, the committee boasted that 'the females have knit several hundred pairs of stockings, besides sewing, repairing cloathes etc'.[102] Alongside the report in the *Gazette* ran an advertisement, repeated in the following year's report: 'knitting in wool and worsted done on reasonable terms'. The intention was not to restrict the inmates' work to making or repairing the garments of the Asylum alone: work for outside contractors was more profitable. In the wider Poor Law system this was known as 'farming the poor', an old method of reducing costs and generating income. At this early stage, girls were likewise being offered as servants, 'to be had on trial for a year', with boys as apprentices on a similar trial basis.[103] This too was standard workhouse practice. At this point, it would seem, no employment could be found for the boys *inside* the Asylum.

Putting out children as apprentices, of course, also had the effect of lifting the lid on conditions within the Asylum which was not something the guardians necessarily wished for. In 1817, for example, three girls were sent to Mrs Francis Harrison, a stay-maker in Bromsgrove Street, to continue their training in clothes making. The mistress subsequently claimed that the three girls left the Asylum affected with 'the itch', an implicit criticism of conditions in their former home. Once the story reached the press, the Asylum committee was forced to leap to its own defence. Medical evidence, they reported, showed that the young women did indeed have 'the itch', 'but there was no sign of its inveteracy'. And

---

100　June Edwards was still in post in 1848, though her father was not, when Francis White was writing his gazetteer. Cf. White, *History, Gazetteer and Directory of Warwickshire*, p. 28; J.M. Bourne, *Patronage and Society in Nineteenth-Century England*, London, 1986, p. 23.

101　Langford, *A Century of Birmingham Life*, Vol. II, p. 81.

102　*Aris's Gazette*, 24 September 1798.

103　See J. Humphries, *Childhood and Child Labour in the British Industrial Revolution*, Cambridge, 2010, pp. 256–305.

Mrs Harrison herself was accused of exacerbating the condition by sleeping all three girls (plus one other) in the same bed.[104] It was very difficult to win a public argument with Poor Law guardians, but it was equally true that, though they might win the legal argument, it was nigh impossible for the guardians on the Asylum committee to win the moral one. Concerns over the treatment of the poor had a habit of becoming fixed in the public mind, and the fact that the individuals concerned were children only added to them. In the hands of a political agitator like George Edmonds, a story of ill-treatment or poor conditions in the Asylum was the perfect opportunity to galvanise popular opinion. So the tale of the three girls with 'the itch' continued to do the rounds, long after the guardians' appeared to have scotched it. Edmonds accused the committee of failing to provide regular medical provision in the Asylum and the mistress, Mrs Brueton, of 'experimentalizing upon the poor children' by the use of 'mercurial girdles' in the Asylum, indicating that 'the itch' was endemic in the institution.[105] This probably referred to the soaking of a belt, usually of linen, in a solution of mercury, lemon juice and egg white as a treatment for what was, in fact, either scabies or impetigo.[106]

It was not difficult for the Asylum managers to keep their female inmates busy with domestic duties and needlework; nor were domestic situations hard to find, once the girls were old enough. Providing suitably industrial work for the Asylum boys, however, was a considerably more challenging proposition. Yet it did not take the committee long to make such an arrangement. In February 1800 the Birmingham parishes entered into an agreement with Thomas Phipson, a Birmingham pin manufacturer with a large works in New Street, for the employment of the boys.[107] As Shill points out, it was an industry that only slowly took to mechanisation of its processes.[108] In his *Wealth of Nations* Adam Smith used pin production to illustrate the advantages of the division of labour.[109] Pin-making, then, was a perfect example of a labour-intensive manufacture that lent itself to the employment of unskilled children. The work required from the Asylum boys involved putting heads on the pins, and then sticking them in rows on paper. Since the Asylum itself did not have space for such a workshop, land adjacent to it was rented for the

---

104 *Aris's Gazette*, 19 July 1819.

105 *Edmonds' Weekly Recorder*, 26 August 1819.

106 R. Hooper, *A New Medical Dictionary*, Philadelphia, 1817, p. 204.

107 Archives and Collections, Library of Birmingham. GP B/2/1/1 Birmingham Guardians' minutes, 19 February 1800.

108 R. Shill, *Workshop of the World: Birmingham's Industrial Heritage*, Stroud, 2006, pp. 6–8.

109 A. Smith, *An Inquiry into the Nature and Causes of the Wealth of Nations*, Vol. I, London, 1776, pp. 7–9.

erection of a factory.[110] In its first ten years of existence (from July 1797 to July 1807) the Asylum generated an income of £576 4s 4d from a variety of trades, including pin-making, knitting, oakum-picking (for the youngest children) and the manufacture of straw bonnets.[111] As the Asylum committee reported to the Society for Bettering the Condition of the Poor in 1809, the older girls undertook domestic duties, 'which reduces the establishment to a governess, schoolmaster and mistress, and one domestic servant'.[112] The knitting and cloth work was itemised for the society's report thus:

> Stockings knit for workhouse, more than 1,000 pairs. Ditto for the Asylum, with footing others and mending. Making children's linen, repairing cloaths, bedding etc.

The Asylum committee, however, was careful to stress that this was not simply a matter of budgets and profits. It was as much about setting the children on the path to social usefulness: 'Their habits of labour induces chearfulness and renders them more welcome to manufacturers who may in future employ them.' The committee considered that the labour undertaken was light: 'None are oppressed with hard labour so as to produce deformity, which was not uncommon while under the care of livelong nurses in the neighbouring villages.'[113] Nevertheless, the money made out of child labour made the Asylum practically self-supporting and, by 1819, it had cleared all the costs of land purchase and building work. The overseers were, as a result, able to declare in that year 'a considerable decrease in parish debt'.[114] Income from asylum labour in 1824–5 amounted to no less than £427, compared to £68 from the workhouse.[115] By 1817 the wages of all five of the servants at Summer Lane were also paid out of the profits of the manufactory,[116] and much of the cost of any necessary building work was also funded this way.[117] But this was not a situation which was allowed to continue indefinitely. In 1818, following the scandal described in chapter 8, the guardians moved to centralise the profits for the good of the whole union and not simply the Asylum for the Infant

---

110 Archives and Collections, Library of Birmingham. GP B/2/1/1 Birmingham Guardians' minutes, 25 June 1800.

111 *Ibid.*, 9 October 1804; *Aris's Gazette*, 19 November 1804.

112 T. Barnard (ed.), *Of the Education of the Poor*, London, 1809, p. 215.

113 *Aris's Gazette*, 19 November 1804.

114 *Aris's Gazette*, 29 March 1819.

115 *Aris's Gazette*, 27 June 1825.

116 Archives and Collections, Library of Birmingham. GP B/2/1/2 Birmingham Guardians' minutes, 28 October 1817.

117 Archives and Collections, Library of Birmingham. CP B/660983 Birmingham Overseers' Minutes, Vol. 2, 24 December 1816.

Poor. All attempts to run the Asylum as an independent institution ended at this point.

Industrial employment in the Asylum was as vulnerable to wider economic conditions as it was anywhere else, especially in the years following the end of the Napoleonic Wars. In July 1819, just as the Asylum reached capacity, the guardians reported that a fall in demand and in particular the depressed state of the pin trade, had reduced the children's working hours by a half.[118] Whatever the disadvantages of manual labour, it did, at least, keep the children active. By 1822 as the economy recovered, however, as many as 257 of the children, out of a total of 324, were being found work of some kind. Figures produced by the Asylum committee at this date show that 128 boys and 29 girls were heading pins, 82 girls were plaiting straw and 18 girls were making 'British lace'.[119] The overall profits for the year amounted to an impressive £683 1s 6d. By 1827 this list of trades had diversified still further, though a smaller proportion of the children were actually at work. Of the 293 boys and girls resident in January 1827 some 73 were in the pin shop, 31 were making 'Nottingham lace', 22 were stringing beads, 21 were manufacturing 'small articles in wire' and 7 were cutting glass, presumably for the beads.[120] This brought in a far from negligible profit of £8 3s a week.

Initially the children worked for eight hours a day: from 8 o'clock until midday and from 1 o'clock until 5 o'clock, with an hour set aside after this (from 5.30 to 6.30) for schooling, as was noted above.[121] The youngest children (under seven years of age) were not required to work and therefore four hours of schooling could be allocated, two hours in the morning and two in the afternoon. This, at least, was the situation in the early 1830s. Already by this date some members of the Asylum committee, most notably John Cadbury, were beginning to voice disquiet over the hours of labour and its effect upon the children. Requests for shorter hours, allowing more time for exercise and recreation, were made in January 1820,[122] in June and December 1831 and again in 1836.[123] On this latter occasion the surgeons requested a reduction of two hours, from eight to six hours a day, to allow an hour's recreation. They recommended, in addition, that no labour should commence before breakfast and that lace-making be

---

118 *Edmonds' Weekly Recorder*, 3 July 1819.

119 *Aris's Gazette*, 1 April 1822.

120 Archives and Collections, Library of Birmingham. GP B/2/1/3 Birmingham Guardians' minutes, 30 January 1827.

121 Archives and Collections, Library of Birmingham. CP B/660985 Birmingham Overseers' Minutes, Vol. 4, 6 December 1831.

122 Archives and Collections, Library of Birmingham. GP B/2/1/2 Birmingham Guardians' minutes, 25 January 1820.

123 Archives and Collections, Library of Birmingham. GP B/2/1/3 Birmingham Guardians' minutes, 10 August 1836.

discontinued. It was, they thought, 'utterly useless to the girls after they had left the Asylum' and it was certainly true that lace-making had never been a significant part of the local economy. As was usually the case with the Poor Law, the surgeons got their way where the guardians alone had previously failed. From June 1836 the older girls (aged between eleven and fourteen) were taken out of lace-making and were switched to playground duties instead, looking after the infants while they were playing outside.[124] Lace-making was entirely discontinued soon afterwards; two of the overseers, on one of their regular inspections, noted with pleasure 'the cessation of lace making at the Asylum and the greater relaxation consequently allowed to the girls, several of whom he saw happily engaged in the healthful amusement of skipping.'[125]

The shift in the union's attitude towards the children in its care over the space of only a few years in the late 1820s and early 1830s was marked. Slowly but surely, exercise, play and education were moving in and child labour was moving out, no doubt influenced by significant national campaigners against child labour such as Richard Oastler, Lord Ashley, Frances Trollope and Leonard Horner. But this change also had a gendered dimension. By 1839 it appears that only the boys were still being employed in industrial activity and this for no more than four hours a day, instead of eight.[126] By October 1839, the guardians reported that ninety boys were still heading pins, with a further fourteen employed either as tailors or shoemakers:

> The tailors have completed whole suits for the boys in which they appeared at the late Fair. Two men instruct the shoemakers, and in consequence not a pair of shoes has been purchased during the quarter.[127]

The expectation was that these boys would find gainful employment in these two trades once they left the Asylum behind; every town, no matter how small, needed tailors and shoemakers. The small number of boys who remained in the workhouse in Lichfield Street had once been similarly employed.[128] By the summer of 1840, no more than a third or so of the 355 children in the Asylum were now in employment. Of these 70 were making pins, 24 were tailors and

124 Archives and Collections, Library of Birmingham. CP B/660986 Birmingham Overseers' Minutes, Vol. 5, 3 June 1836.

125 Archives and Collections, Library of Birmingham. CP B/660986 Birmingham Overseers' Minutes, Vol. 5, 28 March 1837.

126 Archives and Collections, Library of Birmingham. GP B/2/1/4 Birmingham Guardians' minutes, 14 January 1839.

127 Ibid., 3 October 1839.

128 Archives and Collections, Library of Birmingham. GP B/2/1/2 Birmingham Guardians' minutes, 8 April 1823.

24 shoemakers, with a further 24 girls employed in domestic work. Three more were making straw bonnets, since the uniform of the Asylum females now demanded it. With appropriate instruction the girls were able to make 131 bonnets in twenty-eight days, enough both for use in the institution and for sale.[129] If manual labour was still considered appropriate activity for the older Asylum children, it was now considerably reduced in hours. The Birmingham Statistical Society reported in 1838 that boys were now employed for only four hours per day in pin-making, and the girls three hours in domestic work. The division between schooling and work, however, was a decidedly blurred line, particularly in the case of the girls. As we have already seen, their training also involved sewing and knitting, which may well have been directed to the repair of workhouse or Asylum clothes.[130] But since the emphasis had shifted to view healthy exercise as an intrinsic part of growing up, there was now 'an extensive new playground' to accommodate the changed circumstances.[131] Not that the playground was solely a place for play; it too became a new location for social improvement, and what the children did there was never a matter of personal choice alone. As such, the asylum committee undoubtedly had one eye on how play was organised and conducted at Birmingham Infant School. The improvement in the overall health of the children was put down, not only to the new dietary emphasis on more milk, but also 'in drilling the boys, by marching them in the playground, an exercise highly conducive to health and pleasing to the children'.[132] Nor was play an entirely neutral activity. If skipping was just the kind of pastime the overseers liked to see, bandycock, a rough and ready version of hockey, was certainly not:

> They require attention to be paid to the bandy game played by the boys, which is dangerous to the children and likely to break the windows, and they recommend that the boys be allowed a number of hoops and sticks, which they think would be beneficial to the children's health and not so dangerous.[133]

For all its ambitions, the Asylum was hardly able to keep its young inhabitants healthy any more effectively than the poor homes they had left behind. Indeed,

---

129 Archives and Collections, Library of Birmingham. GP B/2/1/4 Birmingham Guardians' minutes, 7 July 1840.

130 Archives and Collections, Library of Birmingham. MS 1683/1 Birmingham Statistical Society for Education, Supporting Evidence, 1838, p. 33.

131 Archives and Collections, Library of Birmingham. GP B/2/1/4 Birmingham Guardians' minutes, 3 October 1839.

132 *Ibid.*

133 Archives and Collections, Library of Birmingham. CP B/660987 Birmingham Overseers' Minutes, Vol. 6, 19 February 1839.

by 1839, the surgeons were coming to the conclusion that the very presence of large numbers of children in one place 'always conduces to a bad state of health in the individuals so collected'.[134] The terms 'wasting' or 'decline', they decided, were too indiscriminate a description of the infections that laid them low, but this did not make the doctors any more equipped to deal with them. If the conditions within the Asylum could not be directly linked to the poor health of the children, then an explanation had to be found in the environment around them. When first erected, the Asylum had few neighbours for company and even in 1831 it was described as having little but gardens and brick-kilns nearby.[135] There was also an unidentified Protestant burial ground in the vicinity. In September 1831 the governor was complaining that boys were climbing a mound of earth in the burial ground to call to the children over the wall in the Asylum.[136] The Birmingham parishes had considered using this graveyard for the burial of cholera victims in 1832, but a request to that effect had been turned down by the trustees.[137]

The Asylum committee commented in 1836 that 'the area around the asylum is becoming more populous, and less adapted for a healthy residence for the children'.[138] By 1838, despite having spent £1,000 on the Asylum in the space of two years, the guardians were once more expressing concerns about poor accommodation and inadequate night attendance at the Asylum.[139] The surgeons, on the other hand, had decided that it had been built in the wrong location in the first place. The house, they said, sat in a low valley, 'exposed to the prevalent winds with scarcely the shelter of a tree'.[140] Added to that, the place was damp, cold and insalubrious, partly the result of the clay substratum which lay underneath it and which explained the nearby brickworks. The committee of physicians and surgeons, who reported on the town's health in 1841, were similarly concerned with the 'wet waste land' surrounding the Asylum.[141] Nor was it any longer in a semi-rural location: the towns of Birmingham and Aston were making a pincer movement upon it. The sense of rural separation which

---

134 Archives and Collections, Library of Birmingham. GP B/2/1/4 Birmingham Guardians' minutes 30 January 1839.

135 Archives and Collections, Library of Birmingham. CP B/660985 Birmingham Overseers' Minutes, Vol. 4, 28 June 1831.

136 *Ibid.*, 27 September 1831.

137 *Ibid.*, 23 February 1832.

138 *The Philanthropist and Warwickshire, Worcestershire and Staffordshire Gazette*, 6 October 1836.

139 *Birmingham Journal*, 8 October 1836.

140 Archives and Collections, Library of Birmingham. GP B/2/1/4 Birmingham Guardians' minutes, 13 February 1838.

141 Poor Law Commissioners, Sanitary Inquiry (England), *Report on the State of the Public Health in the Borough of Birmingham*, London, 1842, p. 2.

had recommended the area in 1797 no longer applied. For once the union surgeons were pushing at a half-open door. By this date the guardians had already decided that it was high time to move the whole Poor Law operation to a new site.[142] The cost of doing so was considerably under-estimated, however, and the Asylum continued to operate until 1852. Mary Nejedly has recently described how the building at Summer Lane continued to struggle with over-crowding as the numbers reached 422 children in 1849. The medical officer, Dr Green, worried about the effects of this on the children's health and Nejedly speculates, probably accurately, that Green's report was decisive in the decision to relocate the children to the new workhouse site on Western Road.[143]

We ought, finally, to put the Asylum in its wider context, for, though the logic behind it seemed irresistible in 1796, it was in many ways a unique institution in its day. Indeed, Birmingham's 'superior and intelligent management with regard to the infant poor' was singled out for particular praise by Charles Pelham Villiers in his report to the Poor Law Commission in 1834. The combination of basic schooling for the children of the poor, thought Villiers, with instruction in 'sundry trades, has been proved by experience to be extremely favourable to them in after life.'[144] Nationally there were day schools with comparable educational aims to the Asylum, for example, those founded (for boys and girls) in 1791 by Rev. William Gilpin at Boldre in the New Forest. There were also industrial schools, such as those founded in Kendal in 1799, at Lewisham in 1796 and at Oakham in 1797, and there were National and British Schools, set up by Andrew Bell and Joseph Lancaster, to provide a cheap education for the offspring of the 'industrious classes'. There was the Birmingham Infant School, and others which catered for young children, such as the free school opened in Weston (later Weston-super-Mare) in 1795. There was also a scattering of orphanages, and charitable schools such as the Blue Coat, which boarded pupils. Many of these are described, usually in glowing terms, in the reports of the Society for Bettering the Condition of the Poor.[145]

Mostly closely linked in institutional terms was the Foundling Hospital in London, established by Captain Thomas Coram in 1742, to take in the abandoned, neglected and orphaned children of the capital. Such was the fame of the institution, and its considerable financial backing, that it evolved from

---

142 Archives and Collections, Library of Birmingham. GP B/2/1/4 Birmingham Guardians' minutes, 28 May 1839.

143 M. Nejedly, 'Earning their Keep: Child Workers at the Birmingham Asylum for the Infant Poor, 1797–1852', *Family and Community History*, 20:3, 2018, p. 214.

144 *Report from His Majesty's Commissioners for Inquiring into the Administration and Practical Operation of the Poor Laws*, Appendix A, Parliamentary Papers, XXIX, 1834, p. 7a.

145 Barnard (ed.), *Of the Education of the Poor*, pp. 231–2.

a private to a public charity. Ancillary, though considerably less successful orphanages were later founded in 1756, one for the north of England at Ackworth in Yorkshire and one for the Midlands at Shrewsbury.[146] But there was nothing quite like the Asylum on Summer Lane, whose aims were both educational and industrial, which was funded directly out of the Poor Rate. Founded on a principle of support for 'orphan and destitute children', the Asylum did not deflect from that mission, even though there were, from time to time, calls for it to narrow and refine its admission policy.[147] The reports of the Society show that little at the Asylum was actually new, except its combination of all the elements. Weaving, spinning and sewing took place at Boldre and at Oakham; shoemaking was undertaken by the boys at Kendal; and plaiting split straw was done by the children at the industrial school at Fincham in Norfolk. The master and mistress of the school of industry at Lewisham lived on the premises, and the school also took children from the workhouse, though it did not board them.[148] But none of these institutions dealt with anything approaching the 300 or 400 children seen at the Birmingham Asylum and none were residential, or specifically governed or created by the Poor Law.

---

146 D.S. Allin, *The Early Years of the Foundling Hospital, 1739/41–1773*, London, 2010.

147 *Edmonds' Weekly Recorder*, 10 July 1819.

148 Barnard (ed.), *Of the Education of the Poor*, pp. 105–11, 179–81, 123–39, 201–7, 182–92.

12

'Bitter, unbroken lamentation'?:
The Treatment of the Mentally Ill Pauper

There was one group of paupers, other than the children, whose afflictions, condition and very presence in the workhouse was considered to be not of their own making. Alone among the inmates, the individuals defined variously as mad, lunatic and insane, elicited unusual compassion and sympathy from the guardians and overseers. Indeed, the change in tone and vocabulary when such patients are being described is most striking. In 1803, for example, when two paupers were being removed from the workhouse to a private asylum, it was because of 'the unfortunate nature of their complaint'.[1] Nor did such tenderness vanish with their exit from Lichfield Street. The pauper lunatics visited in an asylum in June 1819 were described as 'miserable objects' and 'unfortunate beings', and the visiting overseers described themselves as giving way to 'melancholy reflections, excited on witnessing so many of our afflicted fellow beings'.[2] There were strong reasons for this newly awakened compassion. The porphyria which increasingly incapacitated George III from the 1760s onwards clearly showed that madness was not confined to the lower classes, was not self-inflicted and was a national problem. This, together with the attempted assassination of the King in 1800 by James Hatfield, took insanity out of the dark cells of Bedlam and into the public arena. Hatfield was acquitted of treason 'by reason of insanity' by the jury and this led, in part, to the law of 1800, which instigated the provision of 'safe custody of insane persons charged

---

1   Archives and Collections, Library of Birmingham. CP B/660982 Birmingham Overseers' Minutes, Vol. 1, 18 November 1803.

2   Archives and Collections, Library of Birmingham. CP B/660983 Birmingham Overseers' Minutes, Vol. 2, 15 June 1819.

with offences.'[3] After a Commons Select Committee investigated the issue and found a wide disparity of treatment of the mentally ill across the county, a further law in 1808 was passed which gave local authorities the power to establish separate asylums.[4] Madness had, not before time, become a matter for doctors and professional care.

There were, of course, a multitude of reasons why an individual might become afflicted by mental illness, and thus thrown upon the mercy of the Poor Law. The earliest such case recorded in the Birmingham records in 1803 has some hint of diagnosis about it, even if the only treatment offered is financial: 'William Smith, melancholy, four children, 1s.'[5] By 1815 two of the Birmingham surgeons, Edward Townsend Cox and J.M. Ledsam, who inspected the paupers housed at Droitwich Asylum, were beginning to show some degree of differentiation between the patients' conditions. 'More,' wrote Cox, 'have want of intellect than madness, more imbecility of mind than insanity.' The distinction was an important one, for the former cases might safely be brought back to Birmingham. A number of patients were here described as epileptic, which still placed them in the same category as those with mental health problems. Cox's colleague identified a further affliction in the case of one woman by the name of Lawrence, 'who is ill of a complaint to which some delicate women are subject after child birth'.[6] As for the reasons behind mental incapacity, the parish surgeons had various explanations to offer. In 1828 Edward's son, William Sands Cox, was pleased by what he saw as the relatively low incidence of mental illness in the town:

> Upon the whole, given the increased population of the town, we may congratulate ourselves there is not a greater increase of maniachal [*sic*] disease under existing circumstances from the high excitement produced by intemperance.[7]

3   L. Blom-Cooper, 'The Criminal Lunatic Asylum System Before and after Broadmoor', in R. Creese, W.F. Bynum and J. Bearn (eds), *The Health of Prisoners: Historical Essays*, Amsterdam, 1995, pp. 153–4.

4   *An Act for the Better Care and Maintenance of Lunatics, Being Paupers or Criminals in England*, 1808, 48 Geo. III c. 96. In the West Midlands, only Stafford chose to build a county asylum: W. White, *History, Gazetteer and Directory of Staffordshire and the City and County of Lichfield*, Sheffield, 1834, pp. 136–7.

5   Archives and Collections, Library of Birmingham. CP B/380973 Accounts of the Birmingham Workhouse and Out-Relief to the Poor, 11 March 1748.

6   Archives and Collections, Library of Birmingham. CP B/660983 Birmingham Overseers' Minutes, Vol. 2, 9 May 1815.

7   Archives and Collections, Library of Birmingham. CP B/660984 Birmingham Overseers' Minutes, Vol. 3, 3 June 1828. Sands Cox went on to help prevent the spread of cholera in Birmingham in 1832 and was the founder of Birmingham's first Medical School: J.T.J. Morrison, *William Sands Cox and the Birmingham Medical School*, Birmingham, 1926.

In 1836 he went even further:

> Upon the whole it is most gratifying, considering the vast extent of our population, together with their irregularities and habits of intoxication, to which the lower grades of society are subject and, I believe, none more addicted thereto than our own.[8]

The problem, to Cox's mind, was endemic in large urban populations, but was brought on, to a great extent, by alcohol. With King George long since dead and buried, Cox's diagnosis could move on to the social causes of insanity, and putting the blame on drink always went down well with a nonconformist Birmingham audience. As Kostas Makras has recently shown, alcohol was widely seen as the chief cause of male madness and the 1830s saw a series of articles in medical journals, including *The Lancet,* noting the large numbers of men who found themselves in pauper lunatic asylums due to their intemperance.[9]

Given the huge changes over a century or so in the general treatment of the poor, the overall approach to those paupers with mental disabilities altered remarkably little, and what Birmingham did could be duplicated across the country. Those pauper lunatics who were considered dangerous, along with those who might be cured of their affliction, were sent to a specialist institution elsewhere, hitherto the abode of the wealthy insane. Those who were diagnosed as harmless or incurable (but not dangerous to other inmates) remained at, or were returned to, the workhouse.[10] In contrast to its treatment of children, Birmingham did not create a specific institution for the mentally ill until the 1840s, by which time such provision had become compulsory. This state of affairs was as much a matter of finance as anything else. The price of the care and treatment of a patient in a private institution was invariably more than double the cost of keeping him or her in the workhouse. In 1815 the total cost of keeping thirty-four paupers in the Droitwich Asylum amounted to £956, about £28 per person per year. The cost of maintaining twenty mentally ill

---

8   Archives and Collections, Library of Birmingham. CP B/660986 Birmingham Overseers' Minutes, Vol. 5, 27 February 1836.

9   K. Makras, "'The Poison that upsets my reason": Men, Madness and Drunkenness in the Victorian Period', in T. Knowles and S. Trowbridge (eds) *Insanity and the Lunatic Asylum in the Nineteenth Century,* London, 2015, pp. 137–8.

10   Smith terms this 'the mixed economy of care'; L.D. Smith, 'The County Asylum in the Mixed Economy of Care, 1808–1845', in J. Melling and B. Forsythe (eds) *Insanity, Institutions and Society, 1800–1914: A Social History of Madness in Comparative Perspective,* London, 1999, pp. 23–47; A. Shepherd, *Institutionalizing the Insane in Nineteenth-Century England,* London, 2014; N. McCrae and P. Nolan, *The Story of Nursing in British Mental Hospitals: Echoes from the Corridors,* London, 2016, pp. 3–12.

patients in the workhouse in the same year was estimated at £182, or a little over £9 a head.[11] Inevitably this wide differential led to patients being returned to Birmingham when they ought not to have been. In 1834, for example, one such patient was found by the overseers in the women's insane ward at Lichfield Street. The visiting overseer commented:

> One inmate lately removed from Stafford appeared to be attacked with a fit of her disease, which your visitors would describe as a bursting forth of 'a bitter unbroken lamentation'.

On the same visit, in the men's 'idiotic ward' the overseers found a man bound hand and foot in chains, exactly the kind of restraint they would generally have condemned in the private madhouses.[12] To be fair to the workhouse physician, this treatment was probably done as a temporary measure to avoid having to send a violent inmate to an asylum, at least until it was clear that his condition was intractable. The use of such severe mechanical restraint in the Birmingham workhouse insane wards does not appear to have been common, however, as successive reports by overseers, select committees, medical inspectors, commissioners and others, fail to identify more than a handful of such cases. Such practices were widely used across other workhouses in Britain under the Old Poor Law, as the Select Committee on Madhouses discovered in 1816, and there was a growing popular perception that the insane were being systematically ill-treated in the workhouse, a perception that the architects of the New Poor Law were keen to capitalise on.[13]

The problem of patients being discharged too early was not limited to the workhouse, however. The Congregationalist missionary, Peter Sibree, recorded a visit to one such case in 1838:

> Was called upon to sympathise and assist another very distressed family in Woodcock Street. (I think Court 6, House 3.) I had been there before, but their miseries were now at a climax. The husband died in a state of insanity, having been brought out of the Asylum only in part restored. The widow had been distrained for her rent; there was no furniture in the house, and the children were weeping over their dead father.[14]

---

11   Archives and Collections, Library of Birmingham. GP B/2/1/2 Birmingham Guardians' minutes, 18 July 1815.

12   Archives and Collections, Library of Birmingham. CP B/660986 Birmingham Overseers' Minutes Vol. 5, 11 November 1834.

13   *Select Committee Report on Madhouses in England*, Parliamentary Papers, VI, 1816. See also G. Oxley, *Poor Relief in England and Wales, 1601–1834*, Newton Abbot, 1974, p. 71.

14   Archives and Collections, Library of Birmingham. CC1/71 Congregational Church Town Mission, 18 December 1838.

Even when a patient, in the eyes of the doctors concerned, was 'cured', there was little or no period of rehabilitation or assistance. Two months earlier Sibree notes in his diary:

> Called also to see a young man who had been brought out of the lunatic asylum. He was without cloathes, having torn everything to pieces in his delirious moments. I procured him a pair of trowsers and some small comforts with which he seemed greatly pleased.[15]

There is no direct evidence, however, that patients were returned to the workhouse or released into the community purely because of the financial savings that this might produce. Knowledge of mental illness, its causes and the best means to rehabilitate sufferers was, after all, still in its infancy and there are plenty of records of patients for whom return or release appears to have been entirely appropriate.[16] Sibree's observations may reflect undue haste on the part of a penny-pinching parish, but they may equally reflect professional error or bureaucratic incompetence. One thing is certain: at this stage the workhouse could not offer anything like the professional and full-time attention paid for in a dedicated lunatic asylum. More often than not, paupers confined to the lunatic ward at Lichfield Street were looked after by paupers from the other wards. This might have disastrous consequences; in November 1812 one Laurence Hughes fatally stabbed his pauper carer 'in a fit of insanity' and was quickly despatched to the county gaol.[17]

The figure which most concerned the overseers and the guardians of the poor at this stage was the weekly charge per person, and that led to a constant running battle with the keepers of private asylums over the unit cost. In 1812 the charge at the private asylum in Droitwich stood at 9s per week, which the overseers reluctantly agreed to increase to 10s in March 1813.[18] The proprietor, William Ricketts, requested an increase by a further shilling in 1818, at which point the overseers threatened to remove their paupers altogether.[19] Here, as elsewhere, the sheer financial clout of a Poor Law authority allowed it to

---

15 *Ibid.*, 19 October 1838.

16 See, for example, details of Edward Cox's decision on the return of three inmates of Staffordshire Asylum: Archives and Collections, Library of Birmingham. GP B/2/1/2 Birmingham Guardians' minutes, 7 April 1835. See also: A. Scull, *The Most Solitary of Afflictions: Madness and Society in Britain, 1700–1900*, New Haven, 1993; R. Porter, *Mind-Forg'd Manacles: A History of Madness in England from the Restoration to the Regency*, Cambridge, 1987.

17 *Aris's Gazette*, 9 November 1812.

18 Archives and Collections, Library of Birmingham. CP B/660982 Birmingham Overseers' Minutes, Vol. 1, 2 March 1813.

19 Archives and Collections, Library of Birmingham. CP B/660983 Birmingham Overseers' Minutes, Vol. 2, 19 May 1818.

squeeze its supplier, drive down the cost of care and get away with it. Mr Ricketts could ill afford to turn his back on a contract as large as Birmingham's. Even though the weekly charge at Droitwich did eventually rise to 11s, the Birmingham overseers forced Ricketts to reduce his fees again in 1822. Caught up in a bidding war for Birmingham's pauper lunatics, he was obliged to match the fees charged by the Stafford County Asylum or lose his business. The price, therefore, returned to 10s.[20]

Only gradually were concerns over the quality of care taken into account in these negotiations. In 1837 Thomas Lewis, the proprietor of nearby Duddeston Hall, made an offer to Birmingham (of 10s 6d per head) to undercut his rivals. On this occasion, however, the guardians, led by Henry Knight, took into account the positive reports of their patients at Stafford, as well as the cost and disruption of moving them to a new institution.[21] Nevertheless, by a process of slow attrition Lewis eventually did win the contract. Of course, the overseers' insistence on 'not a penny more' took no account of the unstable price of provisions. From the 1790s onwards the cost of bread and potatoes, the staples of institutional food, fluctuated widely, but generally increased. No allowance was made for this in the contract. In 1840 Duddeston Asylum attempted to raise fees by 2s per week, a request which was immediately turned down. In desperation the asylum proprietor sought a compromise, tying the charge to the cost of bread, much as the Speenhamland system had done with levels of relief. If the price of a loaf (of half a peck) exceeded 12½d the charge would rise to 11s; if the cost of a loaf rose above 15d the charge would rise to 12s.[22] This creative solution was also turned down by the Birmingham overseers and Lewis was forced to maintain his fee at 10s (with 1s extra for clothing) and to hold his prices for at least six months.[23]

The financial burden was not necessarily borne in its entirety by the parish. Families of patients (where they could be traced) were means-tested as to their ability to contribute to the cost of care. In October 1823 the family of Hiram Aaron was forced to pay £5 a year towards his accommodation at Droitwich,

---

20   *Ibid.*, 18 January 1822. Smith, 'The County Asylum', pp. 38–9.

21   *Birmingham Advertiser*, 5 January 1837. It was unsurprising that Knight was positive in his praise of Staffordshire asylum, as he was the asylum's physician. White, *History, Directory and Gazetteer of Staffordshire*, p. 137. Lewis did persuade the guardians of Aston to send seventeen of their pauper lunatics to Duddeston Hall, though they continued to chafe at the expense. Archives and Collections, Library of Birmingham. GP AS/2/1/1 Aston Guardians' minutes, 16 May 1837.

22   Archives and Collections, Library of Birmingham. CP B/660987 Birmingham Overseers' Minutes, Vol. 6, 18 August 1840.

23   *Ibid.*, 1 September 1840.

despite their protests.[24] This represented about one fifth of the total bill. Ten years later Charles Salmon was paying 4s per week for the upkeep of his mother in the workhouse. If she was transferred to Stafford Asylum, he was told, the cost would rise to 7s.[25] The evidence of the Congregational town missionaries shows that in many cases families continued to wrestle with the challenges of poverty and mental illness at home, rather than request help, even when such help was theoretically available. Peter Sibree vividly records the afflictions of one family in his diary:

> The husband and father of a pious but very poor family was deranged. The fever had seized his brain and I found him tied to the four posts of the bed raving. He had bitten his children and injured his wife much before he could be restrained.[26]

Over the century and more of this study, the Birmingham authorities made use of a range of private lunatic asylums in the region.[27] The first asylum enlisted was Samuel Proud's madhouse at Bilston (probably the earliest in the area), and an early discharge register (1767–76) shows a number of paupers being transferred to Proud's from 1771 onwards.[28] The parish was still using Proud's in 1785, when Mrs Mary Simpson was declared 'insane and dangerous' and sent there.[29] The absence of overseers' minutes before 1803 prevents us from determining when Droitwich was added to the list of contacts, but the Droitwich Asylum had become a favoured destination by 1799, when the parish accounts record a payment 'for two women in the house with two lunatics to Droitwich 16s 6d'.[30] From this point onwards, or at least for the next twenty-five years, Droitwich was to be the asylum of choice. Droitwich Lunatic Asylum was opened in 1791 by William Ricketts and remained in operation

---

24 Archives and Collections, Library of Birmingham. CP B/660984 Overseers' Minutes, Vol. 3, 28 October 1823.

25 Archives and Collections, Library of Birmingham. CP B/660985 Overseers' Minutes, Vol. 4, 9 July 1833.

26 Archives and Collections, Library of Birmingham. CC1/71 Congregational Church Town Mission, 8 September 1838.

27 L.D. Smith, 'The Pauper Lunatic Problem in the West Midlands, 1818–1850', *Midland History*, 21, 1996, pp. 106–13.

28 Archives and Collections, Library of Birmingham. CP B/662385 Birmingham Paupers' Admission and Discharge Register. See L.D. Smith, 'Eighteenth Century Madhouse Practice: The Prouds of Bilston', *History of Psychiatry*, 3, 1992, pp. 45–52.

29 Archives and Collections, Library of Birmingham. GP B/2/1/1 Birmingham Guardians' minutes, 20 June 1805.

30 Archives and Collections, Library of Birmingham. GP B/3/1/1 Birmingham Guardians' cash books, 16 April 1799.

for eighty years. In 1817 William Ricketts was succeeded as proprietor by his sons, W.H. Ricketts and M. Ricketts. The institution relied heavily upon Poor Law contracts (especially from Birmingham), until the opening of the Worcester Country Asylum at Powick in 1852. Half of Ricketts' ninety inmates were paupers in 1816, the rest being private cases. Droitwich was generally believed to be one of the best private asylums in the country, particularly for its professional care (both the sons were surgeons) and for its lack of physical restraint.[31] Certainly the visitors from Birmingham had little to complain about during their visits, other than their frequent wrangling over the bill. Such inspections were sporadic before 1816, after which reports are much more regular. The increased tempo coincided, unsurprisingly, with the Parliamentary Select Committee on the regulation of madhouses of 1815–16.[32] Numbers sent to Droitwich were small, relative to the overall size of Birmingham's pauper population. In 1815, at the time of one such visit, there were approximately 550 inmates at Birmingham workhouse and the Asylum of the Infant Poor, but only 34 pauper patients at Droitwich. Edward Townsend Cox's report on Droitwich lists them, variously described as 'mischievous', 'dangerous', 'in a low state of mind', and 'very bad'.[33] In Cox's opinion, a number of these patients might be brought back to Birmingham 'especially as you have plenty of room for buildings at the asylum for every purpose'. By this he meant the Asylum for the Infant Poor on Summer Lane, whose semi-rural surroundings (at least at this point) could have been considered beneficial to mental patients. However, there was never any question of the overseers and guardians agreeing to a lunatic asylum close to their home for children. The number of such individuals, 'confined at the public expense' at Droitwich rarely dropped very far below forty. This was exactly the total in June 1819 (twenty-three men and seventeen women). Of these:

> Three men are incurables who are become idiotic, inoffensive in their conduct, and, of course, more easily managed, who may be removed and placed in the lunatic ward in the [work]house.[34]

If a cure was out of the question, therefore, and there was evidence that the patients were at least 'manageable' and 'inoffensive' then the expense of asylum

---

31 W.L. Parry-Jones, *The Trade in Lunacy: A Study of Private Madhouses in England in the Eighteenth and Nineteenth Centuries*, London, 1972, pp. 121–4.

32 *Ibid.*, pp. 15–16.

33 Archives and Collections, Library of Birmingham. CP B/660983 Birmingham Overseers' Minutes, Vol. 2, 9 May 1815.

34 *Ibid.*, 15 June 1819.

fees could be saved and the patients returned to the workhouse. This judgement anticipated by fifteen years the distinction that was drawn between the patients who could and could not be safely accommodated in the workhouse in the Poor Law Amendment Act.[35]

Visits to Droitwich by the overseers or parish surgeons were therefore as much about identifying those who could be brought home and maintained more cheaply in Birmingham as they were about the conditions in the asylum, but the question of care in the asylums was nevertheless regularly addressed. Little was said in criticism of the care and, indeed, more often than not there was praise for the 'care and humanity' of Mr Ricketts and his staff. One recommendation in 1820 indicated a prevailing attitude within the Birmingham parish and may reflect a difference of opinion between the overseers and Ricketts as to the correct therapeutic treatment of the inmates: The visitors wanted the inmates to be given work to do. 'Employment of the body', declared the officers, 'as far as it is practicable with a diseased mind, contributes in a very great degree towards restoring it to health.'[36] The earliest definite indication that Birmingham was considering terminating its contract with Ricketts is in September 1821. This suggestion was not actioned, though there was a visit to assess alternative accommodation at the newly opened Stafford County Asylum in November 1821.[37] Nevertheless, the discussion at this time highlighted what would need to be provided for such patients if they were ever returned en masse to the workhouse.[38] The surgeons recommended not one, but two rooms to be set aside, one for sleeping and one as a day room. Ideally, such rooms should be on the ground floor 'as many are cripples'. They further recommended 'suitable and sufficient attendants', as well as the provision of cribs and a particular kind of bath, what they called 'a floating room with water'. Finally, the surgeons suggested that the day room should open onto a private or retired yard, 'in order that the patients may exercise without being exposed to the gaze and interruption of the other inhabitants of the house'. Such provision would eventually come to Lichfield Street, but not yet. A footnote to this report, perhaps anticipating objections, suggested that the parish might wish to reconsider its opinion about accommodation at the Infant Asylum. This was no more likely to be accepted in 1821 than it had been in 1815.

---

35   D. Mellett, *The Prerogative of Asylumdom: Social, Cultural and Administrative Aspects of the Institutional Treatment of the Insane in Nineteenth-Century Britain*, New York, 1982, pp. 136–7.

36   Archives and Collections, Library of Birmingham. CP B/660983 Birmingham Overseers' Minutes, Vol. 2, 4 January 1820.

37   *Ibid.*, 2 November 1821.

38   *Ibid.*, 18 September 1821.

The guardians had, in the meantime, been contemplating the idea of a new, purpose-built, lunatic asylum on Birmingham Heath, 'near to where the windmill is built'.[39] The attraction of the site was that it was 'sufficiently spacious to admit of patients taking the air and exercise necessary to their recovery', an arrangement urged in the County Asylums Act of 1828. Such a decision would not be made for another thirty years, but even in 1815 the guardians went as far as to invite tenders and plans. An advert to this effect appeared in *Aris's Gazette* in October 1815, indicating the intention to build an asylum 'for 80 patients in three classes', and which was capable of later extension.[40] The architects who submitted designs suggested an overall cost of between £12,000 and £15,000, with the encouragement that such an institution could recoup £500 a year by opening its doors to private patients.[41] At the very least the spacious designs sent in, surrounded by gardens and open space, made Droitwich begin to look very cramped indeed by comparison. Such plans were probably over-ambitious in the financial climate of the mid-1810s and by 1822 the guardians were proposing a much more modest scheme, costing no more than £3,000.[42] Yet the 'peculiar salubriety' of the Heath still retained its appeal, along with the possibility of involving the inmates in the agricultural work currently taking place on the parish farm. This too came to nothing at this time. Droitwich therefore remained, for the moment, the best available option, although it was no longer the sole provider for Birmingham's mental care. By April 1823 there were still twenty men and women at Ricketts', but also two at the Stafford County Asylum and another at Mr Burman's asylum at Henley-in-Arden. The latter, opened in 1795, was one of a number of such houses in the Warwickshire village.[43] Birmingham was still using Burman's for the occasional patient in 1828.[44]

The summer of 1828 represented something of a watershed in Birmingham's relationship with the private asylums. The war of words with the Ricketts over the cost of care had reached crisis point, and the overseers were ordering the complete removal of the Birmingham paupers by Christmas.[45]

39 Archives and Collections, Library of Birmingham. GP B/2/1/2 Birmingham Guardians' minutes, 18 July 1815.

40 *Aris's Gazette*, 16 October 1815

41 Archives and Collections, Library of Birmingham. GP B/2/1/2 Birmingham Guardians' minutes, 23 January 1816.

42 *Ibid.*, 1 January 1822.

43 Parry-Jones, *The Trade in Lunacy*, p. 36.

44 Archives and Collections, Library of Birmingham. GP B/3/1/4 Birmingham Guardians' cash books, 19 July 1828.

45 Archives and Collections, Library of Birmingham. CP B/660984 Birmingham Overseers' Minutes, Vol. 3, 3 June 1828.

Facing a potential emergency, letters were dashed off to all the asylums in the local area, to Henley, Lichfield, George Boddington's asylum at Sutton Coldfield, Thomas Bakewell's Spring Vale asylum at Stone, and to Stafford.[46] In addition, inspections were made of a number of these institutions, but with less than encouraging results. Driffold House at Sutton Coldfield replied that it was 'not in their power' to receive any of the Birmingham inmates, whilst the one in Lichfield was given a far from clean bill-of-health. 'I am persuaded the parish of Birmingham', commented William Sands Cox, 'would not for one moment entertain the idea of sending their unfortunate paupers to a place of that description.'[47] The only institution which was large enough to receive the Birmingham patients, it seemed, was Stafford County Asylum, and preparations were therefore made for the transfer by the end of the summer. The journey from Droitwich to Stafford would not have been easy in the early nineteenth century; especially given the delicate condition of the passengers. Four overseers were deployed to supervise the transfer, and the carriage normally used to transport prisoners provided the means. The owner of the hotel in Droitwich, Mr Ellis, took the thirty-seven paupers to the Crown Inn at Stourbridge, and so by stages to Stafford.[48] By the beginning of December 1828 all the Birmingham paupers were safely installed in their new home. They had, it seemed, landed on their feet, for the conditions there were clearly far superior to what they had enjoyed at Ricketts' establishment.

The asylum at Stafford had opened on 1 October 1818, the earliest of the county asylums in the West Midlands. Within a couple of months of opening, according to Leonard Smith, Stafford was looking to establish a contract with Birmingham, offering prices of 10s per week for incurables and 12s for curable patients.[49] There is no indication in the Birmingham records that such an offer was initially taken up. Nevertheless, compared to the small private madhouses in the region, Stafford was spacious, professionally run, and designed with the Lunacy Acts, and increasingly fussy inspectors, in mind. An inspector himself, Dr Sands Cox, was almost beside himself with pleasure when he inspected the place in December 1828.

46   L.D. Smith, 'To Cure those Afflicted with the Disease of Insanity: Thomas Bakewell and Spring Vale Asylum', *History of Psychiatry*, 4, 1993, pp. 107–27.

47   Archives and Collections, Library of Birmingham. CP B/660985 Birmingham Overseers' Minutes, Vol. 4, 22 July 1828.

48   *Ibid.*, 26 August 1828.

49   L.D Smith, *Cure, Comfort and Safe Custody: Public Lunatic Asylums in Early-Nineteenth-Century England*, London, 1999. p. 76.

The interior is most advantageously situated; it stands on an eminence, commands an extensive prospect, possesses commodious grounds and garden, a portion of which is partly cultivated by the assistance of the convalescent patients. The interior of the building is judiciously arranged; the different apartments are spacious, lofty and well-ventilated ... The bedrooms particularly are clean, the beds thrown open every morning during the day. The galleries or day rooms are warmed in cold weather by patent air stoves and presented an appearance of order and regularity ... The keepers, both male and female, are clearly intelligent and kind towards the unfortunate inmates.[50]

Stafford was everything, in short, that Droitwich and Lichfield Street were not. Such care and attention came at a price, but reduced packages were usually available to keep parish overseers happy, and it was possible to take an annual subscription. By 1825 Stafford was charging 25s per week for patients from outside the county, but Birmingham would certainly not have paid this amount.[51] The parish accounts remain silent over what was actually being paid, but at any rate the numbers concerned had dropped, as facilities for their care at Birmingham improved. There were only sixteen Birmingham patients at Stafford in September 1833,[52] and no more visits were made after September 1834.[53] After 1834, under the terms of Section 45 of the Poor Law Amendment Act, inmates deemed dangerous could only be held in a workhouse for a maximum of fourteen days.[54] Birmingham parish was therefore forced to revert to using the private asylums once more for its intractable cases. This new opportunity brought new competitors for the 'trade in lunacy' into the field. Duddeston Hall, a former hotel and pleasure park to the north of Birmingham, had opened in 1835 under the proprietorship of Thomas Lewis. The institution was described as newly open, 'with extensive garden and pleasure grounds' in July of that year, and it quickly won itself a contract with Birmingham.[55] Mr Lewis wrote to the overseers to advertise his services as early as April 1835 and, as we have already seen, renewed his offer at the end of 1836.[56] It was the first time an asylum of this size (by 1844 Duddeston Hall had eighty inmates, sixty

50   Archives and Collections, Library of Birmingham. CP B/660985 Birmingham Overseers' Minutes, Vol. 4, 2 December 1828.

51   Smith, *Cure, Comfort and Safe Custody*, p. 76.

52   Archives and Collections, Library of Birmingham. CP B/660985 Birmingham Overseers' Minutes, Vol. 4, 10 September 1833.

53   Archives and Collections, Library of Birmingham. CP B/660986 Birmingham Overseers' Minutes, Vol. 5, 2 September 1834.

54   K. Jones, *A History of the Mental Health Services*, London, 1972, pp. 124–5.

55   *Birmingham Advertiser*, 30 July 1835.

56   Archives and Collections, Library of Birmingham. CP B/660986 Birmingham Overseers' Minutes, Vol. 5, 28 April 1835.

of them paupers) had been within easy reach of the town and it is likely that patients still at Stafford were transferred here by 1837 or soon after.[57] But Mr Lewis found Birmingham just as demanding a customer as Mr Ricketts had done. We have already noted Duddeston's vain attempt to increase its charges in 1840. Thomas Lewis lost the battle, but had he been privy to the discussions between the overseers he might have pressed his case more keenly. They were struggling to find any viable alternative: Stafford was (presumably) too expensive in most cases, and Droitwich no longer met their increasingly strict criteria. The parish surgeon certainly found Mr Lewis's plea persuasive.

If Duddeston asks more, it is better to agree than to move them. It is impossible to find any asylum in the neighbourhood of Birmingham where the comforts of the inmates are better attended to than at Duddeston.[58]

Certainly the surviving regulations from Duddeston, dating from 1844 and reproduced in full by Parry-Jones, suggest an institution which was carefully and professionally run.[59] But by this date Birmingham workhouse had considerably improved the conditions for those pauper lunatics who stayed at home. Peter Sibree, who alone of the Congregationalist missionaries referred to mental illness, described in some detail the transfer of a young man from his home to Duddeston Asylum in January 1839. Sibree's account reflected the traumatic effect of such an event both on the patient and his family.

Attended an insane young man with his brother to the lunatic asylum, Duddeston, at the request of his parents, who were too much afflicted with his melancholy situation to go with him. I had frequently visited him in his lucid intervals, but, having last night risen against his brother and recently strangled him before help could be obtained, it was decided prudent by the medical men that he should be put under confinement. We had no difficulty getting him into the car and I endeavoured to soothe his mind by telling him there was mercy in every place and that he would find it where he was going. But when he got to the house and found himself in a place of confinement, he made a desperate attempt to escape and ran from the keeper's care to the door, where a struggle took place, and they both fell violently to the floor.[60]

---

57 Parry-Jones, *The Trade in Lunacy*, p. 190. Patients from workhouses across Warwickshire and Worcestershire were moved to Duddeston after 1835. L.D. Smith, 'Duddeston Hall and the "Trade in Lunacy", 1835–65', *Birmingham Historian*, 8, 1992, pp. 16–22.

58 Archives and Collections, Library of Birmingham. CP B/660987 Birmingham Overseers' Minutes, Vol. 6, 1 September 1840.

59 Parry-Jones, *The Trade in Lunacy*, pp. 190–2.

60 Archives and Collections, Library of Birmingham. CC1/71 Congregational Church Town Mission, 21 January 1839.

It remains to consider the case of the mentally ill patients detained in the workhouse itself. The poorhouse in Lichfield Street had probably housed people with disabilities of mind, as well as body, from the day it first opened its doors, and this would have included inmates with some form of senile dementia. Eighteenth and nineteenth-century categories of mental illness such as idiot, lunatic and imbecile did not generally allow for such a group to be separately distinguished or treated. The earliest detailed account of accommodation at the workhouse in 1816 lists a 'women's insane ward' with eleven beds, containing eleven women and four children, and also a room on the top floor, the women's garret, for the 'deranged'. The latter had seven beds and twelve inmates.[61] No separate provision for males is indicated, and there were no day rooms, separate from the dormitories. There had been little, if any, change to this situation by 1824, when the parish surgeons were requesting a swing and a shower bath 'for the use of the insane patients'.[62] The latter was not simply a matter of cleanliness; the shower bath, be it hot or cold, was a proven way of pacifying patients who were in an 'excited' state. The lack of separate day rooms was still an issue in 1832, despite numerous requests by overseers and surgeons alike. Sands Cox recommended:

> the propriety (if practicable) of a day room for lunatics. As you must be well aware of the great inconvenience, the whole being confined day and night in the sleeping apartments, more particularly during the winter months, when they cannot go out into the open air.[63]

The oppressive atmosphere of round-the-clock occupation was especially evident in the women's ward, which even lacked a water-closet.[64] By 1831 a ward had been appropriated for those termed 'dirty lunatics',[65] but in general the existing accommodation was unable to separate more severe cases from the rest. On one visit to the house in April 1832 the overseers found in the men's lunatic ward:

> a poor man who has been and still continues in a very violent state of derangement. He almost incessantly keeps talking night and day, using occasionally dreadful language.

---

61 Archives and Collections, Library of Birmingham. CP B/660983 Birmingham Overseers' Minutes, Vol. 2, 24 December 1816.

62 Archives and Collections, Library of Birmingham. CP B/660984 Birmingham Overseers' Minutes, Vol. 3, 4 May 1824.

63 Archives and Collections, Library of Birmingham. CP B/660985 Birmingham Overseers' Minutes, Vol. 4, 23 March 1830.

64 *Ibid.*, 21 December 1830

65 *Ibid.*, 22 February 1831.

It was probably the bad language, rather than the disruption, that led to the suggestion of a separate room for 'noisy lunatics', achieved by partitioning one section of the men's ward.[66] Help, however, was at hand. The guardians had recently purchased an adjacent property at 42 Steelhouse Lane, with a view to extending the workhouse, and this was to include new insane wards.

> This property happens to be close to the lunatic ward, where thirty persons sometimes are obliged to sleep. It is also close to the tramps' ward, which is also close and confined.[67]

James Plevins was paid £272 5s 10d for building the new wards in November 1833.[68] The extension included new day rooms and bedrooms for men and women, along with a 'spacious' yard for exercise, separate from the other inmates of the house. There was also a ward for 'refractory' cases. Not that expansion allowed every case to be concentrated here. In March 1835 there were twenty-eight males and eight females in the new wards, but still twenty-five women in the old building in three distinct apartments.[69] These patients were taken care of by a keeper and assistant keeper in the men's insane wards and by two nurses in the women's ward and in the women's 'insane attic'.[70] This considerable expense in the provision of new facilities and the employment of specialist carers contradicts Brundage's judgement that decent treatment of the ill in workhouses was usually the unintended 'result of inefficiency and corruption' and that the workhouses of the period were distinguished by 'the total absence of professional staff'.[71] Hodgkinson acknowledges that treatment of the mentally ill in Birmingham was 'more progressive than … the Poor Law Unions'.[72]

A report to the Warwick Quarter Sessions in 1836 listed 30 males and 37 females in the Birmingham insane ward, but this only included the more

---

66   *Ibid.*, 3 April 1832.

67   *Midland Representative & Birmingham Herald*, 19 November 1831.

68   Archives and Collections, Library of Birmingham. GP B/3/1/5 Birmingham Guardians' Cash Books, 2 November 1833.

69   Archives and Collections, Library of Birmingham. CP B/660986 Birmingham Overseers' Minutes, Vol. 5, 31 March 1835.

70   The Poor Law Commissioners' Report of 1842 notes that a nurse in the women's insane ward in Birmingham was paid an annual salary of £10, a remarkably large sum, which indicates that the nurse in question was treated as a professional person and was certainly not a pauper. *Ninth Annual Report of the Poor Law Commissioners, Appendix A: Reports of Assistant Commissioners, No. 2, Mr Power and Mr Weale's Report on Birmingham*, Parliamentary Papers, London, 1843, pp. 139–40.

71   A. Brundage, *The English Poor Laws, 1700–1930*, Basingstoke, 2002, p. 18.

72   R.G. Hodgkinson, *The Origins of the National Health Service: The Medical Services of the New Poor Law, 1834–71*, London, 1967, pp. 190–1.

severe cases. 'Many others, in a less deranged state', the report went on, 'are distributed among the ordinary paupers, and assisting in the occupations of the house.' Overall in the county 133 pauper patients were confined in workhouses, compared to 32 in county asylums, 14 in public hospitals and 31 in private madhouses. A further 36 were said to be 'not in confinement'.[73] Despite Section 45 of the 1834 Poor Law Amendment Act, the county's workhouses evidently continued to shoulder the greatest burden in the treatment of mental health. But, as Peter Bartlett has suggested in his national study of the Poor Law in the nineteenth century, this should not merely be interpreted as the result of parsimony on the part of the guardians and the overseers.[74] By the mid-1830s the parish authorities had, in fact, gone as far as it was possible on the current site to create separate space for the mentally ill. The building work undertaken in 1831 meant that the lunatic wards, alongside the new infirmary wards, were the only parts of the Lichfield Street complex not condemned as 'dilapidated' in the guardians' new Workhouse Committee report of July 1839. In this, at least, improvements had taken place and it proved that, in contrast to the experience described by Driver in Huddersfield, the treatment of the insane was 'an important local issue in its own right' in Birmingham.[75] It was, in fact, the rest of institution that was falling apart.

In 1844, under pressure from the Metropolitan Commission in Lunacy that was seeking to remove the mentally ill from the nation's workhouses, the Poor Law commissioners appointed the medical supervisor of Gloucester County Asylum, Samuel Hitch, to investigate the conditions in the insane ward of Birmingham workhouse.[76] Hitch, as an asylum doctor, was naturally unsympathetic towards the efforts of the workhouse staff, criticising the isolated location and poor furnishing of the facilities and the mixing of the sexes and those with differing degrees of mental illness. He was, however, unable to find any grounds on which to criticise the condition of the wards or the treatment of the inmates by the staff. Nevertheless, he recommended that several of the patients be transferred to an asylum, such as the one he worked in.[77] The drive by both sets of commissioners to remove the mentally ill to separate institutions culminated with the passage of the Lunatic Asylums Act in 1845. For an interim period Thomas Green was appointed as medical officer to the insane wards in

---

73 *Aris's Gazette*, 1 August 1836.

74 P. Bartlett, *The Poor Law of Lunacy: The Administration of Pauper Lunatics in Mid-Nineteenth-Century England*, London, 1999, pp. 51–5.

75 F. Driver, *Power and Pauperism: The Workhouse System 1834–1884*, Cambridge, 1993, p. 159.

76 *Report of the Metropolitan Commissioners in Lunacy to the Lord Chancellor*, London, 1844, pp. 98–9, 234–5.

77 National Archives, MH 12/13288/18261 S. Hitch, *Report of the Insane Poor Confined in the Workhouse Birmingham*, 31 October 1844.

Birmingham workhouse, which were improved still further on the basis of the recommendations of Hitch's report.[78] The Birmingham Borough Lunatic Asylum was eventually established in 1850, with Green as superintendent, with many of the workhouse inmates transferred there in the following months.[79] As Smith has recently demonstrated, however, the harmless, the elderly and those seen as incurable, continued to be cared for in the workhouses, long after the establishment of the Borough Lunatic Asylum.[80] Serious cases deserved specialist care. For everyone else, the workhouse was sufficient.

---

78   Archives and Collections, Library of Birmingham. GP B/2/1/4 Birmingham Guardians' minutes, 27 January 1845; GP B/2/1/5 Birmingham Guardians' minutes, 22 July 1845.

79   Archives and Collections, Library of Birmingham. BCC/1/AF/1/1/1 Birmingham Lunatic Asylum Committee minute book, 1845–1850.

80   L.D. Smith, '"A Sad Spectacle of Hopeless Mental Degradation": The Management of the Insane in West Midlands Workhouses, 1815–1860', in J. Reinarz and L. Schwarz (eds), *Medicine and the Workhouse*, Woodbridge, 2013, pp. 113–16. See also F. Hughes, 'The Cost of Caring: Expenditure on County Asylum Services in Shropshire and Middlesex 1850–1900', *Local Historian*, 45:4, 2015, pp. 312–14.

13

Putting the Poor to Work

In March 1819, the employment committee of the Birmingham guardians declared:

> We are not without hope that some more extended plan for the general employment of our poor may, at no very distant period, be accomplished. When that is the case we shall be happy to have the mills assigned to obscurity. In the meantime, we think they should be continued, though upon a smaller scale, as a memento that an establishment which professes to be a house of industry has at least one species of work performed within its walls.[1]

There could be no better demonstration of the modest, and regularly frustrated, ambitions of the body which ran the Birmingham Poor Law. Putting work into the workhouse was much easier said than done however. No proper manufactory could possibly be run in the way a workhouse was, with a constantly expanding and contracting number of workers, with a largely unskilled, unpaid (and uninterested) workforce, with employees ranging in age from eight to eighty and with little or no scope for capital investment. Any attempt to impose even the most modest kind of business model upon workhouse labour collided, sooner or later, with these stark realities. For the Birmingham workhouse to keep at least some of its charges in active employment required considerable ingenuity and adaptability. Nevertheless, the thrust of the 1601 Poor Law Act had always been to 'put the poor to work' and the expectation that this should be part of social provision survived well into the eighteenth century. Over the period covered by this study, a variety of means, internal and external, were found to employ those inmates who were capable of employment. Machinery was installed in the house, workshops erected or commandeered, or labour colonies set up, with or without the assistance of outside agencies. Rarely were individual measures

---

1   Archives and Collections, Library of Birmingham. GP B/2/1/2 Guardians' minutes, 23 March 1819.

long-term, reflecting as they did temporary economic circumstances, changing political times and differing ideas of how the workhouse should be organised and who should be in it.

As we have already seen, when Birmingham workhouse was first built (in 1734 or 1735), those paupers who were able to work were employed in making pack-thread. We cannot say for certain how long this occupation kept them busy, because little in the way of records survive for the period between the 1730s and the arrival of the first guardians in 1783. Related work was still being carried on in 1771, when the overseers were eager to inform potential customers that 'mop yarn has been manufactured in the workhouse for some years'.[2] The suggestion, put forward in 1767, at the time of negotiations over the cutting of the Birmingham Canal, that the workhouse poor might be employed 'in loading, unloading and weighing of coal' does not appear to have been pursued, however.[3] The proposal may well have been made chiefly to emphasise the social benefits of the Canal Bill and to win the ratepayers' support for it, rather than with any real intention to use the paupers for such demanding work.

In addition to the manufacture of pack-thread or mop yarn, the domestic side of workhouse life could always be relied upon to employ a number of the pauper women. A job description for the workhouse mistress, drawn up in 1775, showed that women were employed in the laundry, in changing the bed linen, cleaning the rooms and stairs and in making up the cloth into clothes and sheets.[4] The last of these activities might supply items for outside customers, but that would come much later. In addition, a few women were selected to work as nurses, either in the infirmary or in visiting the sick poor. By 1784, when the guardians first began to consider a long-term strategy for employment, it appears that little of it was going on in the house at all. A few men, it would appear, were being employed by the Street Commissioners to sweep the streets in the winter of 1786.[5] Since paupers should be employed, the guardians and the parish 'receive some certain advantage from this labour', necessary alterations would have to be made to the existing buildings to allow for it.[6] Such requests were still being made a year later, when mop-yarn and necessary utensils were being purchased.[7] None of these workers were paid, of course, but it was

---

2   *Aris's Gazette*, 23 December 1771.

3   *Aris's Gazette*, 2 February 1767.

4   *Aris's Gazette*, 30 January 1775.

5   Archives and Collections, Library of Birmingham. MS 2818/1/2 Street Commissioners' minutes, Vol. 2, 7 December 1786.

6   Archives and Collections, Library of Birmingham. GP B/2/1/1 Birmingham Guardians' minutes, 23 February 1784.

7   *Ibid.*, 29 March 1785.

widely accepted across the Poor Law system that some inducement or reward needed to be offered to encourage their efforts. Those helping in the kitchen might expect a larger allowance of food; those employed elsewhere in the house might receive tea or coffee, sweetened with sugar, luxuries denied the regular paupers. James Oram, himself a former guardian, referred to this practice in 1835, though he questioned how the workhouse was able to consume some 170 pounds of tea and 172 pounds of coffee in the course of a single year.[8] The difficulty for the authorities was how to avoid those perquisites being seen as an entitlement and how to prevent them being traded on the black-market, either within the workhouse or outside it. The enquiry into the running of the house under George Hinchcliffe in 1818 and the activities of Ann Martin (*see* chapter 8) which were consequently revealed showed how easy it was to spirit away workhouse stock and earn a considerable sum of money.

Subsequent to the 1818 scandal, the system of 'perquisites' had largely been abandoned by the mid-1830s, to be replaced by 'gratuities'. Again it must be stressed that these payments were by no means wages, or not for those permanently accommodated in the house, at least. What they represented, we may surmise, was an inducement to work and a reward for effort. It was a little cash that the residents might carry with them into the outside world. The 1834/35 guardians' accounts record a little under £280 paid in gratuities, predominantly to the 'nurses and others employed in the house'.[9] The rest was paid to the 'shoe-menders', the men at the mills (discussed below) and almost £10 given to those leaving the house. Nevertheless, these were trivial sums compared to the £3,575 paid in wages to the out-poor working on the roads, the sand-mine and in breaking stones. In addition, as the vestry clerk, William Brynner, told the Poor Law Commission in 1834, the able-bodied engaged in employment in the house were entitled to 'a larger portion of food than the aged and impotent'.[10] Whether this could also be considered an inducement to work, or a realistic appraisal of what a working man or woman needed in the way of extra calories, is a question open to debate.

The anonymous pamphleteer who complained about the state of the workhouse in 1782 had already spotted flaws in the system then in operation, though his solution, to build an entirely new workhouse elsewhere, would lie dormant for another seventy years. Want of proper employment in the house, he argued, meant that a number of men, women and children were sent out to work in the town's factories.

---

8   *Birmingham Journal*, 9 May 1835.

9   *Birmingham Advertiser*, 2 July 1835.

10   *Report from His Majesty's Commissioners for Inquiring into the Administration and Practical Operation of the Poor Laws*, Appendix G, Parliamentary Papers, XXIX, 1834, p. 289g.

But the opportunities and temptations to bad practice, which being so much at large gives them, has been found exceedingly injurious, particularly in the case of the girls and the women, where morals are almost sure to be corrupted, and who are thereby disqualified for domestic service.[11]

This argument, that factory work corrupted the morality of women, was one frequently deployed in the town and not only in relation to the poor. It is remarkable, in a place so reconciled to industrialisation and where whole families found jobs in the factories, how often this opinion was heard, though it was one, more often than not, drowned out by the sound of machinery. As for the women of the town previously employed in the manufactories, the pamphleteer went on, they had been put out of work by the cheap labour from the workhouse and had turned to prostitution instead. The guardians had always to bear in mind the impact of their measures upon the real economy in the world outside Lichfield Street. There was little point in widening employment opportunities for the inmates, when it only served to lengthen the queue for admission. Many of the guardians were also gunsmiths or brass founders themselves and while they wished to inculcate the moral and economic benefits of work for the inmates, they had no desire to put their own manufactories out of business.

By the mid-1790s the workhouse was also providing overnight accommodation for inmates who had managed to gain employment working in the town's factories. But in September 1795 the overseers pulled up this particular drawbridge.

Because of the abuse by paupers, those who go to work in the manufactories now must leave the house entirely. They are no longer to be boarded and lodged in the workhouse.[12]

Yet decisions taken in the vestry, both negative and positive, were rarely irrevocable. By 1814 the overseers and guardians were once again happy to provide overnight accommodation in the house, if the inmates were able to gain some form of employment during the day:

There are a number of stout men and young women in the workhouse, who have been admitted for want of employment and to prevent them resorting to an improper mode for a living. Inhabitants and manufacturers are requested to interest themselves in procuring employment for them. Their wages, while they remain in the house, will be

---

11   Anon., *The Present Situation of the Town of Birmingham Respecting its Poor, considered. With a Proposal for Building a New Workhouse*, Birmingham, 1782, pp. 5–6.

12   *Aris's Gazette*, 14 September 1795.

of little consequence, the object being to prevent their living in idleness at the expense of the parish.[13]

The Old Poor Law was at its most puzzling and most open to criticism in cases like this. Parochial funds were being used, not only to support the unemployed (as they were designed to do), but also to supplement low incomes, either by providing the wage-earners with accommodation in the house or paying them additional weekly relief. It was, in a sense, the urban equivalent of what came to be known as the Speenhamland System, after the Berkshire parish where the level of relief was tied to the price of bread, in order to prop up agricultural wages.[14] In a manufacturing town such as Birmingham, low wages might well result in cheaper products and the unscrupulous employer could thus undercut his competitors by using poor relief to top up the low wages he was paying.

The governor of the Aston parish workhouse, Thomas Lewis, had no doubt that this practice was widespread in Birmingham, when he spoke to the assistant commissioner in 1834:

> From his own knowledge he can state that what are called 'small masters' in the town, i.e. those employing one or two journeymen ... were in the constant habit of employing men who were receiving allowances from the parish, and that many in consequence were able to undersell other masters who were paying the full wages themselves; he could not say whether the practice was continued, but that the inducement to it was perhaps greater than ever, since the demand for cheap labour and cheap productions was never so general as in Birmingham at present.[15]

For the most part, however, work in the workhouse was designed to be carried on within its walls. Yet the problem of inside employment was perennially one of space in the increasingly crowded confines of the house. It may have been possible to make room for a few women to weave and sew clothes (and that was undoubtedly going on) but production on a more industrial scale required dedicated workshop space. Whenever the guardians recommended the purchase of additional property, as they did on a number of occasions between 1784 and 1788, full parish meetings invariably vetoed the idea as the

---

13   *Aris's Gazette*, 12 December 1814.

14   S. Fowler, *Workhouse: The People, the Places, the Life behind Doors*, Richmond, 2007, p. 208; S. King, *Poverty and Welfare in England 1700–1850: A Regional Perspective*, Manchester, 2000, p. 59.

15   *Report from His Majesty's Commissioners for Inquiring into the Administration and Practical Operation of the Poor Laws*, Appendix A, Parliamentary Papers, XXIX, 1834, p. 31a.

ratepayers always resisted any additional expenditure in this period.[16] By 1789, however, by a process of slow attrition, the guardians achieved their demands and in March of that year announced in the press that 'a spacious building is now erected for employing a considerable number of in-pensioners (about one hundred pair of hands)'. Tenders were invited by 25 March, 'when that building is complete'.[17] The intended workshops probably occupied two houses in Lichfield Street, which had recently been purchased by the overseers, adjacent to the existing workhouse. The solution the parish had in mind was to farm out the poor, that is, to pay an individual to employ all the available workhouse labour in the workshops in Lichfield Street. The employer would then profit from the sale of whatever items they made. The guardians were, at the same time, considering a similar scheme, thinly disguised as apprenticeship, as a means of finding work for many of the younger inmates. William Griffin made such an offer to the guardians in 1789, but they found the man 'so full of his own consequence, and his demands so high' that the proposal came to nothing.[18] In response to the invitation made on 9 March, two tenders were submitted for a cloth or clothing manufacture, one from George Robinson and a second from Josiah Robins, a worsted maker in Digbeth.[19] Robinson's scheme was designed to include children as well as adults.

The two proposals were made public in *Aris's Gazette* and a town meeting summoned to decide between them. The town meeting still played a major part in Birmingham's political life and was not yet so riven by factionalism as to be unmanageable and counter-productive. Recourse to such a meeting and the publication of the two tenders indicates the importance the authorities attached to the principle of 'farming out'. It was a new step for Birmingham and therefore required some measure of public consultation. 'Farming out', the privatisation of workhouse labour, was a system regularly used by parishes in the hope of reducing costs and most of the West Midlands parishes experimented with it at some point. One wave of 'farming out' occurred in the 1780s, when the parishes of Bromsgrove and Walsall adopted it and another in the mid-1820s, when authorities as far apart as Meriden, Kinver and Wednesbury advertised for such contracts. Sutton Coldfield attempted something similar and Aston too claimed to be farming out its paupers in 1803, though this probably

---

16   Archives and Collections, Library of Birmingham. GP B/2/1/1 Birmingham Guardians' minutes, 25 April 1785.

17   *Aris's Gazette*, 9 March 1789.

18   Archives and Collections, Library of Birmingham. GP B/2/1/1 Birmingham Guardians' minutes, 29 May 1789.

19   *Ibid.*, 21 October 1789.

applied to the outdoor, not the indoor, poor.[20] In September 1789, just as the workshop at Lichfield Street was completed, the Birmingham overseers visited Wolverhampton workhouse to assess how the system was operating there.[21] There were two principal methods of putting it into operation. One was to appeal for an external contractor to bid for the inmates' labour, supplying equipment and tools and supervising the workshop, in return for the entire profits made from their work. Birmingham ventured in this direction at the Asylum for the Infant Poor (as has been seen in chapter 11) and it was regularly tried at prisons. The other method was to make the workhouse master's salary dependent upon 'setting the poor to work', turning him into a workshop supervisor. A third system, less commonly seen, was to pay the master a per capita sum, reflecting the number of inmates. There was no obligation, under this last model, to set them working.

The two proposals were outlined in the *Gazette* and published (in the case of George Robinson) in 'Articles of Agreement', dated 17 June 1789.[22] The rival schemes provide a rare insight into how farming out could be made to work in practice, as well as two radically different models of workhouse labour. Under Josiah Robins' plan, the parish was to provide the workshop space, along with 'wheels, reels, cards etc.' and to supply additional shopping (workshop space), should it be needed. The inmates would work from 6 o'clock in the morning (7 o'clock in the winter) until 7 o'clock in the evening, with half an hour for breakfast and an hour for dinner. The early start meant that the workers would be required to sleep in separate wards from the other inmates. All the wages earned (the agreement does not specify what the rate of pay was to be) would be paid by the contractor into a central fund, which would be released partly to cover his expenses and partly for general parish purposes. The inmates themselves, so it seems, would see none of it. The problem, as with all workhouse labour, was finding sufficient numbers with knowledge or experience for the work to be undertaken. The contract with Robins allowed him to pay 'overlookers' as necessary (out of his profits) and to appoint others from the workhouse to train their less experienced colleagues. These trainers were to wear different clothes to distinguish them and sleep in separate apartments. The workforce could also be supplemented from outside the workhouse, for under this tough new regime anyone receiving out-relief and who was capable of work was required to enter the house or lose their allowance. It was an early example of what later came to be known as the 'workhouse test'. Finally, it was

---

20 *Abstract of answers and returns made pursuant to the Act of 43 George III relative to the expense and maintenance of the poor in England*, Parliamentary Papers, XIII, 1803–4, p. 534.

21 *Aris's Gazette*, 7 September 1789.

22 'Articles of Agreement', *Aris's Gazette*, 17 June 1789.

up to the contractor to identify what skills his new workforce possessed and to find traders who were willing to pay for what was made. The contract itemised the trades in some detail and made it clear that the inmates were only to be engaged in part of the production process, which would then be completed in the town's clothing workshops:

> viz … the shopkeepers for the making of sale shirts, quilting etc; … thread-makers for flax-spinning; … bag or wick yarn-makers for hurd-spinning; … worsted-makers for jersey-spinning; … brush-makers for wool-spinning; …pattern tye-makers for stiching; and … such other of the manufacturers who shall choose to have any part of their work done at the workhouse.

Such was the arrangement proposed by Josiah Robins. It would run initially for twelve months and then (all being well) indefinitely.[23] The list of manufacturing processes, it has to be said, was remarkably, if not absurdly, optimistic and would require a considerable amount of technical expertise and equipment.

George Robinson's plan envisaged that 'adult' paupers would be paid one shilling a week and children under eight years sixpence a week. There was also to be an initial three-month period without pay. This, we may guess, was the 'sweetener' to get the proposal a favourable hearing. But the longest clause and the one upon which the arrangement stood or fell, was the impact of 'setting the poor to work' upon the rates. If the number of levies each year could be reduced to eight, then all the tools and implements in the manufactory would become the property of the contractor. And for as long as the levies were reduced to six collections each year, George Robinson was to be paid £200 per annum.[24] No more explicit link between the cost of poor relief and the pockets of the ratepayers could possibly have been made.

Put to a vote at a town meeting in October 1789, however, George Robinson's proposal was rejected and that of Josiah Robins, which the overseers recommended, was almost unanimously approved.[25] The decision was no doubt influenced by the fact that Robinson was asking for a £500 advance before commencing operations, whilst Robins was not. We do not know, of course, how even-handedly the two plans were presented to that meeting, or whether Robinson's careful, though complicated, link between levies and labour was fully fleshed out. Even then, formal agreement did not prevent a furious debate in the local press over the relative merits and costs of the two schemes.[26]

---

23   *Aris's Gazette*, 26 October 1789.

24   *Ibid.*

25   *Aris's Gazette*, 2 November 1789.

26   *Aris's Gazette*, 9, 16 and 23 November 1789.

A year later, the writer and bookseller, William Hutton, was still fuming at the overseers' support for Josiah Robins over George Robinson.[27] For Hutton, Robinson's rejection had been as much about sectarianism as cost. 'No man,' an overseer had told him, 'would be suffered to conduct parochial business who did not believe in the Trinity'. Needless to say, there is no external evidence to suggest that Robinson's Unitarian beliefs were a factor, though we might bear in mind that this was less than a year before the Church and King Riots in the town (of July 1791) targeted Unitarian dissidents such as Joseph Priestley and William Hutton himself.[28] That accusation of high-handed Anglicanism could certainly not have been made a generation later, when the complaint was of the undue dominance of the Unitarians in public affairs.

There is no indication in the records of how long Josiah Robins remained in charge of fabric production, though it is clear that clothing continued to be made at Lichfield Street for some years. In 1796 Eden describes the presence of 'various manufactures' in the house, 'chiefly weaving, spinning, wool-combing and flax-dressing'.[29] By the middle of the 1790s, however, it is clear that all was not well. The rules drawn up in 1789 had one, probably fatal, flaw in them. Since the paupers were not paid personally for their labour, there was little inducement for them to work productively, only the threat of punishment if they did not. The contract thus had a stick, but it did not have a carrot. In addition, as the Birmingham economy ground to a halt under the impact of recession and the war with France, the market for new clothes contracted. By the end of 1792 the workhouse paupers had been redirected to more tried-and-trusted trades. A notice from November of that year advertised 'any quantity of wick-yarn', together with 'a regular supply of pounded ironstone'.[30] Stone-breaking was, by the nineteenth century, a regular activity in workhouse yards, usually to provide gravel for roads. This early and solitary reference to the breaking of ironstone reflects the fact that the material was valuable in a town so dependent on the metal trades. By 1796 a newly appointed manufacturing committee was wrestling with the consequences, as well as endeavouring to isolate 'some of the most refractory and idle from those who are more governable'.[31] Had the workhouse manufactory been a real business, it would undoubtedly have gone to the wall in the 1790s, as many others in the real

27   *Swinney's Birmingham Chronicle*, 18 November 1790.

28   J. Atherton, 'Rioting, Dissent and the Church in Late Eighteenth-Century Britain: The Priestley Riots of 1791', unpublished PhD thesis, Leicester, 2012.

29   F.M. Eden, *The State of the Poor*, Vol. III, London, 1797, p. 737.

30   *Aris's Gazette*, 19 November 1792.

31   Archives and Collections, Library of Birmingham. GP B/2/1/1 Birmingham Guardians' minutes, 28 June 1796.

economy certainly did, but the guardians could always play the moral card, when the economic one was trumped:

> Those who are able to work are employed in the manufactories of the house, and though no great profit may immediately result from articles manufactured, yet its effects are ultimately advantageous in respect both to the order of the house and the decrease of the number of poor; their weekly average has amounted to 465.[32]

A detailed breakdown of workhouse costs (from August 1795 to August 1796) appended to this report from the employment committee made it clear that the balance sheet was even worse than the committee admitted, however. The largest single item in the debit column was from the manufactory, which had cost a penny under £598 to run in that single year alone, while the sale of produce made by the paupers amounted to only £235. It was at this point that the superintendent of the manufactory, Andrew Inglis, resigned and we can well understand why.[33] Ambiguous as the language of the committee is in praising 'the order of the house', it shows that the guardians had, at last, grasped the reality of the situation. Workhouse labour would probably never make a profit, but if it discouraged idle applications for relief, or reminded inmates that their rights also carried responsibilities, it was not entirely useless. But if one wanted to see truly productive labour, one needed to visit the Asylum for the Infant Poor. Like it or not, child labour was far more lucrative. The Poor Law accounts for 1824/25 show that workhouse labour produced income of £68, compared to £427 from the Asylum.[34] What made the situation worse was that the recession of the mid-1790s had added considerably to the ranks of the unemployed and increased the numbers of able-bodied in the house, just at a time when it was least equipped to deal with them. It was with a sense of desperation that the parish looked for potential employers to find work for 'a number of useful hands, who from the scarcity of employment and the severity of the last winter are in the workhouse or in relief'.[35] Two months later the overseers were advertising for 'a person to superintend the work of the healthy poor ... that has been used to spinning, weaving and such business'.[36] This allusion to mainly female occupations reflected an unusual imbalance in the numbers of inmates at this time. In September 1795 the workhouse contained

---

32   Archives and Collections, Library of Birmingham. GP B/2/1/1 Birmingham Guardians' minutes, 30 August 1796.

33   *Ibid.*, 30 November 1796.

34   *Birmingham Journal*, 18 June 1825.

35   *Aris's Gazette*, 22 June 1795.

36   *Aris's Gazette*, 31 August 1795.

219 women, 112 children and only 72 men.[37] It is unlikely that unemployment was adversely affecting women in these years, more likely that many of the female inmates were single mothers with young children.

There was one more attempt to farm out the workhouse paupers along the lines outlined above. This came in 1803, when the governor, George Hinchcliffe, entered into an agreement with the guardians to set the poor to work and the initial seven-year contract was renewed up to 1817. The unpleasant fall-out from this arrangement was described in chapter 6, but it was certainly beneficial to Mr Hinchcliffe himself, at least up to the moment when he was summarily dismissed. His contract, initially set at £100 per annum, increased by £10 a year and by 1817 it had reached £230 (this was in addition to his annual salary). As previously stated, in 1803–4 the pauper labour at this time was said to include 'picking of oakum, carding and spinning wool, spinning jersey and flax, making stocking yarn, weaving hurden and linseys'.[38] One little workshop, however, continued to operate productively throughout much of this period, independent of the sewing and weaving shops. Both inmates and outworkers were always in need of shoes and here was a task that could be performed relatively easily in-house. Shoemaking had been carried on in the workhouse almost as far back as records survive and as early as 1740 payments are recorded for leather and 'leather bodies'.[39] The man supplying the leather, a Mr Rann, was also supplying the meat and was responsible for looking after the workhouse cows. Lack of decent footwear (which might mean stockings as well as shoes) was probably the single most common reason for being unable to work and parish overseers spent money providing the out-poor with shoes. In 1774, for example, the overseers at Edgbaston purchased or mended twenty-nine pairs of shoes or clogs.[40] If shoes could be made cheaply in-house, it would drive down costs markedly. The making and mending was mostly done by boys under adult instruction and supervision. In 1817 Samuel Bailey was being paid 24s a week to train up the boys.[41] A trainer's services would always be required, since the lads would move on to apprenticeships elsewhere once the overseers found them a suitable employer and new recruits would arrive to replace them. At some point after 1817, however, the shoe shop closed, probably because it

37   *Aris's Gazette*, 14 September 1795.

38   *Abstract of answers and returns made pursuant to the Act of 43 George III relative to the expense and maintenance of the poor in England*, Parliamentary Papers, XIII, 1803–4, p. 257.

39   Archives and Collections, Library of Birmingham. CP B/380973 Accounts of the Birmingham Workhouse and Record of Out-Relief to the Poor, 1739–48.

40   Archives and Collections, Library of Birmingham. CP ED/661512 Edgbaston Overseers' accounts, Vol. 4.

41   Archives and Collections, Library of Birmingham. GP/B/2/1/2 Birmingham Guardians' minutes, 28 October 1817.

was having an adverse effect on the town's shoemakers. It was, after all, one of the duties of the parish to advance the cause of real employment and putting cobblers out of work was not a good indication of this. For a small business, a contract to supply the workhouse could mean the difference between survival and redundancy and so the guardians vowed to buy shoes 'from the little makers in the town'.[42] The boys would have to be found other work to do. The result of this was entirely predictable. As the overseers lamented in 1821:

> The young persons in the house are either unemployed at all, and thus contracting habits of idleness, or employed in labour that is unproductive of any benefit to the parish.[43]

And so the workhouse lads, never more than a dozen or so, were back mending (rather than making) shoes for the inmates and for the children in the Asylum and repairing others worn down by the sand wheelers at Key Hill. It was not the most exciting of tasks, but it was, without doubt, a trade. It might even lead to a job.

In 1818, after the departure of George Hinchcliffe, Birmingham workhouse underwent a sea-change, one which affected indoor employment as well as living conditions. But before investigating these changes it is worth reflecting on the position reached thus far. Employment in the house had swung between profit and loss, but had generally involved most of the women (those not employed as nurses, ward-keepers or cleaners) in cloth making of some kind. The men, more often than not, had been offered work outside the workhouse. In 1818, with the contract with George Hinchcliffe at an end, the women were knitting stockings and mending the clothes of inmates, while the men and boys (always more difficult to employ) were said to be picking oakum or wool.[44] Oakum was an ever-present ingredient of workhouse life across the country. Ship and boat makers, as well as builders, were in constant need of what they called 'caulking' to seal the gaps between wood and brick and the best form of caulking proved to be oakum: tarred rope which had been teased out and untwisted by the well-worn fingers of paupers and prisoners.[45] Oakum could be (and was) sold, but the heaps of untangled thread hardly made a fortune. Oakum-picking was far more important as a means of giving idle

---

42 Archives and Collections, Library of Birmingham. GP B/2/1/2 Birmingham Guardians' minutes, 2 June 1818.

43 Archives and Collections, Library of Birmingham. CP B/660983 Overseers' minutes, Vol. 2, 30 August 1821.

44 Archives and Collections, Library of Birmingham. GP B/2/1/2 Birmingham Guardians' minutes, 2 June 1818.

45 A. Brundage, *The English Poor Laws, 1700–1930*, Basingstoke, 2002, pp. 80–1.

hands something to do. Money for old rope, they called it. And here was a real irony: the inmates of Birmingham workhouse, who had begun their labour in the 1740s by twisting string into pack-thread, were now, sixty years later, untwisting rope into string.

Oakum-picking looks like the meaningless drudgery so beloved of the Poor Law Board after the 1834 Amendment Act, but Birmingham had not quite gone that far, or at least not yet. Two rather more encouraging ideas also emerged in the course of all those heated discussions following the sacking of Mr Hinchcliffe. The first of these proposals, for the manufacture of cloth from flax, was placed before the guardians in June 1818. The preparation of hemp or flax for cloth-making was already being tried in a few houses of industry. James Lee (in 1810) and Samuel Hill, in partnership with William Bundy (in 1817), had patented machines which broke down the plant to produce fibres. Both devices were portable and, as John Claudius Loudon noted in his *Encyclopaedia of Agriculture*, Messrs Hill and Bundy's device was 'well calculated for parish workhouses'.[46] The minutes do not tell us which of the two machines the guardians plumped for, however. It took two years to get the operation off the ground, but was a rare example of the guardians thinking holistically. Flax could be grown on the parish land at Birmingham Heath, dew-rotted in the fields and then delivered to the workhouse, where it was turned by the inmates, first into fibre and then into linen. The first two acres of flax were harvested in the autumn of 1819[47] and small-scale production was underway in the house by the following spring.[48] One man (an experienced worker, not an inmate) did the breaking and twelve girls the spinning. Weavers were then added to the production line and the workhouse had its own cloth, home-grown, home-spun and home-woven. The first year of the experiment produced no less than 1,100 yards of linen, enough to supply the cloth and bed ticking for the whole house.[49] All this in spite of the fact that the little cottage industry had no dedicated workspace. Work went on in two dark and confined rooms and the weavers (mostly elderly women) were unable to keep up with the spinners. But so successful had the experiment become that the guardians were persuaded to part with enough cash for a new building in the workhouse yard to accommodate it.[50] By 1822 fourteen women and six men were breaking, swingling (beating flax to extract the fibres), spinning and weaving for all they

---

46   J.C. Loudon, *An Encyclopaedia of Agriculture*, London, 1825, p. 850.

47   Archives and Collections, Library of Birmingham. GP B/2/1/2 Birmingham Guardians' minutes, 12 October 1819.

48   *Ibid.*, 25 April 1820.

49   *Ibid.*, 17 April 1821.

50   *Ibid.*, 3 July 1821.

were worth and the maximum acreage devoted to flax was increased to five acres.[51] Additional workers were required, of course, for weeding and pulling the flax out on the Heath. Yet for all these encouraging signs, flax production was eventually consigned to that long list of discontinued workhouse projects. No explanation was given for this.

One more new idea also emerged in the course of 1818: corn-milling; it came to fruition more quickly than most and, in workhouse terms, had remarkable longevity. This new mode of employment was announced in the kind of negative language in which workhouse labour was usually described:

> Your Committee being anxious to find employment for the many able bodied men who apply for Parochial Relief under pretence of inability to obtain work have carried into operation a plan submitted to them for effecting that object by the erection of Hand Mills for grinding wheat, six of which are put up in a convenient situation near the Workhouse and will be ready to go into operation in about six or seven days – it is intended to pay the men wages in proportion to the quantity of flour made at such a rate that by a hard day's labour each man may earn 2/-. And your Committee have good grounds for believing that most of those for whom this employment is intended will find other means of obtaining subsistence more agreeable to themselves.[52]

Half a dozen steel crank-mills were installed in a building, rented for the purpose, close to the rear of the workhouse in Steelhouse Lane in November 1818 and those applying for outdoor relief were despatched thither. The mills were not tread-mills of the sort being introduced into county gaols in this period (those at Warwick and Stafford were installed in 1823[53]), but the kind that milled grain by hand, rather than foot, power. Although it is nowhere stated as such, it was important to maintain the distinction between a device meant to stimulate hard work and one for hard labour. Yet for both the productiveness of the mill was always a secondary consideration. The daily grind could earn an employee around two shillings a week, enough to keep a family off the bread-line, but not sufficient to retain workers indefinitely. Wages were paid at the end of each day and the men were 'at liberty to leave whenever they think proper.'[54] Many did exactly that. Of the 110 men sent to the mills between

---

51   *Ibid.*, 25 June 1822.

52   *Ibid.*, 27 October 1818.

53   *Gaols: reports from magistrates and keepers under 4 George IV c. 64, called the Gaols Act*, Parliamentary Papers, XIX, 1824, pp. 202, 228.

54   *Aris's Gazette*, 29 May 1819.

November and December 1818 only 24 were still there in January 1819.[55] Yet the mill committee did not need to be quite so negative. For one thing, the flour produced went to the workhouse to be baked into bread and anything which reduced the institution's enormous food bill could only be a good thing. In financial terms alone, setting aside the moral case for 'putting the poor to work', the scheme can be judged successful. On the debit side stood the wages paid to men working the mills, which amounted to £422 in 1819/20. And to this we must also add the annual rent of the mill premises, which was £25.[56] The same accounts declare a profit of £481 from the sale of 'flour, bran, sharps etc.' The removal of flour or bread from the list of workhouse purchases must also be borne in mind. Three years later, the wages paid to men grinding wheat had fallen to £350 as the general economy began to recover and the number seeking out-relief had dropped.[57] The sale of unwanted 'bran, sharps etc.' was also down to £79. No longer, it seems, was there surplus flour to dispose of.

We know quite a lot about the milling process, because the newly created mill committee had to address serious questions about the quality of the flour, compared to that milled in the town's steam mills and to that produced by the Birmingham Flour & Bread Co., which was already supplying cheap bread from its two mills to charitable institutions. There were also doubts whether the workhouse dough would rise as effectively as bread made with stone-ground flour. Both suspicions proved to be ill-founded. The corn was ground first by hand in the newly purchased steel hand-mills and then a second time (by an experienced miller) using mill stones. This appeared to do the trick and the bread rose accordingly.[58] Whether the need for secondary milling destroyed the point of the whole exercise was not a question the guardians cared to address. In the first four months of the trial the paupers milled a total of 520 bags of wheat, which in turn filled 285 sacks of flour (of 260 pounds each) for the house, enough for all its bread and for the Asylum too. The five tons of bran generated at the same time were sold.[59] Since the workhouse and the Asylum needed only about eighteen sacks of flour a week, the mills were generating quite enough for all concerned and there was even enough flour, at

55 Archives and Collections, Library of Birmingham. GP B/2/1/2 Birmingham Guardians' minutes, 19 January 1819.

56 Archives and Collections, Library of Birmingham. 89104A Birmingham Scrapbook 3, Birmingham Workhouse Accounts, March 1819–April 1820, p. 360.

57 Ibid., 1822–23, p. 357.

58 Archives and Collections, Library of Birmingham. GP B/2/1/2 Birmingham Guardians' minutes, 19 January 1819.

59 Ibid., 23 March 1819.

times, to supply to the out-poor.[60] All this despite the fact that the workhouse and Asylum devoured huge quantities of bread each week. The estimate in 1819 was of a weekly consumption of almost 6,500 pounds, though this surely includes bread supplied as part of out-relief. Bread was certainly needed: the new dietary introduced in 1838 shows that each pauper in the house consumed 5 lbs 4 oz of bread each week, the equivalent of about three of today's large sliced loaves.[61] The process was not without its overheads, of course. The two mill stones cost £10, an 'overlooker' was paid a pound a week and the individual mills themselves cost around £6 each. The figure quoted by *Aris* in June 1819 was that set-up costs (for mills, dressing machines, sacks, mill-stones, scales and fixtures) amounted to £161 18s.[62] The governor of the house still had to buy barm (the foam produced on the surface of beer during brewing) and salt and the baker was paid one shilling a week.[63] The guardians were quick to underline that the baker himself had been a claimant and therefore his wages must be set against the saving in out-relief for him and his family.[64] It was also true that the men employed on the mills were entitled to higher rations than their colleagues. Indeed, it was said at a guardians' quarterly meeting in January 1839 that the cost of maintaining them was twice that of the other inmates and that, by making life in the workhouse more tolerable, it failed to induce them to leave.[65] But once the mill wheels were first set in motion on 24 November 1818, they continued to turn for thirty years or more. What made the operation particularly attractive was that the corn, or at least some of it, could also be grown on the parish land on Birmingham Heath. Over eight acres had been sown with wheat in 1822.[66]

It ought to be emphasised, however, that only a small fraction of the workhouse inmates were ever actually working and many of the aged, infirm or sick were quite incapable of toiling for their supper. To take a typical example from April 1823, there was an average of 459 paupers, men and women, in the house in this month. Of these, 14 men (including the overlooker) were milling, 5 men and 8 women were employed in the flax room, 12 'boys' were making

---

60   Archives and Collections, Library of Birmingham. CP B/660985 Overseers' minutes, Vol. 4, 20 November 1833.

61   Archives and Collections, Library of Birmingham. GP B/2/1/4 Birmingham Guardians' minutes, 17 October 1838.

62   *Aris's Gazette*, 28 June 1819.

63   Archives and Collections, Library of Birmingham. GP B/2/1/2 Birmingham Guardians' minutes, 23 March 1819.

64   *Aris's Gazette*, 28 June 1819.

65   *Aris's Gazette*, 21 January 1839.

66   Archives and Collections, Library of Birmingham. GP B/2/1/2 Birmingham Guardians' minutes, 25 June 1822.

and mending shoes, 'ten of the Poor from the House' worked at the sand mill (with a further 16 or 17 of the 'Out Poor' wheeling the sand to the canal), 5 inmates more were based at the farm, digging and forking, and 20 to 25 had been sent out to work in the town's manufactories. Thus, at most, only 70 or so of the male inmates were able-bodied enough for work.[67] In April 1832, out of 471 in the house, only 8 men were going out to work and 4 or 5 men and boys were repairing shoes.[68] Some others, mainly women, were needed for domestic work, nursing or as ward-keepers, but this was still a proportionally small number. The 1841 workhouse regulations sought to keep at least some of the elderly inmates busy by requiring them to superintend and manage their younger companions.[69]

If able-bodied paupers were thin on the ground, reinforcements arrived daily in the shape of the casual poor, or what the minutes called trampers or tramps. These were far from modest numbers. In the first quarter of 1832 a total of 1,952 tramps received a night's accommodation, an average of some twenty-one each night.[70] The tramps were given, on application, bed and board at the house (which included supper and breakfast), but for these meals they were required to do a couple of hours' work on the mills in the morning.[71] For this to be effective, however, it was necessary to bring the mills into the house and this happened at the end of 1829, when the premises currently being rented were given up.[72] The move had the added advantage of putting a stop to the mysterious disappearance of bags of flour into the town. By 1836, not only were the mills making a small profit, they also continued to be a deterrent on applications for relief and, as the house committee proudly stated: 'In no case ... have the advantages been more evident than in the diminution of the number of tramps.'[73] But for those who still found the lure of the workhouse irresistible, seven new steel mills were installed in December 1837 to keep them busy.[74] The Aston guardians also installed corn mills in the union workhouse

67   *Ibid.*, 8 April 1823.

68   *Midland Representative & Birmingham Herald*, 7 April 1832.

69   Archives and Collections, Library of Birmingham. 64250 BCOL 41.11 *Rules and Regulations of the Guardians of the Poor of the Parish of Birmingham*, Vol. 2, Birmingham, 1841, p. 24.

70   *Midland Representative & Birmingham Herald*, 7 April 1832.

71   Archives and Collections, Library of Birmingham. GP B/2/1/3 Birmingham Guardians' minutes, 27 July 1830.

72   *Ibid.*, 26 January 1830.

73   *Ibid.*, 24 February 1836.

74   Archives and Collections, Library of Birmingham. CP B/660986 Overseers' minutes, Vol. 5, 19 December 1837.

at Erdington in February 1838.[75] The allegation was made at the time, refuted by the Aston guardians, that this kind of mill was 'more laborious than the treadmill in the county jail.' Hand-mills had also been used at Sutton Coldfield parish workhouse for some years before that.[76]

Finally, there is also outdoor employment to consider. No cash books survive for the ten years between 1818 and 1828, but once they resume we can get a good idea of how this external labour was organised. The farm at Key Hill and the sand mine are discussed elsewhere in this book, but we need to add them to the list. Effectively they operated as an early form of labour colony, employing men in manual labour and paying them an (almost living) wage. From the late 1820s until 1835 men were employed as sand wheelers, digging out sand from the quarry at Key Hill and taking it to the sand wharf on the Birmingham Canal. Others were occupied nearby, breaking stones or (from 1833 to 1835) in the gravel mine. By 1838, however, after the sale of Key Hill, stone-breaking represented the sole surviving employment for the out-poor. The resulting gravel was sold to the Street Commissioners for the surfacing of roads.[77]

Together the sale of sand, gravel and broken stone contributed £1,852 to Birmingham's Poor Law income for the year ending March 1834.[78] More significantly, the transfer of men to the labour colonies at Key Hill removed all able-bodied males from the workhouse entirely. By October 1836 the guardians were told at their quarterly meeting that only eight able-bodied persons (two male and six female) remained in the house as servants.[79]

If work at Key Hill represented a semi-permanent method of employing the out-poor and able-bodied males, other means were found to meet temporary spikes in unemployment. Inevitably such work required a partnership with other bodies. In 1816, during the post-Waterloo recession, when trade was said to be 'depressed' and applications for relief 'increasing to an alarming degree', the overseers worked in tandem with the Street Commissioners to find work for as many as 200 or 300 of the 'labouring classes'.[80] In December 1816 the *Gazette* reported that the work involved paving, carting gravel, digging culverts, 'or work of a similar description'.[81] Single men received a weekly wage

75   Archives and Collections, Library of Birmingham. GP AS/2/1/1 Aston Guardians' minutes, 20 June 1838.

76   Sutton Coldfield Reference Library. Sutton Coldfield Select Vestry Minutes 1819–33, 27 November 1829, p. 349

77   *Aris's Gazette*, 25 June 1838.

78   *Birmingham Journal*, 5 July 1834.

79   *Birmingham Journal*, 15 October 1836.

80   Archives and Collections, Library of Birmingham. MS 2818/1/4 Street Commissioners' Minutes, Vol. 4, 9 September 1816.

81   *Aris's Gazette*, 2 December 1816.

of six shillings, seven shillings for a married man 'and an additional sum for his wife and each child'. Similarly, in an imaginative example of a private-public partnership, in 1817 a band of men was recruited from the workhouse to lower a hill 'behind Mr Shakespeare's glass house' on Birmingham Heath. For this task (estimated at £35) the parish put up £7 and the remainder was paid by Mr Shakespeare himself.[82] This kind of arrangement had the combined benefit of discharging a number of able-bodied men from the house, freeing up beds and providing them with six to eight weeks' paid work. In 1827 some men were switched from sand-wheeling to 'lower the hill on the Bristol Road'.[83] At times of high unemployment, when Birmingham's economic output fell, the condition of its roads appears to have risen.

The surviving cash books also describe infrastructure work being undertaken in the 1830s, as the guardians sought to keep able-bodied men at work outside the workhouse. In June 1833 some men were employed as street sweepers[84]; by October of that year others were put to work 'lowering Albion Street'.[85] In the following year, the unemployed men were engaged at the road works in Bell Barn Road,[86] in sweeping the streets[87] and later in the same year on what was called 'the old parish garden'.[88] Finally, as Key Hill sand mine was about to make way for Key Hill Cemetery, men were employed digging and levelling at the new burial ground in preparation for its official opening. The formation of labour colonies such as this did not go unchallenged. The men deployed on the Bristol Road were said to have been earning nine or ten shillings a week, with an additional one shilling for each child not yet able to earn. It was not enough in the eyes of two labourers, who went on strike and physically threatened one of the guardians.[89] In general, though, it was not the money alone, nor the back-breaking work, which engendered confrontation, but the stigma of the labour colony itself. To the Birmingham reformers of the early 1830s the sand-mine became a symbol of a wider malaise in British society, its political and economic stagnation, and it revealed an unacceptable tightening in the operation of the Local Act. As the Tory *Monthly Argus* asked in October 1832:

---

82 Archives and Collections, Library of Birmingham. CP B/660983 Overseers' Minutes Vol. 2, 15 August 1817.

83 *Birmingham Journal*, 15 May 1827.

84 Archives and Collections, Library of Birmingham. GP B/3/1/5 Birmingham Guardians' cash books, 12 June 1833.

85 *Ibid.*, 28 October 1833.

86 *Ibid.*, 30 June 1834.

87 *Birmingham Journal*, 5 July 1834.

88 Archives and Collections, Library of Birmingham. GP B/3/1/5 Birmingham Guardians' cash books, 24 November 1834.

89 *Birmingham Journal*, 5 May 1827.

The stone-breaking slaves at Walmer Lane, Broad Street and Gas Street cannot earn, winter and summer, more than six shillings a week. Can a man, his wife and six children – the average of the stone-breaking families – exist upon this small pittance?[90]

At the heart of the debate was a simple question: what level of pay was high enough to avoid the charge of 'white slavery', but low enough to encourage the men to look for more permanent paid work elsewhere?

As with the sand at the wharf, stone could accumulate quicker than the parish could find a use or a buyer for it. In 1837 the overseer of the work – appropriately called Mr Stone – complained of a surplus and urged the overseers:

...to send as few men as possible to break stones, and particularly to refuse employment to such men, who, for several years past are in the habit of working for the parish and do not try to obtain work elsewhere.[91]

Mr Stone repeated his request nine months later, informing the committee that he had paid no less than £40 to the stone breakers the previous week.[92] At times of high unemployment, which the late 1830s undoubtedly were, even the artificially low wages offered by the parish were better than none at all. This, overall, was probably as much as the parish could achieve with its motley crew of workers. Some perfectly good ideas had come and gone, but the link between relief and labour had never been entirely severed. By the 1830s, in addition to outdoor labour, the cash books show that workhouse inmates were continually employed either as nurses, at the mills or in making shoes. By then the guardians had also recognised that giving such workers financial 'gratuities' via the workhouse master helped to keep the wheels turning. There was now a carrot as well as a stick.

Even though C.P. Villiers offered his judgement in 1834 on the Birmingham workhouse that 'it can hardly be said to offer any very striking contrast to the system of management in other places', this study of the Birmingham workhouse has demonstrated that, with capable management, the Old Poor Law could adapt to the needs of the rapidly industrialising nation.[93] It struggled, as all welfare systems have done, with the ethical, the financial and

---

90   *Monthly Argus & Public Censor*, October 1832, p. 332.

91   Archives and Collections, Library of Birmingham. CP B/660986 Overseers' Minutes, Vol. 5, 25 August 1837.

92   *Ibid.*, 22 May 1838.

93   *Report for His Majesty's Commissioners for Inquiring into the Administration and Practical Operation of the Poor Laws*, Appendix A, Parliamentary Papers, XXIX, 1834, p. 7a.

the practical issues of relieving the distress of the poor whilst preventing the emergence of a dependency culture among them. That it proved so innovative in its approaches to putting the poor to work, providing an asylum for the education of the infant poor, its medical services and treatment of the mentally ill, is testament to the emerging principles of public service and evangelical duties among the overseers, guardians and employees of the Birmingham workhouse. It is to be regretted that the experience of Birmingham workhouse across a century was so undervalued by Villiers and that only the example of the management of the Asylum for the Infant Poor was praised, as, in many ways, the work of the Birmingham workhouse before 1834 was as responsive to the changing economic and social circumstances of the city as the new Poor Law was monolithic and inflexible.

Afterword

Ian Cawood

In his excellent recent biography of C.P. Villiers, the young Assistant Commissioner sent to gather information on the administration of Birmingham and Warwickshire's workhouses in 1832, Roger Swift notes Villiers' highly positive impression of the administration of the Birmingham workhouse and its ancillary establishments. But Swift concludes that this did not prevent Villiers from questioning the efficacy of the Old Poor Law even here. Villiers was concerned that the subsidising of labourers' wages with contributions from the poor rates encouraged improvidence, fecklessness and promiscuity as the workers were thus guaranteed an income no matter how hard they worked and provided with the means for subsistence even in times of illness or unemployment, thus rendering thrift unnecessary. Perhaps worst of all, this action actually enabled employers to reduce wages, knowing that the poor rate payers would supply the necessary supplement to prevent militancy or staff leaving in search of better wages. By providing the effective and integrated services which, as this book demonstrates, may have almost constituted a 'welfare state in miniature'[1] before 1834, Birmingham was, in Villiers' eyes at least, only succeeding in encouraging further pauperism and dependency among the lower orders, as well as placing unreasonable burdens on those who had worked hard to achieve a level of wealth at which they then became financially responsible for the maintenance of these services.[2] This was, of course, music to the ears of those such as Nassau Senior and Edwin Chadwick who sought to rein in state and local expenditure, impose the

---

1   M. Blaug, 'The Poor Law Report Re-examined', *Journal of Economic History*, 24:2, 1964, p. 229.

2   R. Swift, *Charles Pelham Villiers: Aristocratic Victorian Radical,* London, 2017, pp. 17–23.

principle of 'less eligibility' and end outdoor relief of the able-bodied.[3] Those far-sighted innovations in Birmingham, which even Villiers admitted were beneficial to 'the moral feeling of the working classes' such as the Asylum for the Infant Poor and the General Dispensary, were not given significant attention in the subsequent Report of the Royal Commission, nor in the clauses of the Poor Law Amendment Act, passed in August 1834. The agenda of the stern Benthamites would not permit such nuance and the New Poor Law system notoriously provided a minimal service in both child care and health provision, only supplemented by charitable institutions and the commitment and hard work of individual doctors, teachers, matrons and other staff, motivated by their attachment to the emerging British civic ethos of 'public service', which, thankfully, mitigated many of the worse consequences of the New Poor Law.[4]

Chris Upton, who completed this book shortly before his death in 2015, was determined not to retread old scholarly debates on the causes of the Poor Law Amendment Act. He demonstrates, very effectively, that there was much continuity of practice in Birmingham after 1834 and that, if there is a watershed to be found in the history of Birmingham welfare, it should be the building of the new workhouse on Western Road which opened on 29 March 1852. It was then, as Alistair Ritch also showed in his MPhil thesis, that the classification of paupers was more strictly enforced, on the lines that Chadwick and Senior recommended, and when children were moved from the Asylum for the Infant Poor into the main building with far less dedicated staff and suitable facilities.[5] Chris was also keen, as anyone who has read the minute reconstruction of the previous chapters can recognise, to tell the story of the workhouse from the perspective of the people involved. But he did not wish to engage in pointless, historical score-settling. He does not paint the poor as blameless victims of a parsimonious central authority, nor the workhouse and other officials as jobsworths and salary-men (or -women). Chris was no Dickens, thrusting his characters into exaggerated conditions of dreadful hardship to wring the hearts of the reader, knowing that such manipulation of the historical record was possibly even worse than what E.P. Thompson called 'the immense condescension of posterity'.[6] If anything, Chris was far closer in his writing to the style of Anthony Trollope: accurate in detail, yet able to place

---

3   M.A. Crowther, 'The Workhouse', *Proceedings of the British Academy*, 78, 1992, pp. 183–4; J.D. Marshall, *The Old Poor Law, 1795–1834*, London, 1968, pp. 17–22.

4   J.L. Perry and A. Hondeghem, 'Introduction', in J.L. Perry and A. Hondeghem (eds), *Motivation in Public Management: The Call of Public Service*, Oxford, 2008; B.J. O'Toole, *The Ideal of Public Service: Reflections on the Higher Civil Service in Britain*, London, 2006, pp. 32–6.

5   A.E.S. Ritch, '"Sick, aged and Infirm": Adults in the New Birmingham Workhouse', unpublished MPhil thesis, University of Birmingham, 2010.

6   E.P. Thompson, *The Making of the English Working Class*, London, 1963, p. 12.

this into the broader agendas of the age (and not merely those subsequently imposed by academic historians); appreciative of the circumstances of those powerless *and* the powerful – and those merely passing by. Who else would be able to elicit sympathy for George Hinchcliffe, the governor dismissed in 1818 as a result of the outcry following the discovery of the selling of workhouse goods for private profit? Instinctively we would regard such corrupt misuse of public office as wholly without possible defence, but, as Chris explains, the very guardians who hounded Hinchcliffe out of his post and to an early grave, were those who had appointed Hinchcliffe and permitted him to make as much profit as he and his staff could, as long as he kept the poor rate down. Their economical, yet ethically unsound, system had been exposed by George Edmonds and so they had used poor old Hinchcliffe as a convenient scapegoat to hide their own responsibility for the abuse.

Chris's determination to assess fairly the work of the Birmingham workhouse system was informed, at least in part, by the ambiguous attitude shown by scholars towards this culturally crucial event in the history of welfare, state formation and 'governance'. Although the intentions of the new system were deliberately and institutionally cruel, many scholars, especially the 'welfare state whigs' who proliferated in the high noon of social history in the 1960s and 1970s, argued that at least the state was now accepting some responsibility and intervening directly in areas previously left to local preference.[7] The inconsistencies of coverage and quality of the poor law system across the nation were finally eliminated and excessive abuses in areas such as Middlesex in the old system and in Unions such as Andover and Huddersfield in the new system were exposed and eradicated.[8] The new system was unjust, but it was at least *uniformly* unjust. Furthermore, power over the quality of the care provided by the Poor Law now rested in the hands of the state, not the local elites and vested interests. If one could gain control of the apparatus of the state, or at least influence those in control to reform it, then it would be possible to implement a new, kinder, less punitive system.[9] Unsurprisingly, those looking

---

7   See, for examples, D. Roberts, *Victorian Origins of the British Welfare State,* New Haven, 1960; M. Bruce, *The Coming of the Welfare State,* 3rd edn, London, 1966; W.C. Lubenow, *The Politics of Government Growth: Early Victorian Attitudes toward State Intervention, 1833–1848,* Newton Abbott, 1971; D. Fraser, *The Evolution of the British Welfare State,* London, 1973; E. Evans, *Social Policy, 1830–1914: Individualism, Collectivism and the Origins of the Welfare State,* London, 1978.

8   For the Middlesex case see A. Eccles, *Vagrancy in Law and Practice under the Old Poor Law,* Aldershot, 2012, pp. 81–4; for the Andover scandal see N. Longmate, *The Workhouse,* London, 1974, chapter 10, pp. 119–35; for the Huddersfield case see F. Driver, 'The English Bastile: Dimensions of the Workhouse System, 1834–1884', unpublished PhD thesis, University of Cambridge, 1987, pp. 356–64.

9   S. Webb, *The Reform of the Poor Law,* London, 1891.

for the antecedents of the National Health Service, with its guaranteed national standards of provision, centralised administration and parliamentary oversight were forced, even if rather reluctantly, to acknowledge that the NHS could not have emerged without the administrative, technical and political experience of the New Poor Law.[10]

Chris would have none of this, however. For him, the desire to create a teleology of the 'emergence of the welfare state' resulted in a historical distortion as bad as that achieved by Senior and Chadwick in their selective use of the assistant commissioners' reports in 1833/34. Both 'welfare state whigs' and Benthamite reformers had chosen to ignore any example of the good practice that had been achieved in towns such as Birmingham before 1834, as it failed to suit their centralising agendas. The New Poor Law was and is rightly condemned by contemporaries, reformers and historians as it did not address the differing needs of the varied regions of Britain such as the service-based economy in London, the manufacturing of the Midlands and the North and the agrarian South-West.[11] But equally, the limitations of a National Health Service in thrall to successive Conservative governments who starve it of funds and a public seemingly unwilling to pay for the necessary welfare services required by an ageing population have become increasingly apparent in the twenty-first century.[12] What was and is needed, Chris believed after writing this book, was a system which was supervised centrally, but which allowed local providers to adjust the service to suit the needs of their communities. Hence, Birmingham with its young, growing population in the mid eighteenth century needed an Asylum for the Infant Poor, but the dangers of early industrial life required adequate medical provision for those unable to afford doctors' fees. Any historian of Birmingham (and Chris was the leading historian of the city for more than two decades) knows about the significance of the 'Civic Gospel' – a commitment to the care of one's neighbours and the improvement of one's community, famously articulated by George Dawson in the 1860s.[13] Yet, as Chris's book shows, these ideas were present in the town, for a variety of social and cultural reasons, long before Dawson started preaching at the Church of the Saviour in Edward Street in 1845. As the history of welfare since 1834 has demonstrated, the average British citizen was and is far less likely to be

---

10   P. Thane, *Foundations of the Welfare State*, 2nd edn., London, 1996; B. Harris, *The Origins of the British Welfare State: Social Welfare in England and Wales, 1800–1945*, Basingstoke, 2004.

11   A. Digby, *British Welfare Policy: Workhouse to Workfare*, London, 1989, pp. 29–41.

12   M. McCartney, *The State of Medicine: Keeping the Promise of the NHS*, London, 2016; M. Exworthy, R. Mannion, M. Powell (eds), *Dismantling the NHS?: Evaluating the Impact of Health Reforms*, Bristol, 2016.

13   A.B. Rodrick, *Self-Help and Civic Culture: Citizenship in Victorian Birmingham*, Aldershot, 2004, pp. 134–73.

endlessly generous towards people he or she has never met and places he or she was or is unlikely to visit; and the continued vicissitudes of the NHS are caused by the simple ambiguity between local and national identities. While the nation refuses to pay for adequate standards of care for the elderly, communities continuously run marathons, donate time, money and services, sponsor their friends and children and cheer on the work of local hospices and day centres.

Readers of this book will be able to attest that Chris did not, however, regard the system of the 'old' workhouse as even adequate, let alone perfect. He agreed with Lynn Hollen Lees' judgement that the Old Poor Law was 'neither uniformly harsh or benign.'[14] His appreciation of the role of key whistle-blowers, dedicated public servants, scrutiny by the press and by systems of local, national and charitable inspection was tempered by an understanding that their respective confessions, commitment, articles and reports were fundamentally random and appeared as a result of a series of chances or personal choices. How many workhouse supervisors witnessed abuse and did not speak out (or chose to copy the practice for their own gratification)? How many matrons, teachers and doctors chose to spend as little time with their charges as possible and to do as little as possible, for as much salary as possible, while in the workhouse, infirmary or asylum? How many scandals like that of George Hinchcliffe were never reported, by journalists who thought there was no public appetite for the story, blackmailed the perpetrators instead or chose not to upset their proprietors or sources of information? And finally, how many overworked church missionaries, state employees or guardians and overseers simply failed to recognise the symptoms of ill-treatment and neglect among the poor? If a 'lunatic' pauper was kept in chains and one was assured by his 'carer' that this was to prevent him from hurting himself and others, was it not highly likely that one of these unqualified and untrained inspectors would simply have accepted this cruel act as merely a necessary evil? Chris understood that all that we know of the past is that which survives to the present and even that fragmentary and serendipitous material is frequently partial, illegible and unreliable, even sometimes downright wrong. But he was driven to put as many pieces of the impossible puzzle together as he could. Trying to write academic history may, as one wit has observed, be similar to trying to nail jellyfish to the wall, but Chris was indefatigable and he had many, many nails.

Ultimately, Chris wrote this book, not in order to preach the dogma of any system of welfare provision, but merely to illustrate that all systems have benefits and pitfalls and that any alleviation of mass distress takes considerable time, thankless effort and generous funding. It is possible, of course, to argue

---

14   L. Hollen Lees, *The Solidarities of Strangers: The English Poor Laws and the People, 1700–1948,* Cambridge, 1998, p. 19.

that Birmingham had created a system of welfare in the eighteenth and early nineteenth centuries that is largely irrelevant to the needs of our society today. The economic sources of wealth and poverty have changed immeasurably since 1852. The structure of society has continuously evolved and regressed in countless, subjective ways in the century and a half since the Old Workhouse closed its doors for the final time. Politics has lurched from Liberal Political Economy to Democratic State Socialism to Individualistic Conservatism, while leaving adherents who vary in their fanaticism of all three systems trailing in its wake. Organised religion has mostly been displaced from the centre of British public life. The people who operated, oversaw and lived in the old Birmingham workhouse were not like us. They looked different (with fewer teeth, smaller bodies and blemished skins), they thought differently (largely of the relative consequences and attractions of Sin) and they behaved in a different way to almost every reader of this book if he or she swapped material conditions with them. As their time recedes, however, Chris encourages us to reach out to them and to appreciate their lives as far more challenging and filled with obstacles than the ones which we live. He asks us to sympathise with their daily struggles, their weaknesses and their petty concerns, but not to patronise them nor to express pity for people we will never meet. But he believed that if the old Birmingham workhouse ever did any good for any of the people who entered its doors, it was because it did manage, from time to time, sometimes almost by accident, to be responsive to the needs of the people of the town. Such an interpretation, at once both simple and complex, was based on his lifetime's approach to the history of his beloved home region. Start with the people and their lives and see what they can tell you about the world in which they lived and ignore what anyone else has said unless it helps you to understand them.

In the process of researching this book, Chris once told me that in the cholera epidemic of 1832, the worst outbreak of 'plague' since the Great Plague of 1665, in which tens of thousands died in Manchester, London and Glasgow, less than thirty people died in Birmingham. Astonished, I asked him why that was. He replied that he had no real idea as no one had ever bothered to study a case where something *hadn't* happened. Together we investigated and proved that Birmingham had a far better organised, motivated and funded civic response in 1832 than any other city in Britain at the time.[15] This remarkable discovery, which flew in the face of all accepted historical judgements of early nineteenth-century local government, had been conveniently forgotten as the proponents of the incorporation of Birmingham (which came in 1838) preferred to paint a picture of the town as inefficient, corrupt and morally degraded. In a similar

---

15   I. Cawood and C. Upton, '"Divine Providence": Birmingham and the Cholera Pandemic of 1832', *Journal of Urban History*, 39:6, 2013, pp. 1106–24.

fashion, Chris was keen to overturn lazy generalisations about the original Birmingham workhouse with a detailed case study of all aspects of the lives of paupers in a large city, as did Philip Anderson in his 1980 study of Leeds workhouse and Eric Midwinter in his thesis on Lancashire.[16] He was conscious that a survey of workhouse experience, published by the National Archives ten years ago, did not contain a single reference to Birmingham.[17] Like Anderson and Midwinter's work, Chris's book demonstrates that, while the failure of the Old Poor Law was undeniable in rural England and the parish as a unit of administration was largely inadequate, as a system for facilitating relief in accordance with the expectations of the period, the Birmingham Poor Law authorities had responded effectively to the challenges of industrialisation and urbanisation.[18] Such a desire to point out inconvenient truths about Birmingham and its history motivated Chris's work throughout his career, but most particularly in this, his final book.

It has been an honour to co-edit this book with Fiona and to write this Afterword in Chris's memory, in the same way that it was a pleasure, every day, to work alongside someone simultaneously so humble, so silly and so wise for seventeen years. I hope Chris's history of the original Birmingham workhouse opens doors to those who wish to reappraise Birmingham's early industrial past and that it inspires everyone who reads it to go and know more about the complex, contradictory and confusing world of modern provincial England's history. If it does, can I recommend that you read more of the work of my dear, late colleague, Dr Chris Upton, Reader in Public History at Newman University in Birmingham. I can guarantee that you will not be disappointed.

16   P. Anderson, *Leeds Workhouse Under the Old Poor Law*, Leeds, 1980; E. Midwinter, 'Social Administration in Lancashire, 1830–1860' unpublished PhD thesis, University of York, 1966.

17   S. Fowler, *Workhouse: The People, the Places, the Life behind Doors*, London, 2007.

18   P.M. Solar, 'Poor Relief and English Economic Development before the Industrial Revolution', *Economic History Review*, 48:1, 1995, pp. 1–22.

Appendix

Anonymous notes recorded on a copy of the *Regulations of Birmingham Workhouse*, dated 1830[1]

The management of all parish affairs is in the hands of 12 overseers and 108 guardians who are re-elected or changed every three years by the rate payers. The form of appointment is very simple – a parcel containing separate slips of paper, with the names approved of for Guardians is delivered to Scrutineers on a day appointed at the Public office – and the Majority of votes so taken decides the appointments.

Out of these guardians so appointed Sub-Committees are formed for superintending every branch of management.

The Workhouse is within the Town – but there is a considerable tract of Land or Farm on Birmingham Heath which is cultivated by the paupers and the produce accounted for in the yearly statements.

There is also attached a sand mine in the suburbs of the Town – held by the Overseers, at which the sand (chiefly used for casting and building) is got by the paupers and wheeled about a quarter of a mile to the side of the canal, in order to be then conveyed by Boats into the town.

Stone breaking – for the use of the Streets and Roads, is another very considerable source of employment, and the Work is paid for out of the Road rate (or Commissioners' Levy) according to its value.

---

1   Archives and Collections, Library of Birmingham. MS 2126/EB9/1829 Regulations of Birmingham Workhouse (with anonymous annotations), 1830.

And they also have a flour mill, near the house, in Steel House Lane, which is worked by hand.

Connected with the Workhouse is an excellent establishment called the Asylum – for the reception of the young children – who are instructed in reading and Working – until situations can be procured for them, as apprentices to trade.

Present state for 1830

In the House	Men	198	
	Women	195	
	Children	85	= 478
In the Asylum	Children	340	
Total		818	

Employment

From 13 to 17 men are regularly and daily employed at the Mill to grind flour – several are employed about the house – and the remainder wheel sand, break stones, and sweep, and clean the streets according to circumstances.

Of the children – a few of the boys go out to work in the day, and bring home (to the Workhouse) the wages which they earn at the Manufactories – however, they are placed out apprentices as soon as situations can be obtained.

The Women are mostly engaged in household work of all kinds.

At the Asylum 124 Children are employed in making pins – 11 at Glass polishing, and 56 in Working Lace.

All applicants for casual relief are sent to Work at the Sand Mine – or Stone breaking – and sometimes Road making at One Shilling a Day.

Average cost per head per Week in the Workhouse: Two Shillings and eleven pence.

Average cost per head per Week in the Asylum: One shilling and eleven pence half-penny.

Average cost of clothing of each individual per Week: about three pence half penny.

Bibliography

Newspapers and Periodicals

Aris's Birmingham Gazette
Birmingham Advertiser
Birmingham Journal
Birmingham Local Notes & Queries
Edinburgh Review
Edmonds' Weekly Recorder (or Register)
Gentleman's Magazine
Leeds Mercury
Midland Representative & Birmingham Herald
Monthly Argus & Public Censor
The Philanthropist and Warwickshire, Worcestershire and Staffordshire Gazette
The Sunday Referee
Swinney's Birmingham Chronicle

Parliamentary Records

An Act for the Relief of the Poor, 1575, 18 Elizabeth c. 3.

An Act for the Relief of the Poor, 1601, 43 Elizabeth I c. 2

An Act for the due execution of divers laws and statutes heretofore made against rogues, vagabonds and sturdy beggars, and other lewd and idle persons, 1609, 7 James I c. 4

An Ordinance for the Relief and Employment of the Poor, and the Punishment of Vagrants and other disorderly Persons in the City of London etc, 1647

An Act for Amending the Laws relating to Settlement, Employment and Relief of the Poor, 1723, 9 George I, c. 7 (Workhouse Test Act 1723, also known as Knatchbull's Act)

Reports from Committees of the House of Commons, first series, IX, 1774–1802

An Act for Providing a Proper Workhouse..., 1783, 23 George III c. 54 (Birmingham Poor Relief Act 1783)

Birmingham Inclosure Act, 1797, 38 George III c. 54.

An Act for the Better Relief and Employment of the Poor in the Several Parishes ... of the City of Coventry, 41 George III, 1801

Abstract of answers and returns made pursuant to the Act of 43 George III relative to the expense and maintenance of the poor in England, Parliamentary Papers, XIII, 1803–4

An Act for the Better Care and Maintenance of Lunatics, Being Paupers or Criminals in England, 1808, 48 George III c. 96

An Act for the Regulation of Parish Vestries, 1818, 58 George III c. 69

An Act to Amend the Law for the Relief of the Poor, 1819, 59 George III c. 12

Select Committee Report on Madhouses in England, Parliamentary Papers VI, 1816

Gaols: reports from magistrates and keepers under 4 George IV c. 64, called the Gaols Act, Parliamentary Papers, XIX, 1824

An Act for Better Regulating the Poor within the Parish of Birmingham, 1831, 23 George III c. 54

Report from His Majesty's Commissioners for Inquiring into the Administration and Practical Operation of the Poor Laws Parliamentary Papers, XXIX, 1834

Report on the State of the Public Health in the Borough of Birmingham, London, 1842

Ninth Annual Report of the Poor Law Commissioners, Appendix A: Reports of Assistant Commissioners, No. 2, Mr Power and Mr Weale's Report on Birmingham, London, 1843

Report of the Metropolitan Commissioners in Lunacy to the Lord Chancellor, London, 1844

Printed Primary Sources

Anonymous, *The Present Situation of the Town of Birmingham Respecting its Poor, considered. With a Proposal for Building a New Workhouse*, Birmingham, 1782

Anonymous, *Regulations for Conducting the Affairs of the Birmingham Workhouse*, Birmingham, nd. [1820?]

Barnard, T. (ed.), *Of the Education of the Poor*, London, 1809

Camden, W., *Britannia*, London, 1586

Chapman's Birmingham Directory, Birmingham, 1801

Dickens, C., *Our Mutual Friend*, London, 1865

Durnford, C. and Hyde East, E., *Term Reports in the Court of the King's Bench from Michaelmas Term 1794 to Trinity Term 1796,* London, 1802

Eden, F.M., *The State of the Poor*, 3 vols, London, 1797

Edmonds, G., *George Edmonds' appeal to the labourers of England: an exposure of aristocrat spies, and the infernal machinery of the poor law murder bill*, London, 1836

Finigan, T.A., *Journal of Thomas Augustine Finigan,* Birmingham, 2010

Freeth, J., *The Political Songster or A Touch on the Times,* Birmingham, 1790

Gissing, G., *New Grub Street*, London, 1891

Hooper, R., *A New Medical Dictionary*, Philadelphia, 1817

Hutton, W., *The History of Birmingham*, 6 edns, Birmingham, 1781–1836

Johnson, H.C. (ed.), *Warwick County Records Vol. VIII, Quarter Sessions Order Book 1682–90*, Warwick, 1953

Johnson, H.C. and Williams, N.J. (eds), *Warwick County Records Vol. IX, Quarter Sessions Proceedings 1690–96*, Warwick, 1964

Kempson, J., *Map of the Town and Parish of Birmingham*, Birmingham, 1808

Knight, E., *Observations on the Relief of Cases of Out Poor in the Parish of Birmingham*, 1838

Loudon, J.C., *An Encyclopaedia of Agriculture*, London, 1825

Pratt, S.J., *Harvest Home, Consisting of Supplementary Gleanings, Original Dramas and Poems, Contributions of Literary Friends and Select Re-publications*, Vol. 1, London, 1805

Pugin, A.W., *Glossary of Ecclesiastical Ornament and Costume*, London, 1844

Ratcliff, S.C. and Johnson, H.C. (eds), *Warwick County Records Vol. I, Quarter Sessions Order Book 1625–37*, Warwick, 1935

Ratcliff, S.C. and Johnson, H.C. (eds), *Warwick County Records Vol. II, Quarter Sessions Order Book 1637–50*, Warwick, 1936

Ratcliff, S.C. and Johnson, H.C. (eds), *Warwick County Records Vol. III, Quarter Sessions Order Book 1650–57*, Warwick, 1937

Ratcliff, S.C. and Johnson, H.C. (eds), *Warwick County Records Vol. VII, Proceedings in Quarter Sessions 1674–82*, Warwick, 1946

'H.W.S.', *Plain Truth, or a Correct Statement of the Late Events Relative to the Birmingham Workhouse*, Birmingham, n.d. [1818?]

Sidney, S., *Rides on Railways*, London, 1851

Smith, A., *An Inquiry into the Nature and Causes of the Wealth of Nations*, Vol. I, London, 1776

Thackeray, W.M., *Vanity Fair*, London, 1848

Thomson and Wrightson's New Triennial Directory of Birmingham, Birmingham, 1808

Timmins, S., *Birmingham and the Midland Hardware District*, London, 1866

West, W., *The History, Topography and Directory of Warwickshire*, Birmingham, 1830

White, F., *History, Gazetteer and Directory of Warwickshire*, Sheffield, 1850

White, W., *History, Gazetteer and Directory of Staffordshire and the City and County of Lichfield*, Sheffield, 1834

White, W., *Our Jubilee Year 1895: The Story of the Severn Street and Priory first-day-schools, Birmingham*, London, 1895

Willich, A.F.M., *Domestic Encyclopaedia*, London, 1802

Wrightson and Webb's Birmingham Directory, Birmingham, 1833

Yarranton, A., *England's Improvement by Sea and Land*, London, 1677

Manuscript Collections

Archives and Collections, Library of Birmingham

BCC/1/AF/1/1/1 Birmingham Lunatic Asylum Committee minute book, 1845–1850

CC1/61–CC1/71 Congregational Church Town Mission records

CP B/286011 Birmingham Town Book, 1727–35

CP B/380973 Accounts of the Birmingham Workhouse and Record of Out-Relief to the Poor, 1739–1748

CP B/660982–CP B/660987 Birmingham Overseers' Minutes, 6 vols. 1803–40

CP B/662385 Birmingham Paupers' Admission and Discharge Register

CP ED/5/1/1–8 661511–16, 663087–8 Edgbaston Overseers' accounts, 1713–1812

CP Y/661613 Yardley Parish Vestry Minutes, 1833–51

DRO 86/109 Handsworth Vestry minutes, 1784–1822

GP AS/2/1/1–2 Aston Guardians' minutes, 1836–42

GP B/2/1/1–4 Birmingham Guardians' minutes, 1783–1845

GP B/2/9/1/1 Birmingham Guardians' Estates Committee minutes, 1837–40

GP B/2/9/2/1 Birmingham Guardians' Estates and Law Committee minutes, 1841–48

GP B/2/9/3/1 Birmingham Guardians' Estates and Law Committee minutes, 1849–53

GP B/3/1/1–7 Birmingham Poor Law Union Cash Books, 1799–1847

GP B/12/2/1 Examination of Paupers re their Place of Settlement, 1838–46

GP B/19 Birmingham Pauper Admission and Discharge Register, 1767–76

GP KN/1/2/4–13 Kings Norton Guardians' minutes, 1847–72

GP KN/2/1/1 Kings Norton Guardians' minutes, 1836–41

MS 252/5 Account of teachers' salaries, Old Meeting Sunday School, 1813

MS 464/1–2 Title deeds relating to property in Lancaster Street, otherwise Walmer Lane, 1759

MS 662/2–3 Timmins collection

MS 897 Pershouse Collection, Vol. 1

MS 1683/1 Birmingham Statistical Society for Education, 1838 Report

MS 2126/EB9/1829 Regulations of Birmingham Workhouse (with anonymous annotations), 1830

MS 2818/1/2–4 Street Commissioners' minutes, 1786–1822

MS 3001/2/31 Levy made to John Thornton, churchwarden and John Chattock, overseer for Bromwich Hide, to raise money for a workhouse in Aston Parish, Deeds of Castle Bromwich, 1700

MS 3069/13/3/31 Collections and manuscript notes of W.B. Bickley

MS 3219/6/195/2 Papers of James Watt Jr. re: Aston

MS 3219/6/198/47 Papers of James Watt Jr. re: Aston

MS 3255 Thomas Augustine Finigan's Journal, 1837–8

MS 3456 Poems of George Davis, 1790–1819

MS 3629/13 [471911] Register of Children at the Protestant Dissenting Working Charity School, Vol. 1, 1798–1835

MS 3782/12/59/152 Matthew Boulton Papers

QS/B Birmingham Quarter Sessions records, 1839–1971

Sutton Corporation Old Documents

UC1 /11/2/1 Old Meeting Sunday School minutes, 1787–1818

49736 BCOL 41.11 vol. 2, *Orders and Rules to be Observed in the Birmingham Workhouse*, Birmingham, 1784

64250 BCOL 41.11 vol. 2, *Rules and Regulations of the Guardians of the Poor of the Parish of Birmingham*, Birmingham, 1841

64374 Birmingham Institutions B/1

65627 BCOL 41.1 vol. 4, Edmonds, G., *Letters to the Inhabitants of Birmingham*, Birmingham, 1819

89104A, Birmingham Scrapbook 3, Birmingham Workhouse Accounts, 1819–23

202322 Birmingham Miscellaneous M/1

National Archives

MH 12/13288/18261 Hitch, S., *Report of the Insane Poor Confined in the Workhouse Birmingham*, 31 October 1844

Shakespeare Birthplace Trust

ER1/75/5 Order of the County Sessions for a House of Correction at Stratford, January 1725/6

Sutton Coldfield Reference Library

Sutton Coldfield Select Vestry Minutes, 1819–33

Warwickshire County Record Office

DRB 115/3 Sutton Coldfield Select Vestry minutes, 1798–1825

DRB 52/34 Sutton Coldfield Select Vestry minutes, 1826–63

DRB 0100/93 Sutton Coldfield Select Vestry orders, 1816–36

QS0039/3–5 Warwick Quarter Sessions minutes, 1690–1756
QS0040/1/8 Warwick Quarter Sessions order book, 1709–18
QS1/63 Coventry Quarter Sessions records

Secondary Texts

Allin, D.S., *The Early Years of the Foundling Hospital, 1739/41–1773*, London, 2010

Anderson, P., *Leeds Workhouse Under the Old Poor Law,* Leeds, 1980

Atherton, J., 'Rioting, Dissent and the Church in Late Eighteenth Century Britain: The Priestley Riots of 1791', PhD, University of Leicester, 2012

Atkinson, J.R., *Victorian Biography Reconsidered: A Study of Nineteenth-Century 'Hidden' Lives,* Oxford, 2010

Bartlett, P., *The Poor Law of Lunacy: The Administration of Pauper Lunatics in Mid-Nineteenth-Century England*, London, 1999

Bebbington, D.W., *Evangelicalism in Modern Britain: A History from the 1730s to the 1980s*, London, 1989

Beier, A.L., *The Problem of the Poor in Tudor and Early Stuart England*, London, 1983

Blaug, M., 'The Poor Law Report Re-examined', *Journal of Economic History*, 24:2, 1964, pp. 229–45

Blom-Cooper, L., 'The Criminal Lunatic Asylum System Before and after Broadmoor', in R. Creese, W.F. Bynum and J. Bearn (eds), *The Health of Prisoners: Historical Essays*, Amsterdam, 1995, pp. 151–62

Boulton, J., 'Indoors or Outdoors? Welfare Priorities and Pauper Choices in the Metropolis under the Old Poor Law, 1718–1824', in C. Briggs, P.M. Kitson and S.J. Thompson (eds), *Population, Welfare and Economic Change in Britain, 1290–1834,* Woodbridge, 2014, pp. 153–99

Bourne, J.M., *Patronage and Society in Nineteenth-Century England,* London, 1986

Briggs, A., *Press and Public in Early Nineteenth-Century Birmingham*, Oxford, 1949

Bruce, M., *The Coming of the Welfare State*, 3rd edn, London, 1966

Brundage, A., *The English Poor Laws, 1700–1930*, Basingstoke, 2002

Carter, P., and Whistance, N., *Living the Poor Life: A Guide to the Poor Law Union Correspondence, c. 1834–1871, held at the National Archives*, BALH, 2011

Carter, P. and Thompson, K., (eds), *Pauper Prisons, Pauper Palaces: The Victorian Poor Law in the East and West Midlands, 1834–1871*, BALH, 2018

Cawood, I. and Upton, C., '"Divine Providence": Birmingham and the Cholera Pandemic of 1832', *Journal of Urban History*, 39:6, 2013, pp. 1106–24

Chambers, J., *A General History of Malvern*, Worcester, 1817

Cherry, G.E., *Birmingham: A Study in Geography, History and Planning*, Chichester, 1994

Chinn, C. (ed.), *Birmingham: Bibliography of a City*, Birmingham, 2003

Crompton, F., *Workhouse Children: Infant and Child Paupers under the Worcestershire Poor Law, 1780–1871*, Stroud, 1997

Crowther, M.A., 'The Workhouse', *Proceedings of the British Academy*, 78, 1992, pp. 183–92

Crowther, M.A., *The Workhouse System 1834–1929: The History of an English Social Institution*, London, 1981

Dent, R.K., *The Making of Birmingham*, Birmingham, 1894

Digby, A., *British Welfare Policy: Workhouse to Workfare*, London, 1989

Driver, F., 'The English Bastile: Dimensions of the Workhouse System, 1834–1884', PhD, University of Cambridge, 1987

Driver, F., *Power and Pauperism: The Workhouse System 1834–1884*, Cambridge, 1993

Eastwood, D., *Governing Rural England: Tradition and Transformation in Local Government, 1780–1840,* Oxford, 1994

Eccles, A., *Vagrancy in Law and Practice under the Old Poor Law*, Aldershot, 2012

Evans, E.J., *Social Policy, 1830–1914: Individualism, Collectivism and the Origins of the Welfare State,* London, 1978

Exworthy, M., Mannion, R. and Powell, M. (eds), *Dismantling the NHS?: Evaluating the Impact of Health Reforms*, Bristol, 2016

Fideler, P.A., *Social Welfare in Pre-Industrial England: The Old Poor Law Tradition.* Basingstoke, 2006

Fowler, S., *Workhouse: The People, the Places, the Life behind Doors,* London, 2007

Fraser, D., *The Evolution of the British Welfare State,* London, 1973

Gagnier, R., *Subjectivities: A History of Self-Representation in Britain, 1832–1920,* Oxford, 1991

Gill, C., *History of Birmingham*, Vol. I., Oxford, 1952

Harling, P., *The Waning of 'Old Corruption': The Politics of Economical Reform in Britain, 1779–1846,* Oxford, 1996

Harris, B., *The Origins of the British Welfare State: Social Welfare in England and Wales, 1800–1945,* Basingstoke, 2004

Hewitt, M., 'Diary, Autobiography and the Practice of Life History', in D. Amigoni (ed.), *Life Writing and Victorian Culture*, Aldershot, 2006, pp. 21–40

Higgs, M., *Life in the Victorian and Edwardian Workhouse*, Stroud, 2007

Hindle, S., *The Birthpangs of Welfare: Poor Relief and Parish Governance in Seventeenth -Century Warwickshire*, Oxford, 2000

Hitchcock, T.V., 'The English Workhouse: A Study in Institutional Poor Relief in Selected Counties 1696–1750', DPhil, St. Anthony's College, University of Oxford, 1985

Hodgkinson, R.G., *The Origins of the National Health Service: The Medical Services of the New Poor Law, 1834–71*, London, 1967

Hollen Lees, L., *The Solidarities of Strangers: The English Poor Laws and the People, 1700–1948*, Cambridge, 1998

Horden, J., *John Freeth (1731–1808): Political Ballad-Writer and Innkeeper*, Oxford, 1993

Hughes, F., 'The Cost of Caring: Expenditure on County Asylum Services in Shropshire and Middlesex 1850–1900', *Local Historian*, 45:4, 2015, pp. 312–20

Humphries, J., *Childhood and Child Labour in the British Industrial Revolution*, Cambridge, 2010

Innes, J., 'Prisons for the Poor: English Bridewells, 1555–1800', in F. Snyder and D. Hay (eds), *Labour, Law and Crime: An Historical Perspective*, Oxford, 1987, pp. 42–122

Jones, K., *A History of the Mental Health Services*, London, 1972

Jütte, R., *Poverty and Deviance in Early Modern Europe*, Cambridge, 1994

Kidd, A.J., *State, Society and the Poor in Nineteenth-Century England*, Basingstoke, 1999

King, S., *Poverty and Welfare in England 1700–1850: A Regional Perspective*, Manchester, 2000

Landau, N., 'Who was Subjected to the Laws of Settlement? Procedure under the Settlement Laws in Eighteenth-Century England', *Agricultural History Review*, 43:2, 1990, pp. 139–59

Lane, J., *Apprenticeship in England, 1600–1914*, London, 1996

Langford, J.A., *A Century of Birmingham Life: Or, A Chronicle of Local Events, from 1741–1841*, 2 vols, Birmingham, 1868

Line, P.L., *Birmingham: A History in Maps*, Stroud, 2009

Longmate, N., *The Workhouse*, London, 1974

Lubenow, W.C., *The Politics of Government Growth: Early Victorian Attitudes toward State Intervention, 1833–1848*, Newton Abbott, 1971

Makras, K., "'The Poison that upsets my reason": Men, Madness and Drunkenness in the Victorian Period', in T. Knowles and S. Trowbridge (eds), *Insanity and the Lunatic Asylum in the Nineteenth Century*, London, 2015, pp. 135–48

Markus, T.A., *Buildings and Power: Freedom and Control in the Origin of Modern Building Types*, London, 1993

Marshall, J.D., *The Old Poor Law, 1795–1834*, London, 1968

McCann, P. and Young, F.A., *Samuel Wilderspin and the Infant School Movement*, London, 1982

McCartney, M., *The State of Medicine: Keeping the Promise of the NHS*, London, 2016

McConville, S., *A History of English Prison Administration*, London, 1981

McCrae, N. and Nolan, P., *The Story of Nursing in British Mental Hospitals: Echoes from the Corridors*, London, 2016

McKenna, J., *In the Midst of Life: A History of the Burial Grounds of Birmingham*, Birmingham, 1992

McNaulty, M., 'Some Aspects of the History of the Administration of the Poor Laws in Birmingham between 1730 and 1834', MA, University of Birmingham, 1942

Mellett, D., *The Prerogative of Asylumdom: Social, Cultural and Administrative Aspects of the Institutional Treatment of the Insane in Nineteenth-Century Britain*, New York, 1982

Midwinter, E., Social Administration in Lancashire, 1830–1860, PhD, University of York, 1966

Morrison, J.T.J., *William Sands Cox and the Birmingham Medical School*, Birmingham, 1926

Morrison, K., *The Workhouse: A Study of Poor-Law Buildings in England*, Swindon, 1999

Nejedly, M., 'Earning their Keep: Child Workers at the Birmingham Asylum for the Infant Poor, 1797–1852', *Family and Community History*, 20:3, 2018, pp. 206–17

O'Toole, B.J., *The Ideal of Public Service: Reflections on the Higher Civil Service in Britain*, London, 2006

Ottaway, S.R., *The Decline of Life: Old Age in Eighteenth-Century England*, Cambridge, 2004

Owen, D., *English Philanthropy, 1660–1960*, Cambridge, MA, 1964

Oxley, G.W., *Poor Relief in England and Wales, 1601–1834*, Newton Abbott, 1974

Parry-Jones, W.L., *The Trade in Lunacy: A Study of Private Madhouses in England in the Eighteenth and Nineteenth Centuries*, London, 1972

Perry, J.L. and Hondeghem, A., 'Introduction', in J.L. Perry and A. Hondeghem (eds), *Motivation in Public Management: The Call of Public Service*, Oxford, 2008, pp. 1–14

Porter, R., *Mind-Forg'd Manacles: A History of Madness in England from the Restoration to the Regency*, Cambridge, 1987

Quickenden, K., Baggott, S. and Dick, M. (eds), *Matthew Boulton: Enterprising Industrialist of the Enlightenment*, Aldershot, 2013

Reid, A., *The Union Workhouse: A Study Guide for Local Historians and Teachers*, London, 1994.

Reinarz, J., *Health Care in Birmingham: The Birmingham Teaching Hospitals 1779–1939*, Woodbridge, 2009

Reinarz, J. and Ritch, A., 'Exploring Medical Care in the Nineteenth-Century Provincial Workhouse: A View from Birmingham', in J. Reinarz and L. Schwarz (eds), *Medicine and the Workhouse*, Woodbridge, 2013, pp. 140–63

Ritch, A.E.S., 'Sick, aged and infirm': Adults in the New Birmingham Workhouse, MPhil, University of Birmingham, 2010

Roberts, D., *Victorian Origins of the British Welfare State,* New Haven, 1960

Rodrick, A.B., *Self-Help and Civic Culture: Citizenship in Victorian Birmingham,* Aldershot, 2004

Scarfe, N., *Innocent Espionage: The La Rochefoucauld Brothers' Tour of England in 1785,* Woodbridge, 1995

Scull, A., *The Most Solitary of Afflictions: Madness and Society in Britain, 1700–1900,* New Haven, 1993

Shave, S.A., *Pauper Policies: Poor Law Practice in England, 1780–1850,* Manchester, 2017

Shepherd, A., *Institutionalizing the Insane in Nineteenth-Century England*, London, 2014

Shill, R., *Workshop of the World: Birmingham's Industrial Heritage*, Stroud, 2006

Shore, H., 'Crime, Criminal Networks and Survival Strategies of the Poor in Early Eighteenth-Century London', in S. King and A. Tomkins (eds), *The Poor in England 1700–1850: An Economy of Makeshifts*, Manchester, 2003, pp. 137–65

Siena, K., 'Contagion, Exclusion and the Unique Medical World of the Eighteenth-Century Workhouse: London Infirmaries in their Widest Relief', in J. Reinarz and L. Schwarz (eds), *Medicine and the Workhouse*, Woodbridge, 2013, pp. 19–39

Simmons, J., *Factory Lives: Four Nineteenth-Century Working-Class Autobiographies*, Plymouth, 2007

Slack, P., *The English Poor Law, 1531–1782*, Cambridge, 1995

Smith, L.D., 'The County Asylum in the Mixed Economy of Care, 1808–1845', in J. Melling and B. Forsythe (eds), *Insanity, Institutions and Society, 1800–1914: A Social History of Madness in Comparative Perspective*, London, 1999, pp. 23–47

Smith, L.D., *Cure, Comfort and Safe Custody: Public Lunatic Asylums in Early-Nineteenth-Century England*, London, 1999

Smith, L.D., 'Duddeston Hall and the "Trade in Lunacy", 1835–65,' *Birmingham Historian*, 8, 1992, pp. 16–22

Smith, L.D., 'Eighteenth-Century Madhouse Practice: The Prouds of Bilston', *History of Psychiatry*, 3, 1992, pp. 45–52

Smith, L.D., 'The Pauper Lunatic Problem in the West Midlands, 1818–1850,' *Midland History*, 21, 1996, pp. 101–18

Smith, L.D., '"A Sad Spectacle of Hopeless Mental Degradation": The Management of the Insane in West Midlands Workhouses, 1815–1860', in J. Reinarz and L. Schwarz (eds), *Medicine and the Workhouse*, Woodbridge, 2013, pp. 103–20

Smith, L.D., 'To Cure those Afflicted with the Disease of Insanity: Thomas Bakewell and Spring Vale Asylum', *History of Psychiatry*, 4, 1993, pp. 107–27

Snell, K.D.M., *Parish and Belonging: Community, Identity and Welfare in England and Wales, 1700–1950*, Cambridge, 2006

Solar, P.M., 'Poor Relief and English Economic Development before the Industrial Revolution', *Economic History Review*, 48:1, 1995, pp. 1–22

Southall, M., *A Description of Malvern and its Concomitants*, London, 1822

Stephens, W.B. (ed.), *A History of the County of Warwick, Vol. 7: The City of Birmingham,* London, 1964

Stephens, W.B. (ed.), *A History of the County of Warwick, Vol. 8: The City of Coventry and Borough of Warwick,* London, 1969

Swift, R., *Charles Pelham Villiers: Aristocratic Victorian Radical,* London, 2017

Tate, W.E., *The Parish Chest: A Study of the Records of Parochial Administration in England,* 3rd edn, Cambridge, 1969

Thane, P., *Foundations of the Welfare State,* 2nd edn, London, 1996

Thompson, E.P., *The Making of the English Working Class,* London, 1963

Webb, S., *The Reform of the Poor Law,* London, 1891

Webb, S. and Webb, B., *English Poor Law History: Part I: The Old Poor Law,* London, 1963

Williams, S., *Poverty, Gender and Life-Cycle under the English Poor Law, 1760–1834,* Woodbridge, 2011

Woodall, J., *Gin, Ale and Poultices....Lasers and Scanners: Solihull Workhouse and Hospital, 1742–1993,* Solihull, 1994

Wrigley, E.A. and Schofield, R.S., *The Population History of England, 1541–1871: A Reconstruction,* Cambridge, 1981

Index